Praise for Strawberry Delights

A Collection of Strawberry Recipes
Cookbook Delights Series Book 15

…"If you enjoy eating fresh strawberries as much as I do, then you will love *Strawberry Delights Cookbook.* It's jammed packed with hundreds of easy-to-make recipes that are both delicious and nutritious. Every time I use this book to bake Strawberry Cobbler, someone asks me for the recipe.

Author, Karen Jean Matsko Hood has come up with some fresh and creative ways to blend the berry into beverages, soups, salads, appetizers, desserts, entrées, and preserves.

You'll never again wonder what to do with all of those strawberries sitting in the freezer!"…

Kimberly Carter
Publicist

…"Strawberries are one of the best known fruits around the world. Throughout literature this colorful fruit has captured the imagination of artists, poets, and storytellers alike.

Now *Strawberry Delights Cookbook* can do the same for your kitchen. You will truly be inspired by the wealth of information, poetry, and more than 280 recipes contained on the pages of this book.

Get this book and have fun inspiring others with your new found delicacies."…

Ed Archambeault
Spokane, WA

Praise for Strawberry Delights

A Collection of Strawberry Recipes
Cookbook Delights Series Book 15

…"*Strawberry Delights Cookbook* is an excellent collection of more than 280 recipes that feature the flavorful flair of the strawberry. This versatile, innovative cookbook will impress even experienced gourmet chefs with its range of dishes and creative uses of the fruit. At the same time, those new to cooking will not find themselves intimidated, for instructions are laid out in a clear manner and are simple to follow. The rewarding experience of making such delicious food will prompt even reluctant cooks into returning to the kitchen again and again. Many of the recipes use strawberry preserves or frozen strawberries, so there is no concern that this cookbook will ever be out of season.

Karen Hood's remarkable cookbook also includes fascinating facts about strawberry nutrition, history, and folklore in addition to information on growing and cultivating your own strawberries–a valuable addition for anyone looking to go green or eat more responsibly. Hood's lovely poems and wide knowledge of cooking, gardening, and the strawberry itself further enhance the collection in the poetry section and the *Did You Know?*... segments sprinkled throughout the book. Plainly, *Strawberry Delights Cookbook* is far more than just a cookbook: it is a versatile companion for any household.

Kim Saunders

…"*Strawberry Delights Cookbook* provides a vast amount of information along with recipes using strawberries divided into organized sections. As a cook and a strawberry enthusiast, I personally enjoy the information and the easy-to-read facts under the *Did You Know?*... questions throughout the cookbook. For the number of pages and the price, the cookbook brings great value to the buyer."…

Dr. James G. Hood
Editor

Praise for Strawberry Delights

A Collection of Strawberry Recipes
Cookbook Delights Series Book 15

…"*Strawberry Delights Cookbook* has fascinating tidbits that will delight and entertain your family. With witty and factual information about strawberries, as well as more than 280 wonderful tasty recipes, this cookbook promises to delight the palate and tantalize the taste buds. Also included is an enormous variety of scrumptious strawberry recipes that promise to deliver a unique experience.

The history and poetry that is included will intrigue and enchant the senses while enjoying the prose."…

Mary Scripture-Smith
Graphic Designer

Strawberry Delights Cookbook was featured on "Good Morning Northwest" on June 29, 2008. The live news program is broadcast on KXLY Channel 4, the ABC TV affiliate in Spokane, Washington. Author Karen Jean Matsko Hood presented an array of cookbook recipes which were posted on news4.com, plus featured a live cooking demonstration.

Strawberry Delights

A Collection of Strawberry Recipes
Cookbook Delights Series Book 15

Karen Jean Matsko Hood

Current and Future Cookbooks

By Karen Jean Matsko Hood

DELIGHTS SERIES

Almond Delights
Anchovy Delights
Apple Delights
Apricot Delights
Artichoke Delights
Asparagus Delights
Avocado Delights
Banana Delights
Barley Delights
Basil Delights
Bean Delights
Beef Delights
Beer Delights
Beet Delights
Blackberry Delights
Blueberry Delights
Bok Choy Delights
Boysenberry Delights
Brazil Nut Delights
Broccoli Delights
Brussels Sprouts Delights
Buffalo Berry Delights
Butter Delights
Buttermilk Delights
Cabbage Delights
Calamari Delights
Cantaloupe Delights
Caper Delights
Cardamom Delights
Carrot Delights
Cashew Delights
Cauliflower Delights
Celery Delights
Cheese Delights
Cherry Delights
Chestnut Delights
Chicken Delights
Chili Pepper Delights
Chive Delights
Chocolate Delights
Chokecherry Delights

Cilantro Delights
Cinnamon Delights
Clam Delights
Clementine Delights
Coconut Delights
Coffee Delights
Conch Delights
Corn Delights
Cottage Cheese Delights
Crab Delights
Cranberry Delights
Cucumber Delights
Cumin Delights
Curry Delights
Date Delights
Edamame Delights
Egg Delights
Eggplant Delights
Elderberry Delights
Endive Delights
Fennel Delights
Fig Delights
Filbert (Hazelnut) Delights
Fish Delights
Garlic Delights
Ginger Delights
Ginseng Delights
Goji Berry Delights
Grape Delights
Grapefruit Delights
Grapple Delights
Guava Delights
Ham Delights
Hamburger Delights
Herb Delights
Herbal Tea Delights
Honey Delights
Honeyberry Delights
Honeydew Delights
Horseradish Delights
Huckleberry Delights
Jalapeño Delights

Jerusalem Artichoke Delights
Jicama Delights
Kale Delights
Kiwi Delights
Kohlrabi Delights
Lavender Delights
Leek Delights
Lemon Delights
Lentil Delights
Lettuce Delights
Lime Delights
Lingonberry Delights
Lobster Delights
Loganberry Delights
Macadamia Nut Delights
Mango Delights
Marionberry Delights
Milk Delights
Mint Delights
Miso Delights
Mushroom Delights
Mussel Delights
Nectarine Delights
Oatmeal Delights
Olive Delights
Onion Delights
Orange Delights
Oregon Berry Delights
Oyster Delights
Papaya Delights
Parsley Delights
Parsnip Delights
Pea Delights
Peach Delights
Peanut Delights
Pear Delights
Pecan Delights
Pepper Delights
Persimmon Delights
Pine Nut Delights
Pineapple Delights
Pistachio Delights
Plum Delights
Pomegranate Delights
Pomelo Delights
Popcorn Delights

Poppy Seed Delights
Pork Delights
Potato Delights
Prickly Pear Cactus Delights
Prune Delights
Pumpkin Delights
Quince Delights
Quinoa Delights
Radish Delights
Raisin Delights
Raspberry Delights
Rhubarb Delights
Rice Delights
Rose Delights
Rosemary Delights
Rutabaga Delights
Salmon Delights
Salmonberry Delights
Salsify Delights
Savory Delights
Scallop Delights
Seaweed Delights
Serviceberry Delights
Sesame Delights
Shallot Delights
Shrimp Delights
Soybean Delights
Spinach Delights
Squash Delights
Star Fruit Delights
Strawberry Delights
Sunflower Seed Delights
Sweet Potato Delights
Swiss Chard Delights
Tangerine Delights
Tapioca Delights
Tayberry Delights
Tea Delights
Teaberry Delights
Thimbleberry Delights
Tofu Delights
Tomatillo Delights
Tomato Delights
Trout Delights
Truffle Delights
Tuna Delights

Turkey Delights
Turmeric Delights
Turnip Delights
Vanilla Delights
Walnut Delights
Wasabi Delights
Watermelon Delights
Wheat Delights
Wild Rice Delights
Yam Delights
Yogurt Delights
Zucchini Delights

CITY DELIGHTS
Chicago Delights
Coeur d'Alene Delights
Great Falls Delights
Honolulu Delights
Minneapolis Delights
Phoenix Delights
Portland Delights
Sandpoint Delights
Scottsdale Delights
Seattle Delights
Spokane Delights
St. Cloud Delights

FOSTER CARE
Foster Children Cookbook
  and Activity Book
Foster Children's Favorite
  Recipes
Holiday Cookbook for
  Foster Families

GENERAL THEME
DELIGHTS
Appetizer Delights
Baby Food Delights
Barbeque Delights
Beer-Making Delights
Beverage Delights
Biscotti Delights
Bisque Delights
Blender Delights
Bread Delights
Bread Maker Delights

Breakfast Delights
Brunch Delights
Cake Delights
Campfire Food Delights
Candy Delights
Canned Food Delights
Cast Iron Delights
Cheesecake Delights
Chili Delights
Chowder Delights
Cocktail Delights
College Cooking Delights
Comfort Food Delights
Cookie Delights
Cooking for One Delights
Cooking for Two Delights
Cracker Delights
Crepe Delights
Crockpot Delights
Dairy Delights
Dehydrated Food Delights
Dessert Delights
Dinner Delights
Dutch Oven Delights
Foil Delights
Fondue Delights
Food Processor Delights
Fried Food Delights
Frozen Food Delights
Fruit Delights
Gelatin Delights
Grilled Delights
Hiking Food Delights
Ice Cream Delights
Juice Delights
Kid's Delights
Kosher Diet Delights
Liqueur-Making Delights
Liqueurs and Spirits Delights
Lunch Delights
Marinade Delights
Microwave Delights
Milk Shake and Malt Delights
Panini Delights
Pasta Delights

Pesto Delights
Phyllo Delights
Pickled Food Delights
Picnic Food Delights
Pizza Delights
Preserved Delights
Pudding and Custard Delights
Quiche Delights
Quick Mix Delights
Rainbow Delights
Salad Delights
Salsa Delights
Sandwich Delights
Sea Vegetable Delights
Seafood Delights
Smoothie Delights
Snack Delights
Soup Delights
Supper Delights
Tart Delights
Torte Delights
Tropical Delights
Vegan Delights
Vegetable Delights
Vegetarian Delights
Vinegar Delights
Wildflower Delights
Wine Delights
Winemaking Delights
Wok Delights

GIFTS-IN-A-JAR SERIES

Beverage Gifts-in-a-Jar
Christmas Gifts-in-a-Jar
Cookie Gifts-in-a-Jar
Gifts-in-a-Jar
Gifts-in-a-Jar Catholic
Gifts-in-a-Jar Christian
Holiday Gifts-in-a-Jar
Soup Gifts-in-a-Jar

HEALTH-RELATED DELIGHTS

Achalasia Diet Delights
Adrenal Health Diet Delights
Anti-Acid Reflux Diet Delights
Anti-Cancer Diet Delights

Anti-Inflammation Diet Delights
Anti-Stress Diet Delights
Arthritis Delights
Bone Health Diet Delights
Diabetic Diet Delights
Diet for Pink Delights
Fibromyalgia Diet Delights
Gluten-Free Diet Delights
Healthy Breath Diet Delights
Healthy Digestion Diet Delights
Healthy Heart Diet Delights
Healthy Skin Diet Delights
Healthy Teeth Diet Delights
High-Fiber Diet Delights
High-Iodine Diet Delights
High-Protein Diet Delights
Immune Health Diet Delights
Kidney Health Diet Delights
Lactose-Free Diet Delights
Liquid Diet Delights
Liver Health Diet Delights
Low-Calorie Diet Delights
Low-Carb Diet Delights
Low-Fat Diet Delights
Low-Sodium Diet Delights
Low-Sugar Diet Delights
Lymphoma Health Support Diet Delights
Multiple Sclerosis Healthy Diet Delights
No Flour No Sugar Diet Delights
Organic Food Delights
pH-Friendly Diet Delights
Pregnancy Diet Delights
Raw Food Diet Delights
Sjögren's Syndrome Diet Delights
Soft Food Diet Delights
Thyroid Health Diet Delights

HOLIDAY DELIGHTS

Christmas Delights
Easter Delights

Father's Day Delights
Fourth of July Delights
Grandparent's Day Delights
Halloween Delights
Hanukkah Delights
Labor Day Weekend Delights
Memorial Day Weekend
  Delights
Mother's Day Delights
New Year's Delights
St. Patrick's Day Delights
Thanksgiving Delights
Valentine Delights

HOOD AND MATSKO FAMILY FAVORITES

Hood and Matsko Family
  Appetizers Cookbook
Hood and Matsko Family
  Beverages Cookbook
Hood and Matsko Family
  Breads and Rolls Cookbook
Hood and Matsko Family
  Breakfasts Cookbook
Hood and Matsko Family
  Cakes Cookbook
Hood and Matsko Family
  Candies Cookbook
Hood and Matsko Family
  Casseroles Cookbook
Hood and Matsko Family
  Cookies Cookbook
Hood and Matsko Family
  Desserts Cookbook
Hood and Matsko Family
  Dressings, Sauces, and
  Condiments Cookbook
Hood and Matsko Family
  Ethnic Cookbook
Hood and Matsko Family
  Jams, Jellies, Syrups,
  Preserves, and Conserves
Hood and Matsko Family
  Main Dishes Cookbook
Hood and Matsko Family,
  Pies Cookbook

Hood and Matsko Family
  Preserving Cookbook
Hood and Matsko Family
  Salads and Salad Dressings
Hood and Matsko Family
  Side Dishes Cookbook
Hood and Matsko Family
  Vegetable Cookbook
Hood and Matsko Family,
  Aunt Katherine's Recipe
  Collection, Vol. I-II
Hood and Matsko Family,
  Grandma Bert's Recipe
  Collection, Vol. I-IV

HOOD AND MATSKO FAMILY HOLIDAY

Hood and Matsko Family
  Favorite Birthday Recipes
Hood and Matsko Family
  Favorite Christmas Recipes
Hood and Matsko Family
  Favorite Christmas Sweets
Hood and Matsko Family
  Easter Cookbook
Hood and Matsko Family
  Favorite Thanksgiving Recipes

INTERNATIONAL DELIGHTS

African Delights
African American Delights
Australian Delights
Austrian Delights
Brazilian Delights
Canadian Delights
Chilean Delights
Chinese Delights
Czechoslovakian Delights
English Delights
Ethiopian Delights
Fijian Delights
French Delights
German Delights
Greek Delights
Hungarian Delights

Icelandic Delights
Indian Delights
Irish Delights
Italian Delights
Korean Delights
Mexican Delights
Native American Delights
Polish Delights
Russian Delights
Scottish Delights
Slovenian Delights
Swedish Delights
Thai Delights
The Netherlands Delights
Yugoslavian Delights
Zambian Delights

REGIONAL DELIGHTS
Glacier National Park Delights
Northwest Regional Delights
Oregon Coast Delights
Schweitzer Mountain Delights
Southwest Regional Delights
Tropical Delights
Washington Wine Country
  Delights
Wine Delights of Walla
  Walla Wineries
Yellowstone National Park
  Delights

SEASONAL DELIGHTS
Autumn Harvest Delights
Spring Harvest Delights
Summer Harvest Delights
Winter Harvest Delights

SPECIAL EVENTS DELIGHTS
Birthday Delights
Coffee Klatch Delights
Super Bowl Delights
Tea Time Delights

STATE DELIGHTS
Alaska Delights
Arizona Delights

Georgia Delights
Hawaii Delights
Idaho Delights
Illinois Delights
Iowa Delights
Louisiana Delights
Minnesota Delights
Montana Delights
North Dakota Delights
Oregon Delights
South Dakota Delights
Texas Delights
Washington Delights

U.S. TERRITORIES DELIGHTS
Cruzan Delights
U.S. Virgin Island Delights

MISCELLANEOUS COOKBOOKS
Getaway Studio Cookbook
The Soup Doctor's Cookbook

BILINGUAL DELIGHTS SERIES
Apple Delights, English-
  French Edition
Apple Delights, English-
  Russian Edition
Apple Delights, English-
  Spanish Edition
Huckleberry Delights,
  English-French Edition
Huckleberry Delights,
  English-Russian Edition
Huckleberry Delights,
  English-Spanish Edition

CATHOLIC DELIGHTS SERIES
Apple Delights Catholic
Coffee Delights Catholic
Easter Delights Catholic
Huckleberry Delights Catholic
Tea Delights Catholic

CATHOLIC BILINGUAL DELIGHTS SERIES

Apple Delights Catholic, English-French Edition
Apple Delights Catholic, English-Russian Edition
Apple Delights Catholic, English-Spanish Edition
Huckleberry Delights Catholic, English-Spanish Edition

CHRISTIAN DELIGHTS SERIES

Apple Delights Christian
Coffee Delights Christian
Easter Delights Christian
Huckleberry Delights Christian

Tea Delights Christian

CHRISTIAN BILINGUAL DELIGHTS SERIES

Apple Delights Christian, English-French Edition
Apple Delights Christian, English-Russian Edition
Apple Delights Christian, English-Spanish Edition
Huckleberry Delights Christian, English-Spanish Edition

FUNDRAISING COOKBOOKS

Ask about our fundraising cookbooks to help raise funds for your organization.

The above books are also available in bilingual versions. Please contact Whispering Pine Press International, Inc., for details.

Please note that some books are future books and are currently in production. Please contact us for availability date. Prices are subject to change without notice.

The above list of books is not all-inclusive. For a complete list please visit our website or contact us at:

Whispering Pine Press International, Inc.
Your Northwest Book Publishing Company
P.O. Box 214
Spokane Valley, WA 99037-0214 USA
Phone: (509) 928-8700 | Fax: (509) 922-9949
Email: sales@whisperingpinepress.com
Publisher Websites: www.WhisperingPinePress.com
www.WhisperingPinePressBookstore.com
Blog: www.WhisperingPinePressBlog.com

Strawberry Delights

A Collection of Strawberry Recipes
Cookbook Delights Series Book 15

Karen Jean Matsko Hood

Published by:

Whispering Pine Press International, Inc.
Your Northwest Book Publishing Company
P.O. Box 214
Spokane Valley, WA 99037-0214 USA
Phone: (509) 928-8700 | Fax: (509) 922-9949
Email: sales@whisperingpinepress.com
Websites: www.WhisperingPinePress.com
www.WhisperingPinePressBookstore.com
Blog: www.WhisperingPinePressBlog.com
SAN 253-200X
Printed in the U.S.A.

Published by Whispering Pine Press International, Inc.
P.O. Box 214
Spokane Valley, Washington 99037-0214 USA

For sales outside the United States, please contact the Whispering Pine Press International, Inc., International Sales Department.

Manufactured in the United States of America. This paper is acid-free and 100% chlorine free.

Book and Cover Design by Artistic Design Service
P.O. Box 1782
Spokane Valley, WA 99037-1782 USA
www.ArtisticDesignService.com

Library of Congress Number (LCCN): 2014 pending

Hood, Karen Jean Matsko
   Title: Strawberry Delights Cookbook: A Collection of Strawberry Recipes: Cookbook Delights Series Book 15

   p.   cm.

ISBN: 978-1-59649-283-7   case bound
ISBN: 978-1-59649-278-3   perfect bound
ISBN: 978-1-59649-280-6   spiral bound
ISBN: 978-1-59649-279-0   comb bound
ISBN: 978-1-59649-281-3   E-PDF
ISBN: 978-1-59210-361-4   E-PUB
ISBN: 978-1-59434-856-3   E-PRC

First Edition: January 2014
1. Cookery (*Strawberry Delights Cookbook: A Collection of Strawberry Recipes: Cookbook Delights Series Book 15*)   1. Title

Strawberry Delights Cookbook

A Collection of Strawberry Recipes
Cookbook Delights Series Book 15

Gift Inscription

To: _____

From: _____

Date: _____

Special Message: _____

_____

_____

_____

_____

_____

_____

_____

_____

*It is always nice to receive a personal note to
create a special memory.*

www.StrawberryDelights.net
www.WhisperingPinePress.com
www.WhisperingPinePressBookstore.com

Dedications

To my husband and best friend, Jim.

To our seventeen children: Gabriel, Brianne Kristina and her husband Moulik Vinodkumar Kothari, Marissa Kimberly and her husband Kevin Matthew Franck, Janelle Karina and her husband Paul Joseph Turcotte, Mikayla Karlene, Kyler James, Kelsey Katrina, Corbin Joel, Caleb Jerome, Keisha Kalani Hiwot, Devontay Joshua, Kianna Karielle Selam, Rosy Kiara, Mercedes Katherine, Jasmine Khalia Wengel, Cheyenne Krystal, and Annalise Kaylee Marie.

To our grandchildren and foster grandchildren: Courtney, Lorenzo, and Leah.

To my brother, Stephen, and his wife, Karen.

To my husband's ten siblings: Gary, Colleen, John, Dan, Mary, Ray, Ann, Teresa, Barbara, Agnes, and their families.

In loving memory of my mom, who passed away in 2007; my dad, who passed away in 1976; and my sister, Sandy, who passed away due to multiple sclerosis in 1999.

To Sandy's three sons: Monte, Bradley, and Derek. To Monte's wife, Sarah, and their children: Liam, Alice, Charlie, and Samuel. To Bradley's wife, Shawnda, and their children: Anton, Isaac, and Isabel.

To our foster children past and present: Krystal, Sara, Rebecca, Janice, Devontay Joshua, Mercedes Katherine, Zha'Nell, Makia, Onna, Cheyenne Krystal, Onna Marie, Nevaeh, and Zada, our future foster children, and all foster children everywhere.

To the Court Appointed Special Advocate (CASA) Volunteer Program in the judicial system which benefits abused and neglected children.

To the Literacy Campaign dedicated to promoting literacy throughout the world.

Acknowledgements

The author would like to acknowledge all those individuals who helped me during my time in writing this book. Appreciation is extended for all their support and effort they put into this project.

Deep gratitude and profound thanks are owed to my husband, Jim, for giving freely of his time and encouragement during this project. Also, thanks are owed to my children Gabriel, Brianne Kristina and her husband Moulik Vinodkumar Kothari, Marissa Kimberly and her husband Kevin Matthew Franck, Janelle Karina and her husband Paul Joseph Turcotte, Mikayla Karlene, Kyler James, Kelsey Katrina, Corbin Joel, Caleb Jerome, Keisha Kalani Hiwot, Devontay Joshua, Kianna Karielle Selam, Rosy Kiara, Mercedes Katherine, Jasmine Khalia Wengel, Cheyenne Krystal, and Annalise Kaylee Marie. All of these persons inspire my writing.

Thanks are due to Sharron Thompson for her assistance in editing and typing this manuscript for publication. Thanks go to Artistic Design Service for their assistance in formatting and providing a graphic design of this manuscript for publication. This project could not have been completed without them.

Many thanks are due to members of my family, all of whom were very supportive during the time it took to complete this project. Their patience and support are greatly appreciated.

Strawberry Delights Cookbook

Table of Contents

Introduction.. 20
Strawberry Information:
    Strawberry Botanical Classification 21-22
    Strawberry Cultivation and Gardening............................. 23-26
    Strawberry Facts.. 27-28
    Strawberry Folklore.. 29-30
    Strawberry History... 31-32
    Strawberry Nutrition and Health 33-34
    Strawberry Poetry.. 35-44
    Strawberry Types... 45-46
Recipe Sections:
    Appetizers and Dips.. 49-64
    Beverages 65-76
    Breads and Rolls.. 77-92
    Breakfasts.. 93-108
    Cakes 109-124
    Candies... 125-138
    Cookies... 139-156
    Desserts.. 157-182
    Dressings, Sauces, and Condiments 183-192
    Jams, Jellies, and Syrups 193-206
    Main Dishes.. 207-220
    Pies 221-234
    Preserving 235-246
    Salads... 247-262
    Side Dishes 263-272
    Soups 273-288
    Wines and Spirits... 289-304
Festival Information 305
Strawberry Associations and Commissions 306
Measurement Charts 307
Glossary 308-312
Recipe Index 313-315
Reader Feedback Form 316
About the Cookbook Delights Series..................................... 317
Order Forms:
    Book Club 318
    Fundraising Opportunities.. 319
    Personalized and/or Translated Order Form 320
    Whispering Pine Press International, Inc., Order Forms 321-322
About the Author and Cook...323-324

Strawberry Delights Cookbook

A Collection of Strawberry Recipes
Cookbook Delights Series Book 15

Introduction

Strawberries are delicious and offer nutrients that the body needs. They are great to use in various recipes and are tasty to eat by themselves.

Strawberries have an interesting history and folklore, some of which I have included in this book. As a poet, I found it enjoyable to color this cookbook with poetry so that readers could savor the metaphorical richness of the strawberry as well as its literal flavor.

Also included in this *Strawberry Delights Cookbook* are some articles on cultivation and botanical information.

The *Cookbook Delights Series* would not be complete without *Strawberry Delights* because strawberries are a common and popular fruit.

We hope you enjoy reading this cookbook as well as trying out all the recipes. This cookbook is designed for easy use and is organized into alphabetical sections: appetizers and dips; beverages; breads and rolls; breakfasts; cakes; candies; cookies; desserts; dressings, sauces, and condiments; jams, jellies, and syrups; main dishes; pies; preserving; salads; side dishes; soups; and wines and spirits.

Do enjoy your reading about strawberries, but most importantly, have fun with those you care about while you are cooking.

Following is a collection of recipes gathered and modified to bring you *Strawberry Delights Cookbook: A Collection of Strawberry Recipes, Cookbook Delight Series* by Karen Jean Matsko Hood.

Strawberry Delights Cookbook

A Collection of Strawberry Recipes
Cookbook Delights Series Book 15

Strawberry
Botanical Classification

Strawberry Botanical Classification

Strawberries make up the genus *Fragaria* of the rose family, *Rosaceae*. The wood strawberry is classified as *Fragaria vesca*, the meadow strawberry as *Fragaria virginiana*, and the beach strawberry as *Fragaria chiloensis*. The fourth principal species from which cultivated strawberries were developed is classified as *Fragaria moschata*.

Strawberries are members of the rose family. They are herbaceous perennials, stoloniferous herbs, meaning that they spread via stolons or runners. They tend to decline a bit faster in the Deep South, where they are usually treated as annuals.

The leaves have three leaflets, and arise from the crown. Leaflets are ovate or broadly oval, obtuse, dentate or coarsely serrate. The runners produce daughter plants at every other node, particularly in the summer, which root where they touch the ground and become independent plants. Flowers are white, about 1 inch across with 25 to 30 yellow stems and 50 to 500 pistils on a raised, yellow, conical receptacle. Borne on a dichasial cyme, the center most terminal flower opens first and is largest, producing the largest fruit. Subordinate flowers are smaller, have fewer pistils, and produce smaller fruit. Flowering occurs over several weeks, and plants may have ripe fruit, developing fruit, and flowers all at once.

Most cultivars are self-fruitful and therefore do not need pollinations for fruit set. However, bee activity is beneficial in transferring pollen to stigmas in an individual flower. A few hundred pollination events must take place to produce a well formed berry.

The strawberry is an accessory fruit, since the edible portion is nonovarian in origin. The true fruits which contain the seed of the strawberry are achenes, which are similar to tiny sunflower seeds. The achenes are the numerous tiny, ellipsoid specks that cover the fruit's surface. They are essential to fruit development because they produce growth regulators that enhance growth of the underlying fleshy tissue. Areas on the fruit surface that are devoid of functional achenes do not grow, causing irregularly shaped fruits.

Strawberry Delights Cookbook

A Collection of Strawberry Recipes
Cookbook Delights Series Book 15

Strawberry Cultivation and Gardening

Strawberry Cultivation and Gardening

Description	Cultivation
Height: 9 inches	*Light Requirement:* full sun
Spread: 9 to 12 inches	*Soil:* moist, fertile, well-drained
Habit: Trailing, mound	*Drought Tolerance:* low
Texture: medium	*Soil Salt Tolerance:* none
Growth rate: moderate	
Leaf: dark green	
Flower: white or pink	
Seed: small, brown	

Soil

Strawberries need full sun and should be grown in deep, fertile, moisture retentive but well drained soil such as loam or sandy loam soil. They do best in slightly acidic soil (pH of 6.2) and will not tolerate pH extremes, such as less than 5.5 or more than 7.0. In heavy soil with poor drainage, strawberries should be planted on raised beds. The beds should be built up 8 to 10 inches; this can be accomplished by taking soil from the aisles between the rows and adding organic material or buying good topsoil. The strawberry beds must be kept weed free because of the shallow root systems. You can hand pull the weeds or remove them by hoeing shallowly. The shallow roots should be disturbed as little as possible. Remove any soil that gets stuck in the crown.

Since strawberries are shallow rooted, a site with access to water is important. Regular irrigation is necessary when you can't count on regular rainfall. To reduce the risk of verticillium wilt, do not plant in soil where tomatoes, potatoes, peppers, eggplant, blackberries, or raspberries have grown in the past three years. Verticillium wilt, nematodes and spider mites can be especially pesky in the lightweight soil of the South and warm West.

Planting your strawberries

In cold winter climates, strawberries should be planted in the spring, as early as possible, March or April in most of the U.S. In warm winter climates, plant from August through November. The plants will fruit in the winter months. In warm winter climates, Day neutrals can be planted in the fall or early spring. A cool, cloudy day is the best for planting sensitive transplants. When you purchase your plants, soak the roots in water for no more than an hour or two and plant immediately. If you cannot plant right away, set the plants in moist sawdust in a plastic bag and store them in the coolest part of the refrigerator. If the roots are very long, trim back about 4 inches. Remove any moldy or black roots before planting. Set plants 12 to 15 inches apart in rows that are 48 inches apart. Mulch the rows with black plastic, except in hot, summer climates where pine needles or straw should be used. Mulching increases productivity, decreases water use and helps to keep the fruit clean.

Dig a hole deep enough for the roots to extend straight down. The soil should be level with the midpoint of the crown. Firm the soil and water thoroughly. Let the runners spread and root to form a solid matted row 15 to 18 inches wide and then clip off those growing longer. It is better for Junebearers if their flowers are removed during the first year. Your efforts will be rewarded the second year with a large crop of berries. The flowers of Day neutrals and Everbearers should be removed for six weeks after planting; then let flowers form. Larger plants with higher yields will be obtained.

Watering

Make sure the plants are well watered for the first two weeks after planting. June and Everbearers need 1 to 1½-inches of water a week. When Junebearers are fruiting, they need 1½ to 2-inches per week. In sandy soil or hot weather, they may need more. Soaker hoses or trickle irrigation is best for strawberries because they keep water off the foliage, which helps prevent problems such as gray mold.

Fertilizer

The amount of fertilizer your plants need depends on the fertility of your soil and the health of your plants. Generally, June and Everbearers should have 2 lbs. of 10-10-10 or 12-

12-12 per 100 linear feet of row, applied six weeks after transplanting, and 2 lbs. per 100 linear feet of row in late August or early September. In the second and subsequent years, fertilizing should be done after harvest. Day neutrals should be fed 2 lbs. of 10-10-10 per 100 feet of row every month, starting a month after planting until September. The second year, apply fertilizer beginning in May at the same rate and frequency. Fertilize your strawberries when the foliage is dry and then water it in. Don't sprinkle fertilizer on the crowns.

Winter Protection

If your garden is in a cold winter region, cover the plants with about 6 inches of clean straw in the fall when the temperatures start falling to around 20 degrees F. and the plants are dormant. Straw mulch shouldn't be used in areas with mild, winter temperatures and large quantities of rain, because the plants will begin growing and rot. In mild climates where some protection is needed, you can mulch with row covers of lightweight fabric instead of straw. This fabric, which can be purchased at nurseries or mail-ordered, allows light to penetrate, producing higher yields. Be sure to remove the fabric in the spring before the plants flower, to ensure good pollination.

Rejuvenating Junebearers

This can be done after their first productive year (the second year after planting) to maintain them for several more seasons. This isn't required, but it helps them from becoming overcrowded and it increases the size of the berries. Mow the foliage to about three inches high just after harvest. Whether you use hedge clippers or a rotary mower, don't damage the plant's crown. Till the winter mulch you pulled off the plants in the spring, into the space between the rows. Apply a 10-10-10 fertilizer at a rate of 5 lbs. per 100 feet of row, then spread an inch of soil over the mowed plants. Irrigate as needed and remove excess runners as they form. In early September, add another 3 lbs. of 10-10-10.

Strawberry Delights Cookbook

A Collection of Strawberry Recipes
Cookbook Delights Series Book 15

Strawberry Facts

Strawberry Facts

The strawberry grows both as a wild plant and as a cultivated plant. Strawberries are the first fruit to ripen in the spring.

Some strawberries, called Everbearers, produce berries throughout the summer and fall. Strawberry plants can be planted in any garden soil, but the richer the soil, the larger the crop. The plant grows best in a cool, moist climate and does not do well in warm temperatures. The plants may be planted in the spring or fall, but if the temperature is too cold, fall planting requires a great deal of care.

The strawberry grows close to the ground on the stem, in groups of three. The greenish-white fruits turn to a rich red color when they ripen. When the strawberry ripens the petals of the flower fall off and all that remains is the calyx, a leafy substance shaped like a star. Not every flower produces fruit.

The strawberry you eat is not really a fruit or a vegetable but is the enlarged receptacle of the flower.

The strawberry plant has about 200 seeds on the outside skin rather than having an outer skin around the seed, as most berries do. They do not, however, normally reproduce by seeds. When the fruit is developing, the plant sends out slender growths called runners. These look like strings. They grow on the ground and send out roots into the soil. The roots produce new plants which grow and bear fruit. Sometimes these plants are taken from the soil and replanted to start a new plantation of strawberry plants. Plants are taken from the soil and replanted to start a new plantation of strawberry plants.

Strawberries were cultivated in ancient Rome and were used as a medicinal herb in the 13th century. The ancient Romans believed that strawberries alleviated symptoms of melancholy, fainting, all inflammations, fevers, throat infections, kidney stones, bad breath, attacks of gout, and diseases of the blood, liver, and spleen.

Strawberries are grown in every state in the U.S. and every province in Canada. California produces 80 percent of the nation's strawberries, providing almost a year-round supply. California strawberry growers and researchers, along with help from the most ideal growing conditions, work together to produce the highest quality strawberries you can buy.

Strawberry Delights Cookbook

A Collection of Strawberry Recipes
Cookbook Delights Series Book 15

Strawberry Folklore

Strawberry Folklore

Strawberries immediately bring to mind the best things in life; warm summers, pretty gardens, and delicious desserts.

They have been used as a flirtatious signal between courting couples, and have been considered an aphrodisiac.

According to zodiac lore, strawberries are ruled by the balance sign Libra. Librans are ruled by Venus, the Goddess of Love, who enjoys pretty flowers and nibbling on rosy fruits. If you are a Libran, then strawberries are the fruit for you! They are considered erotic because of their prolific number of seeds.

Strawberries are undoubtedly one of the ultimate fruits of love. The strawberry was thought to communicate "you intoxicate me with delight" or "you are delicious."

There is a legend about eating a double strawberry that says if you break the strawberry in half and share it with a member of the opposite sex; you will soon fall in love with each other.

Queen Anne Boleyn, the second wife of Henry VIII had a strawberry shaped birthmark on her neck, which some claimed proved she was a witch.

In parts of Bavaria, people still practice the annual rite each spring of tying small baskets of wild strawberries to the horns of their cattle as an offering to elves. They believe that the elves, who are passionately fond of strawberries, will help to produce healthy calves and abundance of milk in return.

In provincial France, strawberries were regarded as an aphrodisiac of the highest quality. Newlyweds traditionally were served a soup of thinned sour cream, strawberries, borage (a European herb whose flavor is reminiscent of cucumber) and powdered sugar.

To symbolize perfection and righteousness, medieval stone masons carved strawberry designs on altars and around the tops of pillars in churches and cathedrals.

Native Americans allegedly invented strawberry shortcake, mashed berries in meal, to make bread the colonists enjoyed, but they apparently used wild strawberries, since strawberries have been cultivated in America only since 1835.

The Fraser clan in Scotland derived its name from French immigrants named Strawberry who came with William the Conqueror in 1066.

Strawberry Delights Cookbook

A Collection of Strawberry Recipes
Cookbook Delights Series Book 15

History of Strawberries

History of Strawberries

The word strawberry is derived from the Old English word *streawberige*. It appears to have received its name from the numerous runners which the plant spreads out into the soil that resemble pieces of straw.

Strawberries have a history that goes back over 2,200 years. Strawberries grew wild in Italy as long ago as 234 B.C. and were discovered in Virginia by the first Europeans when their ships landed there in 1588.

Strawberries are native to North America, and the Native North Americans used them in many dishes. The first colonists in America shipped the larger native strawberry plants back to Europe as early as 1600. Another type of strawberry plant was also discovered in Central and South America, which conquistadores called futilla. Early Americans did not need to plant strawberries, since they were readily available in the wild.

Cultivation began in earnest in the early part of the 19th century when strawberries with cream quickly became a luxurious dessert. New York became a strawberry hub with the advent of the railroad. Crops were shipped in refrigerated railroad cars. Production spread to Arkansas, Louisiana, Florida, and Tennessee. At present, most North American strawberries are grown in California.

As far back as the 13th century, strawberries were used as aphrodisiacs.

During the 1700s, a hybrid variety was developed in France by breeding wild strawberries brought from North America with others from Chile. The first important American variety, the Hovey, was grown in 1834 in Massachusetts.

The Romans prized wild strawberries for their medicinal properties.

The first strawberry festival dates back to 1850.

Strawberries have been grown in California since the early 1900's. Today, over 25,000 acres of strawberries are planted each year in California, and the state produces over 80 percent of the strawberries grown in the United States. On average, each acre produces about 21 tons of strawberries and the state produces one billion pounds of strawberries a year!

Strawberry Delights Cookbook

A Collection of Strawberry Recipes
Cookbook Delights Series Book 15

Strawberry
Nutrition and Health

Strawberry Nutrition and Health

Americans currently consume strawberries all year round. Recent research strongly suggests that consuming them more often will be beneficial to their overall long-term health.

Strawberries are said to be the most powerful fruit as they are very rich in antioxidants.

When selecting strawberries make sure that they are a full red color and avoid any that are uncolored or white.

Ounce for ounce, strawberries have more Vitamin C than citrus fruit. One cup of strawberries gives you a whopping 140 percent of your recommended daily allowance of vitamin C.

Strawberries' versatility and adaptability add interest, lively color, and flavor to either indulgent or healthy recipes. Fresh, frozen, or dried, eaten alone or tossed into cereal, salads, or yogurt, strawberries naturally add a nutritional edge to an ordinary meal or snack.

The strawberry is an incredibly nutrient-dense fruit. In addition to being fat free and low in calories, strawberries have higher levels of vitamin C, folate, fiber, potassium, and other antioxidants than most other fruits like bananas, apples, and even oranges.

Vitamin C and fiber help keep you strong and healthy. Strawberries also contain phytochemicals that help your immune system fight to protect your health. In fact, all berries (blueberries, raspberries, blackberries, cranberries, etc.) are packed with phytochemicals.

Most importantly, they are one of the few sources, along with some other berries, grapes and cherries, for ellagic acid, a compound which prevents carcinogens from turning healthy cells into cancerous ones.

Studies show that strawberries were among the top eight foods that decreased rates of death from cancer. Studies have also shown that eating strawberries improves heart health, enhances memory function, can significantly decrease blood pressure, and aids in the management of rheumatoid arthritis.

Strawberries are available year-round, offering the perfect opportunity for consumers to add great taste and nutrition to their everyday, healthy diet.

Strawberry Delights Cookbook

A Collection of Strawberry Recipes
Cookbook Delights Series Book 15

Poetry

A Collection of Poetry with Strawberry Themes

Table of Contents

Page

Strawberry 36
Strawberry Plants 37
Strawberry Blossoms 38
Earth's Natural Ruby 39
Motherly Gardening 40
June Visitors 41
Nature's Dance 42
Strawberry Syrup 43
Somewhere Between the Spice Bottles 44

Strawberry

The red strawberry appears
from the garden of earth's loam.
Berries begin with a light verdant color
which stand in lush contrast to the rich earth from
where
it sends its runners.
Berries are firm to the touch
and smell of fresh green as they sit
lazily in the sun waiting to ripen
under the rays of early summer.

Earthworms spend their
days work as they burrow around the roots of the straw-
berry plant.
Their tunnels we cannot see but provide
fresh nutrition to the sprightly strawberry stems,
oxygen to nourish and add vigor to
these June plants.

Soon more succulent fruits burst
forth from the landscape to
the delight of the gardeners and
the birds. Ruby berries
to be treasured by the cook.

Karen Jean Matsko Hood ©2014
Published in *Strawberry Delights Cookbook*, 2014
By Whispering Pine Press International, Inc. 2014

Strawberry Plants

A single blossom unfolds on the stem
and then another appears green flat.

Sunrise appears and is greeted with a sunset
each more beautiful than the one before.

Runners sap across the earth
to make more strawberry plants

as the main bundle of green
nourishes more petals of white.

Karen Jean Matsko Hood ©2014
Published in *Strawberry Delights Cookbook*, 2014
By Whispering Pine Press International, Inc. 2014

Strawberry Blossoms

Blossoms unfold,
fragrance explodes.

Hummingbirds cheep,
awaken my soul.

Chickadees argue,
wrens chatter.

The honeybees scold
sheer morning mist.

Pine bark breath
permeates my senses.

Taste the fragrance of the
sweet summer day.

Karen Jean Matsko Hood ©2014
Published in *Strawberry Delights Cookbook*, 2014
By Whispering Pine Press International, Inc. 2014

Earth's Natural Ruby

Earth's natural ruby
grows from a vine
firstborn in the original garden,
its fruit never forbidden or cursed.
One taste of this succulent yield
primes a deep desire
for a sweet taste of heaven
that must not be starved,
but should only be greedily quenched.
Its seedy, firm textured skin easily gives in
to the slightest pressure.
Strawberry's fresh full flavor bursts
wild on the tongue,
quenching thirst and staining
lips a sinful red.
Earth's gift of this precious fruit
should be accepted as penance
for the curse of the ground.

Karen Jean Matsko Hood ©2014
Published in *Strawberry Delights Cookbook*, 2014
By Whispering Pine Press International, Inc. 2014

Motherly Gardening

My mother
Taught me
To garden
To dig with bare hands
In clay and
Loam,
And crawl with
Montana angleworms,
That shine in dim
Rays that reflect
From Big
Sky.

My mind
Wanders
Through the muck,
Reddish, heavy,
Muddy ooze.
Intrigued with
Life
And worms,
Those bugs
Slink through
The gumbo,
Slip
In its
Heaviness.

Great Falls' wind
Reminds
Me to
Plant those
Seeds
Before Chinook
Winds come
To make
More mud.

Wise old mom
Knew that
Earthen mire
Grounded me
In ways
Earthworms
Inch and
Always understand.

Karen Jean Matsko Hood ©2014
Published in *Strawberry Delights Cookbook*, 2014
By Whispering Pine Press International, Inc. 2014

June Visitors

I watch tiny orbs,
   floral buds swell.
First pea-sized marbles sprout,
   then expand to walnut sizing.

All the while the worker ants
   snack on these ballooning spheres,
orbit networks of delight,
   feast on sticky treats.

Sweet feed for their families
   drip from succulent rounds of green,
distend to the moment they burst
   to show off pink petals that unfurl.

Fragrance intoxicates,
   beauty musically exquisite,
voracious visitors expose magnificence,
   peony ecstasy.

Armies of ants return home
   to feed their families
and defend their farm while
   singing birds prime summer.

June visitors.

Karen Jean Matsko Hood ©2014
Published in *Strawberry Delights Cookbook*, 2014
By Whispering Pine Press International, Inc. 2014

Nature's Dance

Hot rays stand above
penetrate canopies of clouds
ever-greening blades of grass,
while wildflowers wilt
to music of a cricket chorus
harmonizing with the colors
of the sand.

Aspen leaves quake in the wind,
tremble and twirl their own soft-shoe style.
Poplar foliage now ground cover,
goldenrod sways in the distance,
cat-tails take their last stand.
All becomes still,
to anticipate the next drama.

Boughs of long-needled pine
ripple in the breeze that swirls,
ice crystals sprout
frosty needles in a glaze.
Pine cones peer through
gossamer-white quills,
waiting for wings to fly.

Blossoms of cherry trees perfume the air,
fragrance delicious to serve a feast.
Hummingbirds ballet on tiny toes
quench their thirst on vernal nectar.
Honeybees jitterbug in frenzied play
delight to the spirit,
sensational notation.

Karen Jean Matsko Hood ©2014
Published in *Strawberry Delights Cookbook*, 2014
By Whispering Pine Press International, Inc. 2014

Strawberry Syrup

Deep crimson mason jars lined in rows.
Carefully sealed golden lids,
Collect dust on uneven birch shelves
Trimmed with yellow paint that peels.

Old, worn hands cracked with age
Squeeze juice from berries picked before.
Strawberries hide behind olive leaves
Framed in carmine gold in forest clearings.

Search that brings
Fond memories,
Bind up our belongings
In the old blue Chevy.

Drive the stick-shift
Down the road,
Up to the foothills
Below Montana's Rocky range.

Right by the road
We stop,
Papa, Mom, and me,
Look through the

Myriad of verdant greens,
To find the tiny crimson berries,
The sweet, scarce,
Unrevealing strawberries.

Karen Jean Matsko Hood ©2014
Published in *Strawberry Delights Cookbook*, 2014
By Whispering Pine Press International, Inc. 2014

Somewhere Between the Spice Bottles

There they are all lined in rows
to stand alphabetically. Parsley,
sage, rosemary and thyme
should actually be parsley, rosemary
sage and thyme in proper order,
but it is the musical tone we favor
and the lyrical notes we savor.

Is there room for tarragon or should
we replace the dill?
Can we find
sweetness among the cinnamon,
tartness among the lemon oil?
Is it the smell of vanilla bean
to prize among the bottles or
simply sweet fragrance that
hides the sour?

Karen Jean Matsko Hood ©2014
Published in *Strawberry Delights Cookbook*, 2014
By Whispering Pine Press International, Inc. 2014

Strawberry Delights Cookbook

A Collection of Strawberry Recipes
Cookbook Delights Series Book 15

Types of Strawberries

Types of Strawberries

There are basically three types of strawberry plants to choose from: Junebearing, Everbearing, and Day Neutral.

From these three types of plants more than 600 different varieties of strawberries are grown, each with its own look and characteristics. Strawberry varieties vary in size, shape, and color. They can be red, maroon, even off-white or yellow.

Junebearing strawberries produce a single, large crop per year during a 2 to 3 week period in the spring. Junebearers are the traditionally grown plants, producing a single flush of flowers and many runners. If you want to do some serious canning, then these strawberries are the ones you want to try. They are classified into early, mid-season and late varieties. The largest fruits are generally from June bearing varieties. This is a list of some of the kinds of Junebearers:

Early Season - Chandler, Earliglow, Sequoia, and Veestar.

Early Midseason - Honeoye, Hood, Kent, Red Chief, and Surecrop.

Midseason - Allstar, Benton, Cardinal, and Shuksan.

Late Midseason - Glooscap, Jewel, Lateglow, Rainier, Sparkle, and Tioga.

Everbearing strawberries are great as you can pick a few strawberries everyday the whole growing season. They produce two to three harvests of fruit intermittently during the spring, summer, and fall. Some kinds of Everbearers are: Fort Laramie, Ogallala, Ozark Beauty, and Quinault.

Day Neutral strawberries will produce fruit throughout the growing season. These strawberries also produce few runners. Everbearing and day neutral strawberries are great when space is limited, but the fruits are usually somewhat smaller than Junebearers. Some kinds of Day Neutrals are: Fern, Hecker, Selva, Tillikum, Tribute, and Tristar.

Local, state and regional strawberry trials are conducted by various governmental agencies and lists are published of the best modern varieties for home or commercial use. Make sure you choose a variety that is adapted to your climate. Consult your County Cooperative Extension or a strawberry nursery.

Strawberry Delights Cookbook

A Collection of Strawberry Recipes
Cookbook Delights Series Book 15

RECIPES

Strawberry Delights Cookbook

A Collection of Strawberry Recipes
Cookbook Delights Series Book 15

Appetizers and Dips

Table of Contents

Page

Strawberry Fruit Salsa and Cinnamon Crisps 50
Strawberry Glazed Meatballs 51
Grilled Fruit Antipasto Plate 52
Strawberry Chevre Spread 52
Cheesy Strawberry Salsa 53
Strawberry Dip... 54
Strawberries with Sweet Cheese 54
Strawberry Pineapple Chicken Bites 55
Chocolate Candy Bar Fondue 56
Strawberry Cheese Ball... 56
Strawberry Cheese Ring 57
Strawberry Supreme Cheesecake Dip... 58
Strawberry Ceviche 58
Strawberry Spring Rolls.. 60
Strawberry and Brie Bruschetta 61
Strawberry Coconut Crème Dip... 62
Red White and Blue Strawberries 62
Fruit and Cheese Quesadillas.. 63
Strawberry Chicken Kabobs 64

Strawberry Fruit Salsa and Cinnamon Crisps

This recipe always goes over well with children, and adults also enjoy its delicious taste. It is a great way to incorporate fruit and fiber into your diet. Whole wheat tortillas may be substituted for plain flour ones.

Ingredients for cinnamon crisps:

- 10 flour tortillas (10-inch size)
- 2   c. cinnamon sugar
      cooking spray, buttery flavored

Ingredients for salsa:

- 2   kiwis, peeled and diced
- 2   Golden Delicious apples, peeled, cored, chopped
- 8   oz. raspberries, mashed
- 1   lb. strawberries, mashed
- 2   Tbs. sugar
- 1   Tbs. brown sugar
- 3   Tbs. fruit preserves, any flavor

Directions for cinnamon crisps:

1. Preheat oven to 350 degrees F.
2. Coat one side of each flour tortilla with cooking spray.
3. Cut into wedges; arrange on baking sheet in a single layer.
4. Sprinkle wedges with desired amount of cinnamon sugar.
5. Spray again with cooking spray.
6. Bake 8 to 10 minutes; cool 15 minutes.
7. Repeat with any remaining tortilla wedges.
8. Serve with chilled fruit mixture for dipping.

Directions for salsa:

1. In a large bowl, thoroughly mix kiwis, apples, raspberries, strawberries, sugar, brown sugar, and fruit preserves.
2. Cover and chill in the refrigerator at least 15 minutes or until ready to serve.

Strawberry Glazed Meatballs

This is a wonderful appetize r that is great for a buffet table.

Ingredients for meatballs:

    1   lb. ground ham
    1   lb. ground pork
    2   eggs, well beaten
    1   c. milk
    2   c. breadcrumbs
        salt and pepper, to taste

Ingredients for sauce:

    1   c. brown sugar, firmly packed
    ½   c. strawberry preserves
    1   Tbs. dry mustard
    1¾ c. water
    ½   c. white vinegar

Directions for meatballs:

1. In large bowl, combine ham, pork, and eggs; blend well.
2. In another bowl, mix milk, breadcrumbs, and salt together.
3. Incorporate into the meat and eggs mixture until all is well blended and clings together.
4. Form into 1-inch meatballs and set aside.

Directions for sauce:

1. Preheat oven to 325 degrees F.
2. In small saucepan, combine sugar, mustard, and preserves and blend well.
3. Add vinegar and water to mixture; stir well to blend.
4. Pour over meatballs.
5. Bake 1 hour, basting frequently.
6. Drain or skim off fat and serve meatballs and sauce in a chafing dish or crock pot, with toothpicks on the side.

Grilled Fruit Antipasto Plate

This is a nice appetizer to serve when having an outdoor barbecue.

Ingredients:

1	Tbs. brown sugar
1	Tbs. white balsamic vinegar
2	Tbs. extra virgin olive oil
2	Tbs. fresh lime juice
2	tsp. vanilla extract
¼	tsp. black pepper, freshly ground
⅛	tsp. salt
⅛	tsp. hot sauce
1	lb. firm bananas, peeled, chopped
1	lb. ripe strawberries, washed, hulled, halved
1	lb. firm apples, cored, sliced
½	lb. peaches, peeled, pitted, sliced
	cooking spray
	mint sprigs, for garnish

Directions:

1. To prepare dressing, combine first 8 ingredients in a small bowl, stirring well with a whisk.
2. To prepare fruit, place whole fruit on grill rack coated with cooking spray, grilling 3 to 4 minutes on each side.
3. Remove from grill and chop, halve, or slice according to ingredient instruction for each fruit.
4. Drizzle fruit with dressing; garnish with mint sprigs.

Strawberry Chevre Spread

This is a wonderfully creamy spread and is great for breakfast or as an appetizer.

Ingredients:

6	oz. Chevre cheese
8	oz. cream cheese

¼ c. nonfat plain yogurt
⅓ c. strawberries, hulled and mashed
1   tsp. almond extract

Directions:

1. In large bowl, combine all ingredients; mix until thoroughly blended.
2. Spoon the mixture into a serving bowl.
3. Refrigerate 2 hours, until slightly firm.
4. Keep chilled until ready to serve on a bed of ice chips to keep fresh.
5. Serve with toast, crackers, or fresh raw fruits for dipping.

Cheesy Strawberry Salsa

Part of this recipe is an easy, make-ahead type of appetizer, which enables the rest of it to be put together quickly at the last minute for the freshest taste possible.

Ingredients:

1   pt. strawberries, sliced
4   Roma tomatoes, seeded, chopped
1   jalapeno pepper, seeded, minced
2   garlic cloves, minced
1   lime, juiced
1   Tbs. olive oil
8   oz. cream cheese, softened

Directions:

1. In a large bowl, combine strawberries, tomatoes, jalapeno pepper, garlic, lime juice, and oil.
2. Toss all together to mix and coat.
3. Cover dish and refrigerate for 2 hours to chill.
4. Place cream cheese in a low salad bowl and cover with chilled salsa before serving.
5. Serve with plain tortilla chips.

Strawberry Dip

This is a great way to use fresh fruit trays as appetizers, and you can simply double the recipe if serving a large crowd.

Ingredients:

    1   c. sour cream
    8   oz. cream cheese, softened
    ½   c. sugar
    1   Tbs. strawberry extract
    ½   c. fresh strawberries
        assorted fresh fruit, cut into dipping-size pieces

Directions:

1. In a medium bowl, place sour cream, cream cheese, sugar, and strawberry extract.
2. With electric mixer, blend until smooth.
3. Chill in refrigerator for 30 minutes.
4. Garnish the dip with fresh strawberries.
5. Place serving bowl onto bed of crushed ice.
6. Serve with assorted fresh fruit pieces.

Strawberries with Sweet Cheese

This is a crowd pleaser and very simple to prepare.

Ingredients:

    ½   c. Mascarpone cheese
    1   Tbs. sugar
    ½   c. whipping cream
    4   c. strawberries, hulled, halved, divided
    8   Tbs. crème de cassis
    4   whole strawberries, for garnish

Directions:

1. In small bowl, beat cheese with sugar and whipping cream. Set aside.

2. Pour 2 tablespoons crème de cassis into each of 4 dessert dishes.
3. Add ¼ of the berries to each dish.
4. Top each dish with ¼ of the cheese mixture and decorate each dish with a whole berry set on top of cheese mixture.
5. Serve immediately.

Strawberry Pineapple Chicken Bites

This is not only a great appetizer, but it can also be used as an entrée simply by adding a half a cup of cubed bell pepper along with the pineapple and a few tablespoons of pineapple juice over top of white rice. Garnish your entrée with a sprinkle of slivered almonds.

Ingredients:

2   Tbs. olive oil
2   lb. skinless, boneless chicken breasts, cut into sm. chunks
1   jar strawberry preserves (12 oz.)
1   jar chili sauce (8 oz.)
1   can pineapple chunks (8 oz.)
1   dash salt
1   dash ground black pepper
    toothpicks, for serving

Directions:

1. Heat olive oil in a skillet over medium-high heat.
2. Add chicken; cook for 5 minutes, until browned on all sides.
3. Reduce heat to medium; pour in preserves and chili sauce.
4. Cook for 10 minutes stirring occasionally.
5. Mix pineapple chunks into skillet.
6. Season with salt and pepper.
7. Continue cooking 2 minutes, until heated through.
8. Serve hot in a chafing dish or a crock pot, along with toothpicks.

Chocolate Candy Bar Fondue

This makes a delicious and rich chocolate dessert that can be made ahead of time and reheated when ready to use.

Ingredients:

    5   med. chocolate candy bars
    1   c. heavy whipping cream
    2   Tbs. corn syrup
    ¼   c. brandy
    12 lg. fresh, whole strawberries, rinsed, stems intact

Directions:

1. Break and melt candy bars in the top of a double boiler.
2. Stirring continuously, add the cream.
3. Immediately add the corn syrup and keep stirring; turn off the heat.
4. Cover until ready to serve.
5. When ready to serve, place strawberries on a tray and serve beside the fondue pot.

Strawberry Cheese Ball

This cheese ball tastes great served with celery sticks or your favorite crackers, and it also makes a great gift to give to others.

Ingredients:

    1   c. pecans, finely chopped
    ½   c. fresh parsley, chopped
    8   oz. Colby cheese, grated
    8   oz. blue cheese, crumbled
    8   oz. cream cheese, softened
    1   tsp. fresh garlic, minced
    1   Tbs. hot sauce
    2   tsp. hot pepper sauce
    1   c. strawberries, hulled, mashed

Directions:

1. Combine pecans and parsley in a small bowl, set aside; reserving 1 tablespoon.
2. In large bowl, combine cheeses, garlic, hot sauce, strawberries, and hot pepper sauce; mix until well blended.
3. Chill mixture in refrigerator for 1 hour.
4. Form chilled cheese mixture into ball shape.
5. Roll ball in pecan and parsley mixture.
6. Serve on center of a salad plate; garnish with reserved tablespoon of pecan and parsley mixture scattered around the ball on plate.

Strawberry Cheese Ring

This is a delicious appetizer for a hungry crowd when served with a basket of assorted crackers, bagel chips, or bread sticks for dipping. If you need a smaller amount, reduce each ingredient by one-half.

Ingredients:

1   lb. sharp Cheddar cheese, grated
1   c. pecans, chopped
¾   c. mayonnaise
1   sm. onion, grated
1   med. garlic clove, minced
½   tsp. hot sauce
1   c. strawberry preserves

Directions:

1. Mix all ingredients, except preserves, together.
2. Spray a 1-quart ring mold with nonstick vegetable spray, pressing mixture into mold, and then chill thoroughly.
3. When ready to serve, unmold onto a serving plate.
4. Spoon the strawberry preserves into center of the ring and serve.
5. Place serving dish on a bed of crushed ice to extend length of time for use. Discard any unused cheese mixture after it has warmed to room temperature.

Strawberry Supreme Cheesecake Dip

Try this delicious, creamy dip with your favorite crackers or chips.

Ingredients:

16 oz. cream cheese, softened
½ c. fresh or frozen strawberries
¼ c. sugar
¼ c. sour cream
1 Tbs. orange liqueur
1 tsp. vanilla extract

Directions:

1. In food processor or blender, add cream cheese, sugar, strawberries, sour cream, liqueur, and vanilla. Blend until very smooth.
2. Chill at least 2 hours.

Strawberry Ceviche

This is a delicious appetizer to make and serve for your special occasion or family get together.

Ingredients for fish:

3 c. strawberry salsa base, recipe follows
4 lb. white fish fillet, cleaned and trimmed, cut into cubes
4 Tbs. kosher salt
8 c. fresh lime juice
2 pt. strawberries
¾ c. cilantro, chopped
1 c. red onion, finely chopped
4 Tbs. fresh basil leaves, chopped
¼ c. dried hominy

Ingredients for salsa base:

1 basket ripe strawberries

2	New Mexico chiles
7	Chile de Arbol
3	lg. Roma tomatoes, quartered
1	Tbs. garlic, chopped roughly
½	c. red onion, diced
½	c. sugar
2	tsp. fresh oregano

Directions for fish:

1. Soak dried hominy in water overnight.
2. Cook hominy in salted water until tender, approximately 1 hour; cool.
3. Toss fish fillet with kosher salt. Let fish drain in nonmetal colander for 1 hour.
4. Transfer fish to a nonmetal bowl, cover with lime juice.
5. Cure for 2 hours, up to 4 hours, depending on personal preference.
6. Drain fish, but do not rinse; transfer to a nonreactive bowl.

Directions for salsa base:

1. Boil strawberries in water until soft and reserve ½ cup of the cooking liquid.
2. Remove the seeds from JUST the New Mexico Chiles.
3. In frying pan, heat all chiles in a little oil until toasted.
4. Simmer chilies in water until soft and reserve the chile liquid.
5. Sauté tomatoes in hot pan with oil until fairly soft.
6. Combine all ingredients in blender and add ¾ cup chile liquid. Purée until smooth.
7. Strain through fine strainer and adjust seasoning with salt and pepper. Cool.
8. Note: If a sweeter taste is desired, add a little of the strawberry cooking liquid. If a spicier taste is desired, add a little more chile cooking liquid.
9. Toss fish with strawberry salsa base and let flavors meld for 30 minutes.
10. Dice strawberries; add berries, cilantro, basil, hominy, and onion to ceviche mixture. Chill 15 minutes and serve.

Strawberry Spring Rolls

Try this sweet and savory appetizer. Enjoy!

Ingredients for dipping sauce:

½ c. strawberries, sliced, stemmed
2 Tbs. rice vinegar
1 Tbs. Asian sesame oil
1 Tbs. sugar
2 tsp. Vietnamese fish sauce
½ tsp. chili flakes

Ingredients for spring rolls:

¾ lb. shrimp, shelled, cooked
¾ tsp. seasoned rice vinegar
8 spring roll wrappers
16 mint leaves
16 cilantro sprigs
¾ c. strawberries, stemmed, quartered
1 c. cucumber, peeled, seeded, cut into strips 2 x ¼-inch

Directions for dipping sauce:

1. In blender or food processor, purée strawberries, vinegar, oil, sugar, and fish sauce until smooth.
2. Add chili flakes; blend until chili flakes are still visible.

Directions for spring rolls:

1. In bowl, toss shrimp with vinegar; set aside.
2. Dip 1 wrapper into very hot water for a few seconds until soft and flexible.
3. Blot on towel to remove excess water.
4. Place 2 mint leaves, 2 cilantro sprigs, 3 pieces strawberry, 3 shrimp, and 3 cucumber strips in a line down the center of wrapper.
5. Fold bottom over filling, fold in sides and roll up into tight cylinder.

6. Fold bottom over filling, fold in sides and roll up into tight cylinder.
7. Repeat with remaining ingredients to make 8 rolls. Serve each roll with 1 tablespoon sauce.
8. Tip: Rolls may be made up to 8 hours ahead.
9. Place in a single layer on plastic wrap-lined pan.
10. Cover with plastic wrap.
11. Refrigerate until needed.

Strawberry and Brie Bruschetta

This is a delicious appetizer to serve for your special occasion.

Ingredients:

12 slices Sourdough Baguette
⅓   c. butter, softened
⅓   c. brown sugar, packed
2   tsp. ground cinnamon
12 oz. Brie cheese
5   c. strawberries, sliced
½   tsp. vanilla extract
1   c. almonds, sliced

Directions:

1. Preheat oven to 375 degrees F.
2. Spread 1 side of each bread slice with butter.
3. Arrange butter side up on baking sheet.
4. In a small bowl, combine brown sugar and cinnamon.
5. Sprinkle 1 teaspoon over each slice of bread; save remaining mixture.
6. Toast bread for 5 minutes.
7. Top each slice with 1 slice of Brie cheese.
8. Place back in oven for 4 to 6 minutes.
9. In large bowl, toss strawberries, vanilla, and remaining sugar-cinnamon mixture.
10. Spoon strawberry mixture over each slice.
11. Sprinkle with toasted almonds.

Strawberry Coconut Crème Dip

This is a delicious dip to serve with your favorite fruits.

Ingredients:

1 c. marshmallow crème
1 Tbs. strawberry preserves
1 c. sour cream
½ c. coconut, toasted

Directions:

1. In small bowl, heat marshmallow crème in microwave for 45 seconds until warm.
2. Stir in preserves and sour cream. Chill.
3. Serve with fresh fruit as a dip.
4. Roll dipped bananas or pineapple in toasted coconut.
5. Note: To toast coconut: In microwave, place coconut on a paper plate; cook on medium-high for 3 minutes.

Red White and Blue Strawberries

This is a perfect appetizer to serve on any patriotic holiday.

Ingredients:

12 each fresh strawberries
24 each fresh blueberries
½ c. yogurt or filling of choice

Directions:

1. Select 12 good quality strawberries; slice each strawberry in half. The green leaves can be kept on if desired.
2. Use a melon ball scoop to remove the center of each half slice of the strawberry and set prepared berries aside.
3. Fill each scooped half slice of strawberry with 1 teaspoon of yogurt or any white filling desired, such as a fruit dip, custard, pudding, or whipped topping.
4. Top each filling with a blueberry. Serve or chill.

Fruit and Cheese Quesadillas

These are wonderful little treats that people of all ages enjoy, and they are healthy at the same time.

Ingredients:

½   c. dried apricots, chopped
1   tsp. orange peel, grated
6   Tbs. strawberry nectar
2   c. part-skim ricotta cheese
6   Tbs. honey, or to taste
1   tsp. ground coriander
12 flour tortillas (7 to 9-inch diameter)
2   c. fresh or canned pineapple, chopped, drained well
1   c. fresh strawberries, hulled, sliced
    mint sprigs, for garnish

Directions:

1. Preheat oven to 450 degrees F.
2. In a bowl, combine apricots, orange peel, and strawberry nectar; let stand until apricots are softened, 20 minutes.
3. In food processor or blender, combine apricot mixture, ricotta cheese, coriander, and honey; blend until smoothly puréed. (At this point, you may cover and refrigerate for up to 2 days.)
4. Arrange 6 tortillas in a single layer on 2 or 3 lightly oiled large baking sheets.
5. Spread tortillas evenly with cheese mixture, covering tortillas to within ½-inch of edges.
6. Evenly cover cheese mixture with pineapple, then strawberries, then top each tortilla with one of the remaining tortillas; press together lightly.
7. Bake 7 to 9 minutes, or until tortillas are lightly browned, switching position of trays halfway through baking.
8. Slide quesadillas onto a board; cut each into 4 to 6 wedges.
9. Arrange on a platter and garnish with mint sprigs and strawberry slices, if desired.

Strawberry Chicken Kabobs

This is a great recipe for a hot summer day. Enjoy!

Ingredients:

1   c. lemon juice
2   cans pineapple chunks, juice reserved (8 oz. ea.)
2   tsp. ground cinnamon
3   skinless, boneless chicken breast halves, cubed
1   c. butter, melted
2   Tbs. brown sugar
1   tsp. ground nutmeg
24 lg. strawberries
    salt and pepper, to taste

Directions:

1. In a shallow glass bowl, combine lemon juice, juice from pineapple can, salt, pepper, and 1 teaspoon cinnamon.
2. Add cubed chicken; marinate 1 hour in the refrigerator.
3. Preheat grill to medium heat.
4. In small bowl, combine butter, 1 teaspoon cinnamon, brown sugar, and nutmeg.
5. Lightly oil grate.
6. Using metal or soaked wooden skewers, arrange chicken, pineapple chunks, and strawberries on each skewer.
7. Brush kabobs with butter.
8. Place on grill and cook 8 to 10 minutes, turning on all sides, until chicken is cooked through and strawberries are sizzling.

Did You Know?....

Did you know that Plant City, Florida, is the winter strawberry capital of the world?

Strawberry Delights Cookbook

A Collection of Strawberry Recipes
Cookbook Delights Series Book 15

Beverages

Table of Contents

Page

Strawberry Smoothie.. 66
Fresh Strawberry Punch... 66
Strawberry Yogurt Swirl... 67
Strawberry and Huckleberry Milkshake....................................... 68
Strawberry Lemonade.. 68
Coral Punch 69
Strawberry and Raspberry Milkshake 69
Strawberry Fruit Shake 70
Strawberry Frappe 70
Strawberry Ice 71
Strawberry Granita.. 72
Strawberry Juice Cocktail 72
Chocolate Strawberry Cordial Yogurt 73
Strawberry Malted Milkshake... 74
Strawberry Milkshake.. 74
Surprise Smoothie 75
Strawberry Slush... 75
Strawberry Frosty 76
Chocolate Strawberry Smoothie 76

Strawberry Smoothie

This strawberry drink can be made year round with frozen strawberries and stashed in the freezer.

Ingredients:

10-12	ice cubes
1	box frozen strawberries
1	c. water
1	c. milk
2	Tbs. sugar
1	tsp. vanilla extract

Directions:

1. Combine strawberries and water in blender; blend until smooth.
2. Add milk, sugar, and vanilla, blending completely.
3. Add ice cubes, 2 at a time; cover and blend after each addition, until smooth, 30 seconds.
4. Serve immediately in chilled glasses.

Yields: 4 to 6 servings.

Fresh Strawberry Punch

This is a delicious punch to serve guests or family for your special occasion.

Ingredients:

1	can pineapple juice (64 oz.)
1	can frozen orange juice concentrate
1	can frozen strawberry concentrate
2	c. sugar
2	qt. water
1	qt. lemon lime soda

⅓ c. lemon juice
3 ripe bananas
1 qt. fresh strawberries

Directions:

1. In large punch bowl, combine pineapple juice, both concentrates, sugar, water, soda pop, and lemon juice.
2. Mix well.
3. In blender, place bananas and strawberries; purée.
4. Add to liquid mixture.
5. Stir well.
6. Add ice and serve.

Strawberry Yogurt Swirl

Try this delicious drink on a hot summer day.

Ingredients:

6   strawberry flavored herbal tea bags
2   c. boiling water
½   c. honey
2   c. ice cubes
1½ c. strawberry yogurt

Directions:

1. In medium bowl, place tea bags.
2. Add boiling water.
3. Steep 4 minutes.
4. Remove tea bags.
5. Add honey and stir.
6. Add ice cubes.
7. Stir until melted.
8. In blender, combine tea mixture and yogurt.
9. Process until blended.
10. Chill and serve.

Strawberry and Huckleberry Milkshake

This Northwest milkshake is a delicious combination for all strawberry and huckleberry enthusiasts.

Ingredients:

- 1   c. fresh strawberries, rinsed, hulled
- 1   c. huckleberries, rinsed, stemmed
- ¾   c. milk
- ½   c. vanilla ice cream
- 3   tsp. brown sugar

Directions:

1. Place strawberries and huckleberries in a blender and purée.
2. Add milk, ice cream and sugar, blending until smooth.
3. Pour into chilled glasses and serve immediately.

Strawberry Lemonade

Strawberries combine with lemonade to make a wonderfully refreshing drink on a hot day.

Ingredients:

- 2   c. strawberries, rinsed, hulled
  lemonade

Directions:

1. Place strawberries in a blender and add lemonade sufficient to make 4 glasses of drink.
2. Strain to remove all the seeds; pour over ice into tall glasses, and serve immediately.

Yields: 4 servings.

Coral Punch

This is a tasty blend of colors and flavors to add to your next festival.

Ingredients:

- 2   cans pineapple juice (46 oz.)
- 1   qt. lemonade
- 3   qt. orange juice
- 1   qt. strawberry nectar
- 2   c. apple juice
- 2   qt. ginger ale

Directions:

1. Combine the juices, nectar, lemonade, and ginger ale in a large punch bowl or container, blend well.
2. Place ice cubes in container or place the punch bowl in a bed of ice to serve.

Strawberry and Raspberry Milkshake

This milkshake is delicious and popular with adults and children alike.

Ingredients:

- 1   c. fresh strawberries, washed, hulled
- 1   c. fresh raspberries, washed
- ¾   c. milk
- ½   c. vanilla ice cream
- 3   tsp. brown sugar

Directions:

1. Place berries in blender and purée.
2. Add milk, ice cream and sugar, blending until smooth.
3. Pour into chilled glasses and serve at once.

Strawberry Fruit Shake

This is an easy-to-make fruit shake. Enjoy the wonderful flavors.

Ingredients:

  1½ c. frozen strawberries, partially thawed
  1   c. plain yogurt
  ½   tsp. vanilla extract
  4   Tbs. frozen pineapple concentrate
      orange or pineapple juice, as needed

Directions:

  1. Place strawberries, yogurt, vanilla, and frozen concentrate into blender.
  2. While blending, add sufficient juice to make ingredients blend to a smooth consistency.
  3. Blend quickly, stopping blender once to push berries down with spoon.
  4. Serve immediately in chilled glasses.

Yields: 2 servings.

Strawberry Frappe

Use the best flavored strawberries you can find, and enjoy this simple drink, which allows one to enjoy the pure taste of strawberries.

Ingredients:

  16 oz. fresh strawberries, rinsed, hulled
  3   tsp. sugar
      milk, to cover berries

Directions:

  1. Fill glass half full with sliced strawberries.
  2. Add milk, just enough to cover berries.

3. Add sugar, blend in glass with hand-held blender on fairly high speed, until all lumps are gone and glass has filled up, or use a blender and purée.
4. Serve immediately in chilled glasses.

Strawberry Ice

This makes a pleasing bright red, thirst-quenching ice on a hot and busy day.

Ingredients:

1   c. sugar
⅔   c. water
6   c. strawberries, washed, hulled
¼   c. lemon juice

Directions:

1. A few hours or a day ahead of making strawberry ice, combine sugar and water in medium saucepan and bring to a boil, stirring to dissolve sugar.
2. Reduce heat and simmer for 5 minutes, then cool to room temperature and refrigerate until cold.
3. When ready to make ice slush, purée the strawberries in a blender producing about 3 cups of purée.
4. In large bowl, combine puréed strawberries, sugar syrup, and lemon juice.
5. Pour mixture into ice cream maker and freeze.
6. When ready to serve, remove the mixture from freezer, break up with fork and blend quickly in a blender.
7. Serve immediately, in chilled glasses and serve with spoon.

Did You Know? . . . .

Did you know that the English and French used the beautiful heart-shaped berries to landscape their gardens?

Strawberry Granita

Granitas are very refreshing, and this strawberry granita is really a great one that everyone is sure to enjoy.

Ingredients:

 1½ c. fresh, ripe strawberries, rinsed, hulled
 ½ c. sugar
 1 Tbs. lime juice

Directions:

 1. Place strawberries, sugar, and lime juice in a blender and purée very smooth.
 2. Strain mixture through a very fine mesh strainer to catch any seeds and force as much of the pulp through as you can. If the strainer clogs, empty the strainer into a glass bowl, clean the strainer, then return the berry purée to it and continue straining.
 3. Strain directly into a shallow container, and place in the freezer when completed.
 4. Freeze for 2 to 3 hours, stirring approximately every 20 minutes to break up any lumps or frozen film, rendering it very smooth.
 5. Serve in chilled stem glasses just before it freezes solid.

Yields: 2 servings.

Strawberry Juice Cocktail

This is a great drink with its combination of citrus juices and strawberries.

Ingredients:

 1 pt. strawberries, rinsed, hulled
 ⅓ c. orange juice
 ¼ c. grapefruit juice
 1⅓ Tbs. lemon juice
 2 Tbs. sugar

Directions:

1. Place strawberries in blender and sprinkle with sugar; let stand for 30 minutes in order to have as much juice as possible.
2. Add orange, grapefruit, and lemon juices to berry and sugar mixture, blending thoroughly.
3. Press this mixture through cheesecloth-lined strainer and chill in refrigerator.
4. When ready to serve, pour into chilled cocktail glasses and garnish each glass with a bright strawberry and slice of orange adhered to the rim.

Yields: 4 servings.

Chocolate Strawberry Cordial Yogurt

This is a quick-to-fix treat, which is really great to cool off with on a hot summer day.

Ingredients:

1   tub chocolate low fat frozen yogurt (64 oz.)
¾   c. fresh strawberries, rinsed, hulled
5   oz. maraschino cherry juice
8   maraschino cherries with stems, drained

Directions:

1. In large bowl, measure and mix together the yogurt, strawberries, and cherry juice.
2. Spoon mixture in batches, if necessary, into blender.
3. Blend each until smooth.
4. Pour into glasses and garnish each with a maraschino cherry.

Did You Know? . . . .

Did you know that strawberries are the only fruit that grow seeds on the outside?

Strawberry Malted Milkshake

Our family loves the classic malted milkshakes, and this great malt taste is delicious with strawberries.

Ingredients:

- 2 c. vanilla ice cream
- 1½ c. fresh strawberries
- ¼ c. milk
- 3 Tbs. malted milk powder
- 1 Tbs. sugar

Directions:

1. Place ice cream, strawberries, and milk into blender and blend quickly.
2. Add the malted powder and sugar; blend until smooth.
3. Pour into chilled glasses and serve immediately.

Strawberry Milkshake

This milkshake is very easy-to-make and popular with the children; also having the ingredients stashed away in your freezer makes it simple.

Ingredients:

- 2 c. vanilla ice cream
- 1 c. milk
- 10 oz. frozen strawberries with juice

Directions:

1. Place vanilla ice cream in blender container; add milk and the thawed strawberries.
2. Cover and blend until mixture is smooth.
3. Poor into chilled glasses.
4. Serve immediately.

Surprise Smoothie

This is a quick, delicious, and healthy breakfast drink that is also very good to serve for a snack.

Ingredients:

    2   c. fresh spinach
    1   Tbs. ground flax seeds
    1   med. banana
    1   c. frozen sliced peaches, unthawed
    1   c. frozen strawberries, unthawed
    1   c. chocolate soy milk

Directions:

1. In blender, place all ingredients.
2. Blend, stopping occasionally to press down fruit with a wooden spoon.
3. Once incorporated, blend 1 minute until thick and smooth.
4. Pour into a tall glass and drink with a straw.

Yields: 1 serving.

Strawberry Slush

This is an easy-to-make drink to enjoy on a nice, hot summer day.

Ingredients:

    3   c. strawberries
    1   c. ice
    1   c. water

Directions:

1. In blender, add all ingredients.
2. Blend until smooth.

Strawberry Frosty

This is a delicious frosty drink to enjoy on a hot summer day.

Ingredients:

- 1   c. strawberries, sliced
- 1   c. milk
- 2   c. strawberry sherbet
- 1   can crushed pineapple or sliced pears, undrained (8 oz.)

Directions:

1. In blender or food processor, combine strawberries, milk, 1 cup of sherbet, and pineapple. Cover; blend until smooth.
2. Pour into 4 glasses.
3. Top each with another scoop of sherbet.
4. Serve immediately.

Chocolate Strawberry Smoothie

This is a very easy-to-make, wholesome drink.

Ingredients:

- 1   Tbs. cocoa powder, unsweetened
- 1   Tbs. wheat germ
- ½   c. strawberries, frozen
- ½   c. soy milk, unsweetened
- ½   c. water
- 2   Tbs. sugar, or to taste

Directions:

1. In blender, place soymilk, water, strawberries, wheat germ, cocoa powder, and sugar.
2. Cover and blend to desired consistency.
3. Note: If you would like a creamier smoothie, add more soymilk or water to your taste.

Strawberry Delights Cookbook

A Collection of Strawberry Recipes
Cookbook Delights Series Book 15

Breads and Rolls

Table of Contents

Page

Strawberry Crumpets 78
Strawberry Pecan Bread 79
Strawberry Bread 80
Strawberry Bagels 80
Strawberry Rhubarb Hickory Nut Bread 82
Strawberry Scones 83
Strawberry Almond Muffins 84
Strawberry Banana Bread 85
Strawberry Cheesecake Muffins 86
Strawberry Chocolate Chip Bread 87
Strawberry Scone Delight 88
Strawberry Whole Wheat Bread 89
Strawberry Almond Bread 90
Strawberry and Apple Muffins 91
Strawberry Bran Muffins 92

Strawberry Crumpets

These are delicious served warm with butter and fresh raspberry jam or homemade jelly.

Ingredients:

    3   c. flour
    2   tsp. dry, active yeast
    2¾ c. warm water
    ½   c. fresh strawberries, washed, hulled, chopped
    1½ tsp. salt
    1   tsp. sugar or honey
    2   Tbs. powdered milk
    1   tsp. baking soda
    2   Tbs. warm water

Directions:

1. A crumpet ring is similar to an egg ring, but some 3 to 4 times larger in volume and about twice as thick. You can use instead a large cookie cutter, or just cook free form.
2. Combine yeast, sugar, and 1 cup warm water in mixing bowl. Cover with plastic wrap; stand in warm place for 10 minutes.
3. Sift flour, powdered milk, and salt into another bowl, blending well.
4. Make a well in center of flour; add yeast water and the additional 1¾ cups warm water.
5. Add strawberries, and then mix all ingredients, making a thick batter.
6. Cover with plastic wrap and let stand in warm place until dough rises and becomes bubbly, 1 hour.
7. Combine baking soda and 2 tablespoons warm water, and add this mix to dough, mixing well.
8. Cover and let mixture stand in a warm place for another 15 minutes.
9. Preheat a heavy based fry pan or skillet to medium heat and place crumpet ring(s) inside.
10. Place enough mixture into the center of each ring to

fill ¾ full. The dough does rise during cooking, and this needs to be allowed for rising.

11. Over medium heat, cook 4 to 8 minutes, until bubbles appear over entire surface and dough appears dry.
12. Remove ring, turn the crumpet over, and cook for a further 30 to 60 seconds to brown the top.
13. Remove from the pan and cool on a cake rack.
14. Note: If you find that the bottom is too dark, you are cooking too quickly.
15. Split and toast the crumpets and serve hot.

Strawberry Pecan Bread

I love pecans and strawberries, and this bread is a delicious combination of both.

Ingredients:

3   c. flour
1   tsp. salt
1   tsp. baking soda
2   Tbs. cinnamon
2   c. sugar
1¼ c. canola oil
4   eggs, beaten
2   c. strawberries, chopped
1   c. pecans, chopped

Directions:

1. Preheat oven to 350 degrees F.
2. Lightly grease three small bread pans.
3. In bowl, sift the flour, salt, baking soda, and cinnamon.
4. In large bowl, cream oil, eggs, and sugar together, blending well. Add dry ingredients to the creamed mixture; mix just until moistened.
5. Spoon batter into prepared pans.
6. Bake 1 hour, or until inserted toothpick comes out clean.
7. Remove from oven, turn out to cool on wire racks.

Strawberry Bread

Strawberries make great fruit bread, and this is a nice bread to serve as a snack or for brunch.

Ingredients:

- 3 c. flour
- 2 c. sugar
- 3 tsp. cinnamon
- 1 tsp. baking soda
- 1 tsp. salt
- 1 pkg. frozen strawberries, thawed, drained
- 4 eggs, beaten
- 1¼ c. canola oil
- 1 c. walnuts or pecans, chopped

Directions:

1. Preheat oven to 350 degrees F.
2. Lightly grease and flour two loaf pans.
3. In large bowl, mix flour, sugar, cinnamon, baking soda, and salt together.
4. Mash strawberries well, add eggs and oil.
5. Combine wet ingredients with flour mixture, blending well.
6. Fold in the nuts and stir gently.
7. Spoon into prepared loaf pans.
8. Bake 1 hour, or until inserted toothpick comes out clean.
9. Remove from oven and let stand 10 minutes; turn out onto wire rack to cool completely before slicing.

Strawberry Bagels

These bagels are sweet and chewy, and you may substitute the dried fruit for any other of your preference for a change of pace.

Ingredients:

- 2 c. warm water
- 4 Tbs. sugar

2   packets yeast
5-6 c. flour
2   tsp. salt
1   c. dried strawberries
2   tsp. raspberry extract
2   Tbs. cornmeal, for baking sheet
1   egg, mixed with 1 Tbs. water, for egg wash
    nonstick cooking spray
    parchment paper

Directions:

1. In small bowl, combine extract and berries to soften; set aside.
2. In small bowl, mix yeast, sugar, and warm water; let sit for 5 minutes, or until bubbly.
3. Add berry mixture to yeast mixture.
4. Mix in 4 to 5 cups of flour, until the dough gets stiff.
5. Turn dough out onto a floured table; knead for 5 minutes, adding flour as needed.
6. Place dough in greased bowl (use nonstick cooking spray) and cover with damp cloth. Let rise until double in size.
7. Punch down dough and divide into 12 balls.
9. Shape each ball into a bagel by placing a hole in center of each with your thumb, and then spin the dough on your finger to widen the hole.
10. After shaping bagels, place on parchment paper to rise for 15 minutes; covering with a tea towel.
11. While the bagels are rising, bring 12 cups of water and 1 tablespoon of sugar to a rolling boil.
12. Boil bagels for 2 to 3 minutes on each side for a total of 5 minutes. Remove bagels from water with a slotted spoon and place on paper towels to drain.
13. Sprinkle cornmeal on the same parchment paper used for rising bagels, and arrange boiled bagels.
14. Brush each boiled bagel with an egg wash, and sprinkle with poppy or sesame seeds if desired.
15. Bake in a preheated oven at 400 degrees F. for 25 to 30 minutes, or until golden brown all over.
16. Remove from oven; place on wire rack to cool.

Strawberry Rhubarb Hickory Nut Bread

The addition of hickory nuts makes this a very interesting and tasty bread.

Ingredients:

½	c. rhubarb, coarsely chopped
½	c. fresh strawberries, rinsed, hulled, crushed
1	c. sugar
1½	c. flour
1½	tsp. baking powder
1½	tsp. baking soda
1	egg
1	Tbs. milk
4	Tbs. butter, melted
½	c. hickory nuts, coarsely chopped

Directions:

1. Preheat oven to 350 degrees F.
2. Lightly butter an 8-inch loaf pan.
3. Let rhubarb and strawberries steep in ½ cup of sugar for 1 hour, or even overnight, stirring occasionally.
4. In small bowl, sift together remaining sugar, flour, baking powder, and baking soda.
5. Beat egg lightly; stir in ¼ cup of juice exuded from fruit.
6. Add milk and melted butter.
7. Mix dry ingredients into the wet, stirring just enough to mix.
8. Drain fruit again; fold into batter. Add nuts, mix gently.
9. Scrape batter into prepared pan.
10. Bake 1 hour.
11. Remove from oven; cool in pan 10 minutes.

Did You Know? . . . .

Did you know that Native Americans called strawberries "heart-seed berries"? They pounded them into their traditional cornmeal bread.

Strawberry Scones

Strawberry scones are great with breakfast, lunch, or as a snack any time of the day.

Ingredients:

   3   c. flour, sifted
   ¾   c. sugar
   4   tsp. baking powder
   1   tsp. salt
   1   c. butter
   5   lg. eggs, slightly beaten
   ½   c. milk
   2   c. strawberries, rinsed, hulled, chopped
   1   egg, for wash
       water

Directions:

   1. Preheat oven to 400 degrees F.
   2. Lightly grease a baking sheet.
   3. In large bowl, sift together flour, sugar, baking powder, and salt.
   4. Cut in butter until texture of coarse meal.
   5. Blend eggs with milk; stir into dry ingredients to form soft dough.
   6. Fold in strawberries.
   7. Turn dough onto floured board and roll or pat into two 8 x 12-inch rectangles, ½-inch thick.
   8. Cut each rectangle lengthwise through center then divide crosswise into 6 rectangles.
   9. Cut each piece into 2 triangles.
   10. Beat 1 egg with 2 tablespoons water for egg wash.
   11. Place on prepared sheet; lightly brush with egg wash.
   12. Bake 20 minutes.

Did You Know? . . . .

Did you know that the strawberry is the state fruit of Louisiana?

Strawberry Almond Muffins

The combination of almonds and strawberries makes for a tasty treat that your family will enjoy, and they will ask for seconds.

Ingredients:

- ½ c. butter, softened
- ¾ c. sugar
- 2 eggs
- ½ c. milk
- 1½ tsp. almond extract
- 1½ c. flour
- 1 Tbs. baking powder
- ½ c. whole wheat flour
- ¼ tsp. salt
- 2 c. strawberries, rinsed, hulled, chopped
- ¾ c. slivered almonds

Directions:

1. Preheat oven to 375 degrees F.
2. Grease or paper-line muffin cups.
3. In large bowl, cream butter and sugar together.
4. Add eggs, one at a time and blend until fluffy.
5. Mix in milk and almond extract.
6. In separate bowl, sift together flours, baking powder, and salt.
7. Add flour mixture to milk mixture.
8. Blend just until combined; fold in strawberries and almonds.
9. Fill prepared-muffin cups ¾ full.
10. Bake 30 minutes, or until golden brown.
11. Remove from oven; turn out onto wire rack to cool.
12. Serve warm or cold with your favorite jam or jelly and butter.

Did You Know? . . . .

Did you know the Italian word for strawberry is fragola?

Strawberry Banana Bread

This bread has strawberries in addition to the bananas for a change of pace, and it also makes a perfect late night snack.

Ingredients:

½ c. butter
1 c. sugar
2 eggs
1½ tsp. vanilla extract
1⅓ c. flour
½ tsp. baking powder
½ tsp. salt
1 c. fresh strawberries, rinsed, sliced
1 ripe banana, mashed
½ c. pecans, chopped

Directions:

1. Preheat oven to 350 degrees F.
2. Lightly grease and flour medium loaf pan.
3. In large bowl, cream together butter, vanilla, and sugar.
4. Add eggs one at a time, beating until fluffy.
5. Sift together flour, baking powder, and salt.
6. Slowly add to creamed mixture, stirring just until blended.
7. Fold in strawberries, bananas, and nuts.
8. Spoon into prepared pan spreading evenly.
9. Bake 1 hour or, until inserted toothpick comes out clean.
10. Remove from oven.
11. Cool 10 minutes.
12. Turn out onto wire rack to cool completely.

Did You Know? . . . .

Did you know that a national survey found that strawberry lovers are said to be health conscious, fun loving, intelligent, and happy?

Strawberry Cheesecake Muffins

Cream cheese makes these muffins both different and delicious.

Ingredients:

4	oz. cream cheese, softened
¼	c. powdered sugar
2½	c. flour
1	Tbs. baking powder
½	tsp. salt
1	egg
1¼	c. milk
½	c. brown sugar
⅓	c. butter, melted
1	tsp. lemon zest
¼	tsp. vanilla extract
¼	c. strawberry jam

Directions:

1. Preheat oven to 375 degrees F.
2. Grease or paper-line muffin cups.
3. In small bowl, blend together cream cheese and powdered sugar until smooth; set aside.
4. In small bowl, beat together egg, milk, brown sugar, butter, lemon zest, and vanilla.
5. In large bowl, sift together flour; baking powder, and salt; add the wet ingredients, mixing just until moistened.
6. Spoon batter into prepared muffin cups to ½ full.
7. Add 1 tablespoon cream cheese mixture and 1 teaspoon of jam on top of each, filling each to ¾ full with remaining batter.
8. Bake 20 minutes, or until golden.
9. Remove from oven.
10. Cool in pan for 5 minutes.
11. Turn out onto wire rack to cool completely.
12. Serve while warm or cooled.
13. Store any remaining muffins in airtight container.

Strawberry Chocolate Chip Bread

This bread is absolutely delicious, and the children especially like the chocolate chips.

Ingredients:

½ c. butter
1½ c. sugar
1   tsp. vanilla extract
1   tsp. salt
1   tsp. lemon juice
4   eggs
½ tsp. baking soda
½ c. sour cream
3   c. flour
½ c. chocolate chips
1   c. strawberry preserves
1   Tbs. red food coloring

Directions:

1. Preheat oven to 350 degrees F.
2. Lightly grease and flour two loaf pans.
3. In large bowl, blend butter, sugar, vanilla, salt, and juice.
4. Beat in eggs one at a time.
5. Dissolve baking soda in sour cream; add to egg mixture.
6. Blend in the flour and fold in chocolate chips, strawberry preserves, and coloring.
7. Pour into prepared pans.
8. Bake 35 to 40 minutes, or until inserted toothpick comes out clean.
9. Remove from oven.
10. Cool 10 minutes.
11. Turn out onto wire rack to cool completely.

Did You Know? . . . .

Did you know that it is a longstanding tradition to serve strawberries at the Wimbledon Tennis Tournament?

Strawberry Scone Delight

Scones are always delicious. Add fresh strawberries, and they are even better.

Ingredients for scones:

2 c. flour
2½ tsp. baking powder
½ tsp. baking soda
1 tsp. salt
¼ c. sugar
1 egg
1 c. sour cream
1 tsp. strawberry extract

Ingredients for strawberry garnish:

fresh strawberries, rinsed, hulled
sugar
scones
whipping cream
powdered sugar
vanilla extract

Directions for scones:

1. Preheat oven to 400 degrees F.
2. Lightly spray a cooking sheet with cooking oil.
3. In medium bowl, combine flour, baking powder, baking soda, salt, and sugar.
4. In small bowl, combine egg, sour cream, and strawberry extract.
5. Make a well in the dry ingredients; add egg mixture.
6. Mix wet into dry slowly to make soft dough.
7. Turn out onto floured board and knead 10 times.
8. Separate dough in half; pat each half into a circle ½ to ¾-inch thick and 6 inches wide.
9. Cut each circle into 6 wedges and place on baking sheet.
10. Bake 20 minutes, or until lightly browned.
11. Remove from oven and place on wire rack to cool.

Directions for strawberry garnish:

1. Early in the day, slice strawberries; add a little sugar to taste; refrigerate until serving time, to allow juice to form.
2. Retain enough whole, perfect strawberries to garnish.
3. Just before serving, whip cream, sweetening with powdered sugar and vanilla.
4. To serve, cut scone in half and place bottom half on plate.
5. Spoon strawberries and some of the juice over top.
6. Spoon whipped cream over top of strawberries, top with other half of scone.
7. Garnish with small spoonful of whipped cream and whole strawberry.

Strawberry Whole Wheat Bread

This is a recipe my whole family loves. It makes great breakfast bread.

Ingredients:

2   c. whole wheat flour
1   tsp. baking soda
1   pinch cinnamon, ground
2   eggs
⅔   c. canola oil
1½ c. sugar
3   c. strawberries, chopped

Directions:

1. Preheat oven to 350 degrees F.
2. Lightly grease and flour a loaf pan.
3. In large bowl, sift together flour, baking soda, and cinnamon; set aside.
4. In large bowl, add oil, sugar, and eggs, mix well.
5. Add flour mixture; mixing well; fold in strawberries.
6. Spoon batter into prepared pan.
7. Bake 1 hour and 15 minutes, or until inserted toothpick comes out clean.
8. Cool 10 minutes; turn out onto wire rack to finish cooling.

Strawberry Almond Bread

This is a delicious strawberry almond nut bread that your family will really enjoy.

Ingredients:

10 oz. frozen sliced strawberries, unthawed
2 eggs
½ c. canola oil
1 c. sugar
1½ c. flour
1½ tsp. cinnamon
½ tsp. baking soda
¼ tsp. salt
1 c. almonds, chopped

Directions:

1. Preheat oven to 350 degrees F.
2. Grease and flour an 8-inch loaf pan.
3. In small bowl, beat eggs, sugar, and oil until fluffy.
4. Add strawberries.
5. In large bowl, sift together flour, cinnamon, baking soda, and salt.
6. Stir in strawberry mixture, mixing until well blended.
7. Fold in almonds.
8. Spoon dough into prepared pan.
9. Bake 1 hour and 10 minutes, or until toothpick test comes out clean.
10. Cool 10 minutes.
11. Turn out onto wire rack to cool completely.

Did You Know? . . . .

Did you know that strawberries were once avoided by pregnant women because it was believed that their children would be born with strawberry birth marks?

Strawberry and Apple Muffins

These muffins are delicious with the fruity and sweet flavors that mingle together.

Ingredients:

2	c. flour
1¼	c. sugar
2	tsp. cinnamon
½	tsp. salt
1½	c. apples, shredded
1½	c. strawberries, chopped
¾	c. coconut
½	c. dates, chopped
½	c. walnuts, chopped
3	eggs, well beaten
1	c. canola oil
½	tsp. vanilla extract

Directions:

1. Preheat oven to 350 degrees F.
2. Paper-line 24 muffin cups.
3. In small bowl, sift together flour, sugar, cinnamon, and salt.
4. In separate bowl, combine apples, strawberries, coconut, dates, and nuts.
5. In small bowl, combine eggs, oil, and vanilla.
6. Add to dry ingredients, mix well.
7. Fold in fruit and nuts blending until just mixed.
8. Spoon into prepared muffin cups, filling ⅔ full.
9. Bake 18 to 20 minutes.
10. Remove from oven.
11. Serve while still warm.

Did You Know? . . . .

Did you know that Strawberry Crater Wilderness is located in Arizona?

Strawberry Bran Muffins

These muffins are delicious, nutritious, and wonderful served right from the oven with butter.

Ingredients:

  1   c. flour
  ⅓   c. sugar
  1½ tsp. baking powder
  ¼   tsp. salt
  1   c. bran cereal
  1   c. milk
  1   egg
  3   Tbs. canola oil
  ¼   c. strawberry jam

Directions:

1. Preheat oven to 400 degrees F.
2. Lightly grease or paper-line 12 muffin cups.
3. In small bowl, sift together flour, sugar, baking powder, and salt; set aside.
4. In large bowl, add bran and milk; stir to combine.
5. Let stand 3 minutes, or until most of moisture is taken up.
6. Add egg and oil; beat well.
7. Add flour mixture, stirring just until combined.
8. Spoon batter evenly into prepared muffin cups.
9. Make deep indentation in top of batter of each muffin.
10. Fill each with 1 teaspoon jam.
11. Bake 20 minutes, or until golden brown.

Did You Know? . . . .

Did you know that the city of Ponchatoula, Louisiana, bills itself as "The Strawberry Capital of the World?

Strawberry Delights Cookbook

A Collection of Strawberry Recipes
Cookbook Delights Series Book 15

Breakfasts

Table of Contents

Page

Streusel Filled Strawberry Coffee Cake 94
French Toast with Strawberries 95
Finnish Soufflé 96
Strawberry Breakfast Sandwich... 96
Buttermilk Pancakes... 97
Strawberry and Chocolate Breakfast Quiche............................... 98
Chocolate Strawberry Waffles.. 99
German Pancakes Oven Style 100
Crêpes 100
Breakfast Strawberry Compote 101
English Muffins... 102
Buckwheat Pancakes... 103
Strawberry Breakfast Sundae 104
Strawberry Omelet 104
Strawberry Breakfast Chops... 105
Strawberry Breakfast Pizza... 106
Strawberry Breakfast Puff 107
Strawberry Crêpes 108

Streusel Filled Strawberry Coffee Cake

This is a wonderful breakfast cake that is fairly easy to make and so scrumptious there won't be a crumb left.

Ingredients for cake:

1½ c. flour
2½ tsp. baking powder
¾   tsp. salt
¾   c. sugar
¼   c. butter
¾   c. milk
1   egg

Ingredients for filling:

½   c. strawberry preserves
1   c. brown sugar
3   tsp. cinnamon
¾   c. nuts, chopped
3   Tbs. butter, melted

Directions for cake:

1. Lightly grease a 9-inch round layer or square pan.
2. In small bowl, sift together flour, baking powder, and salt.
3. In large bowl, cream together sugar, butter, and egg. Add milk and mix well.
4. Slowly add dry ingredients to the egg and milk mixture, beating until smooth.
5. Divide batter in half; spread half the batter in the prepared pan; reserving the other half.

Directions for filling:

1. Preheat oven to 375 degrees F.
2. Combine filling ingredients; divide in half, adding the strawberry preserves to one of the halves and reserve remaining other half.

3. Drop small spoonfuls of the preserves filling over batter in the pan.
4. Top with the reserved batter, then the remaining filling mixture without the preserves.
5. Bake 25 to 30 minutes, or until inserted toothpick comes out clean.
6. Remove from oven.
7. Cut into squares and serve warm with butter.

French Toast with Strawberries

My daughter, Mikayla, likes French toast, and this recipe is designed for a large group but is easily halved for a smaller family.

Ingredients:

8   eggs
6   c. milk
24 thick slices French bread
1   Tbs. butter
4   c. fresh strawberries, hulled, rinsed
1   c. sugar
2   c. sweetened whipped cream

Directions:

1. Place strawberries in large bowl and mash with a potato or pinto bean masher.
2. Add 1 cup sugar as you are mashing berries; mash until all berries are broken apart; set aside to absorb sugar.
3. Beat eggs in a small mixing bowl until light and fluffy.
4. Add milk and mix thoroughly.
5. Heat a griddle or frying pan to medium-high; melt butter on the surface.
6. Dip bread into egg mixture.
7. Brown on the griddle, turning the bread one time to cook the other side.
8. Serve at once with strawberries and whipped cream.

Finnish Soufflé

This is a light and fluffy dish that is baked in a hot oven and will be puffy in the pan, as it is brought to the table straight from the oven.

Ingredients:

- 4   lg. eggs
- 2   c. milk
- 2   Tbs. sugar
- ½   tsp. salt
- ½   c. flour
- ½   tsp. vanilla extract
- 4   Tbs. butter, melted
        fresh strawberries or jam

Directions:

1. Preheat oven to 450 degrees F.
2. Melt butter in a 9 x 13-inch pan.
3. In large bowl, beat together milk, eggs, sugar, flour, salt, and vanilla.
4. Pour batter on top of melted butter.
5. Bake 18 to 23 minutes.
6. Remove from oven and serve directly from the pan with fresh strawberries or preserves and butter.
7. Note: Cut and serve right from the pan, as it will deflate as soon as you cut into it.

Strawberry Breakfast Sandwich

Try this delicious strawberry breakfast sandwich!

Ingredients:

- 1   pkg. low-fat cream cheese, softened (8 oz.)
- 1   Tbs. honey
- 1   tsp. lemon zest, grated
- 4   English muffins, split, toasted

2   c. strawberries, sliced and hulled (10 oz.)

Directions:

1. In food processor or blender, process cheese, honey, and zest until well mixed.
2. Spread 1 tablespoon of the cheese mixture on cut side of 1 muffin half; top with ¼ cup strawberries.
3. Repeat with remaining ingredients to make 8 open-faced sandwiches.

Buttermilk Pancakes

There is nothing like waking up to the aroma of old-fashioned buttermilk pancakes in the morning.

Ingredients:

3   c. flour
3   Tbs. sugar
3   tsp. baking powder
1½ tsp. baking soda
¾   tsp. salt
3   c. buttermilk
½   c. milk
3   eggs
⅓   c. butter, melted
     canola oil

Directions:

1. In large bowl, combine flour, sugar, baking powder, baking soda, and salt.
2. In separate bowl, combine buttermilk, milk, eggs, and melted butter.
3. Heat a lightly oiled griddle or frying pan over medium-high heat.
4. Pour wet mixture into dry mixture; stir until just blended.
5. Pour ½ cup batter onto the griddle. Flip when air bubbles form; brown on that side.
6. Serve hot with butter and syrup or fruit and whipped cream.

Strawberry and Chocolate Breakfast Quiche

Try this delicious quiche. It is definitely a family favorite with the yummy combination of chocolate and strawberries.

Ingredients:

3   eggs
½ c. flour
½ c. milk
½ c. cocoa
¼ tsp. salt
2   Tbs. butter, melted
2   Tbs. sugar
2   Tbs. sliced almonds
2   Tbs. powdered sugar
1   Tbs. butter, melted
3½ c. strawberries, sliced, sweetened with ½ c. sugar
1   c. heavy cream, whipped

Directions:

1. Preheat oven to 450 degrees F.
2. Lightly grease a quiche dish.
3. In large bowl, add eggs; beat well.
4. Stirring constantly, slowly add flour and chocolate.
5. Stir in milk, salt, butter, and sugar.
6. Pour into prepared dish.
7. Bake 12 minutes, or until brown and fluffy.
8. Remove from oven; sprinkle with almonds and sugar; drizzle with butter.
9. Top with berries and whipped cream; cut into quarters.

Did You Know? . . . .

Did you know that California is the largest strawberry producing state? California harvests 83 percent of the strawberries grown in the U.S. on approximately 24,500 acres.

Chocolate Strawberry Waffles

These waffles are actually chocolate waffles, and with the addition of fresh, sweet, summer strawberries in the batter and served over top, they become a mouth watering delight!

Ingredients:

> 3   eggs, separated
> ½ c. chocolate syrup
> 1½ c. flour
> ¼ c. canola oil
> 2   tsp. baking powder
> ¼ c. butter, melted
> ½ tsp. baking soda
> 2   c. sliced strawberries, divided
> 2   Tbs. sugar, divided
> 1   c. whipping cream
> ½ c. sour cream
> ¾ c. milk

Directions:

1. In small bowl, beat egg whites until stiff; set aside.
2. In large bowl, mix the flour, baking powder, baking soda, and 1 tablespoon sugar together.
3. In small bowl, beat egg yolks with sour cream, milk, and chocolate syrup.
4. In another small bowl, mix oil with melted butter.
5. Alternately add sour cream mixture and oil butter mixture to dry ingredients; mix until smooth.
6. Fold in egg whites and 1 cup of sliced strawberries.
7. Pour ½ cup of batter into a lightly greased waffle maker.
8. Cook for 4 or 5 minutes or until the steaming stops.
9. Repeat for the remainder of the batter.
10. In small bowl, whip the cream and the remaining tablespoon sugar until stiff and fluffy, but not dry.
11. Top hot waffles with sliced strawberries and whipped cream. Serve at once.

German Pancakes Oven Style

This is an easy recipe for busy families. Our entire family enjoys this easy-to-make oven puff pancake.

Ingredients:

    4   eggs
    1¼ c. milk
    1   c. flour
    ½   c. butter
         powdered sugar

Directions:

1. Preheat oven to 375 degrees F.
2. Slice butter into a 9 x 13-inch pan and put the pan into the oven until butter starts to sizzle; take the pan out.
3. Combine eggs and milk in blender; pulse 2 to 3 times, adding flour and blending until smooth.
4. Pour mixture into heated pan and return to oven.
5. Bake 15 to 20 minutes.
6. Remove from oven; tip out of pan onto serving platter.
7. Dust with powdered sugar and serve hot with butter, and your favorite syrup, or sliced strawberries and strawberry syrup.

Crêpes

This is a favorite of the Hood Family! The good thing about this breakfast is that everyone in your family can assemble their own and add their favorite fruits and toppings.

Ingredients:

    8   lg. eggs
    2   c. milk
    5   Tbs. butter, melted
    2   c flour, sifted
    1   c. sugar
         fresh strawberries

powdered sugar (optional)
whipped cream (optional)

Directions:

1. In blender, mix eggs, milk, butter, flour, and sugar.
2. In a lightly buttered skillet, on medium-high heat, pour in ½ cup batter.
3. When crêpe looks dry and light brown on the bottom, flip to other side and lightly brown.
4. Place on plate; fill with your favorite fresh strawberries or jam.
5. Top with powdered sugar and sweetened whipped cream if desired.

Breakfast Strawberry Compote

This is a refreshing fruit compote that is easy-to-make ahead of time. Serve with a dollop of yogurt or fresh cream, if desired.

Ingredients:

2   lb. strawberries, halved if large
1   lb. rhubarb, cut into ¾ -inch pieces
¾   c. sugar
3   Tbs. minced crystallized ginger
1   Tbs. fresh lime juice
¾   tsp. lime peel, grated
    yogurt or fresh cream (optional)

Directions:

1. In medium saucepan, combine strawberries and rhubarb.
2. Mix in sugar, ginger, lime juice, and peel.
3. Cook over high heat until sugar dissolves, stirring often.
4. Boil 4 minutes, stirring often.
5. Reduce heat to medium.
6. Simmer, just until rhubarb is beginning to fall apart, about 3 minutes; remove from heat.
7. Stir in remaining strawberries; cool.
8. Chill until cold, at 1 hour and up to 1 day.

English Muffins

Homemade English muffins are the best, and they are delicious with homemade strawberry preserves.

Ingredients:

    3   c. bread flour
    2   tsp. dry active yeast
    1½ tsp. salt
    1   tsp. sugar
    2   c. warm water

Directions:

1. In a large bowl, measure dry ingredients adding most of the warm water.
2. Mix thoroughly, taking great care not to make the dough too wet.
3. Note: To speed up the rising and ensure that the dough is not too moist, you can scrape the dough out of the bowl onto a well floured board and knead for approximately 30 seconds, but it is not necessary.
4. When fully mixed, cover dough with plastic wrap; place bowl somewhere warm to rise, until double in size.
5. Tip dough out onto a floured board; shape until smooth.
6. Divide dough evenly into 12 pieces and shape each into smooth round balls.
7. Note: Muffins can be made larger or smaller just by dividing the dough into different numbers of pieces.
8. Flatten balls of dough to ¾-inch thick.
9. Set aside on a lightly floured surface to rise until double in size.
10. Heat a frying pan to a medium heat and lightly oil.
11. Cook each muffin for 5 to 6 minutes each side, longer if thicker.
12. Cool.
13. To serve, they can be split and slowly toasted.
14. Serve with strawberry jam.

Buckwheat Pancakes

My mom used to make me buckwheat pancakes as a child. I loved them with chokecherry syrup, but they are also enjoyable with strawberry syrup.

Ingredients:

1½ c. flour
½   c. buckwheat flour
1   tsp. salt
1   tsp. baking soda
1   tsp. baking powder
2   c. buttermilk
2   eggs, lightly beaten
¼   c. honey
1   Tbs. butter, melted
½   c. sunflower seeds, toasted

Directions:

1. In large mixing bowl, sift together flours, salt, baking soda, and baking powder.
2. In another bowl, whisk together buttermilk, eggs, honey, and butter.
3. Combine wet ingredients with dry and stir with wooden spoon to combine; batter will be slightly lumpy.
4. Brush hot griddle with oil; pour ¼ cup of batter onto the griddle, leaving 1 inch between pancakes.
5. Immediately sprinkle each pancake with 1 tablespoon of sunflower seeds.
6. Cook one side of the pancake until bubbles begin to break on surface and underside is brown.
7. Flip and brown; do not overcook.
8. Serve with butter and your favorite syrup.

Did You Know? . . . .

Did you know people in ancient times could only hope to dream of strawberries? It was a good sign. For instance, the wife of a young man who dreamt of the sweet fruit was sure to be a sweetheart and bear him many children, all boys.

Strawberry Breakfast Sundae

All children will love this delicious breakfast sundae and it is nutritious too! It is also easy to double or triple this recipe.

Ingredients:

- ½   c. Cheerios cereal
- ½   c. vanilla or strawberry flavored yogurt
- 1   Tbs. strawberry jam
- 2   big fresh strawberries, sliced
- 1   big fresh strawberry, whole

Directions:

1. In the bottom of a parfait glass, place the tablespoon of strawberry jam.
2. Put ¼ cup of Cheerios on top of jam.
3. Cover with half of the sliced strawberries.
4. Put ¼ cup yogurt over strawberries.
5. Cover with remaining Cheerios and repeat the above steps.
6. Garnish top with the whole strawberry.

Strawberry Omelet

This is a change of pace from your every day omelet. Enjoy!

Ingredients:

- ½   c. strawberries, washed, stemmed, and sliced
- 1   Tbs. strawberry preserves
- 1   tsp. brown sugar
- 1   Tbs. butter
- 3   eggs, lightly beaten
- ½   oz. sweet vermouth
-     sour cream
-     whole strawberry, for garnish

Directions:

1. Toss strawberries with preserves and sugar. Set aside.

2. Heat an 8-inch omelet pan over medium-high heat.
3. Add butter, heating until bubbly.
4. Pour in eggs; cook until set on the bottom but still moist.
5. Lift edges gently with rubber spatula and rotate pan to let uncooked eggs run under.
6. Spoon strawberry mixture over half of the eggs.
7. Cook just until eggs fluff.
8. Remove from heat; sprinkle with vermouth.
9. Fold in half to enclose filling. Slide onto serving plate.
10. Top with sour cream and whole strawberry.

Strawberry Breakfast Chops

The unusual combination of strawberries, cayenne pepper, and garlic will help get you motivated in the morning! Enjoy!

Ingredients:

2	pork chops
¼	c. strawberry preserves
4	fresh strawberries, for garnish
1	Tbs. prepared horseradish
1	Tbs. soy sauce
1	Tbs. butter
1½	Tbs. garlic, minced
1	pinch of cayenne pepper

Directions:

1. In small saucepan, combine preserves, horseradish, soy sauce, and garlic.
2. Cook over low heat, stirring often until completely heated.
3. Melt butter in a medium size skillet.
4. Lightly sprinkle some cayenne pepper on both sides of each pork chop. Fry chops until browned on both sides.
5. Continue to cook over medium heat until they are no longer pink, and the juices are clear.
6. Serve with the strawberry sauce poured on top.
7. Garnish with fresh strawberries.

Strawberry Breakfast Pizza

Try this delicious breakfast pizza. Children and adults alike will love it.

Ingredients for crust:

1	c. flour
1	stick butter
¼	c. powdered sugar

Ingredients for filling:

8	oz. cream cheese, softened
½	c. sugar

Ingredients for topping:

1	c. strawberry glaze (8-10 oz. jar)
1	sm. basket of strawberries, ripe, sliced

Directions for crust:

1. Preheat oven to 325 degrees F.
2. In small bowl, combine all ingredients; blend well.
3. Pat into bottom of a pizza pan evenly.
4. Bake until golden brown, 8 to 10 minutes; cool.

Directions for filling:

1. In small bowl, combine cream cheese and sugar.
2. Beat until very smooth and soft.
3. Spread over cooled crust.

Directions for topping:

1. In small bowl, combine glaze and strawberries.
2. Spread on top of pizza.
3. Chill 1 hour. Serve with whipped cream or topping.

Strawberry Breakfast Puff

This is a real treat for breakfast. Try this delicious recipe.

Ingredients:

- 1½ c. plain yogurt
- ¼ c. whipped topping
- 1 Tbs. honey
- 1 tsp. banana extract
- ¾ c. milk
- 3 lg. eggs
- ½ c. plus 1 Tbs. flour
- 1 Tbs. sugar
- 1 Tbs. butter
- 2 c. strawberries, whole, hulled
- ½ med. banana, sliced, sprinkled with lemon juice

Directions:

1. Spoon yogurt into a paper towel-lined strainer.
2. Place over bowl.
3. Refrigerate at least 3 hours or overnight to drain.
4. Preheat oven to 400 degrees F.
5. In medium bowl, combine drained yogurt, whipped topping, honey, and banana extract; set aside.
6. In blender or food processor, combine milk, eggs, flour, and sugar; blend until smooth.
7. Place butter in a 10-inch oven-proof skillet.
8. Place skillet in oven for 3 minutes.
9. Using pot holder to protect hands, swirl butter to cover surface of skillet.
10. Immediately pour in batter; return skillet to oven.
11. Bake 25 to 30 minutes, until puffed and golden.
12. Slide pancake onto rack with spatula; cool 10 minutes; place on plate.
13. Spoon yogurt mixture into center of pancake; top with strawberries and bananas.
14. To serve cut into 6 wedges.

Strawberry Crêpes

Try these delicious crêpes. They are definitely a family favorite.

Ingredients:

3 eggs
½ c. flour
½ c. milk
¼ tsp. salt
2 Tbs. butter, melted
2 Tbs. sugar
2 Tbs. powdered sugar
2 Tbs. sliced almonds
1 Tbs. butter, melted
1 Tbs. lemon juice
3½ c. strawberries, sliced, sweetened with ½ c. sugar
1 c. heavy cream, whipped

Directions:

1. Preheat oven to 450 degrees F.
2. Lightly grease a 9-inch quiche dish.
3. In small bowl, beat eggs well, slowly adding flour and beating constantly.
4. Stir in milk, salt, butter, and sugar.
5. Pour into prepared dish.
6. Bake 12 minutes, or until brown and fluffy.
7. Remove from oven; sprinkle with almonds and powdered sugar.
8. Drizzle with mixture of butter and lemon juice.
9. Top with berries and whipped cream.
10. Cut into quarters.

Did You Know? . . . .

Did you know that 70 percent of a strawberry's roots are located in the top three inches of soil?

Strawberry Delights Cookbook

**A Collection of Strawberry Recipes
Cookbook Delights Series Book 15**

Cakes

Table of Contents

                                                                      Page

Ginger Orange Strawberry Shortcakes 110

Strawberry and Huckleberry Cake 111

Strawberry Peach Delight 112

Strawberry Pecan Roulade 113

Strawberry Jelly Roll Cake 114

Strawberry Chocolate Mousse Cake 115

Strawberry Shortcake Biscuits with Almonds 116

Strawberry Pound Cake 117

Strawberry Chiffon Cake 118

Strawberry Torte Meringue Style 119

Strawberry Torte Ladyfinger Style 120

Strawberry Shortcake 121

Strawberry Angel Cake 122

Strawberry, Blueberry, and Raspberry Tart 123

Strawberry Upside-Down Cake 124

Ginger Orange Strawberry Shortcakes

This makes a refreshing contrast of flavors with the ginger and orange creating a delicious and flavorful combination for this shortcake.

Ingredients:

2	c. flour
2	Tbs. sugar
1	Tbs. baking powder
½	tsp. baking soda
¼	tsp. salt
½	c. butter
2	Tbs. crystallized ginger, finely chopped
1	Tbs. fresh ginger, finely chopped
1	Tbs. orange zest
½	c. sour cream
¼	c. milk
	milk
	sugar
	whipped cream
	fresh strawberries, sliced

Directions:

1. Preheat oven to 425 degrees F.
2. In large bowl, sift together flour, sugar, baking powder, baking soda, and salt.
3. Using pastry blender or 2 knives, cut in butter until mixture resembles coarse crumbs.
4. Add crystallized ginger, fresh ginger, and zest.
5. In small bowl, whisk together sour cream and milk; add all at once to dry mixture, stirring with fork to make soft, slightly sticky dough.
6. Gather into ball and place on lightly floured surface.
7. Knead dough gently 8 times, or until smooth.
8. Let rest 10 minutes on floured surface.
9. Roll out into 8-inch circle and gently lift onto baking sheet.

10. Lightly brush dough with a small amount of milk and sprinkle with sugar.
11. Bake 20 minutes, or until top is golden brown.
12. Remove from oven; place on wire rack to cool.
13. Serve topped with strawberries and sweetened whipped cream.

Strawberry and Huckleberry Cake

Our children love this delicious combination of berries in a moist cake that will disappear quickly.

Ingredients:

> 1½ c. cake flour
> ⅔ c. sugar
> 2   tsp. baking powder
> ½   tsp. salt
> ⅓   c. milk
> 1   egg
> 3   Tbs. butter, melted
> 1   tsp. vanilla extract
> 1½ c. fresh or partially thawed huckleberries
> 1   c. fresh strawberries, hulled
>   sweetened whipped cream or vanilla ice cream

Directions:

1. Preheat oven to 400 degrees F.
2. Lightly grease an 8-inch square baking pan.
3. In large bowl, sift together flour, baking powder, and salt.
4. In medium bowl, beat together sugar, egg, and butter until fluffy; add vanilla and milk.
5. Add wet ingredients to flour mixture, blending just until moistened.
6. Fold in huckleberries and strawberries.
7. Spoon into prepared pan.
8. Bake 30 minutes, or until inserted toothpick comes out clean.
9. Remove from oven; cool in pan on rack.
10. Cut into squares; serve with ice cream or whipped cream.

Strawberry Peach Delight

This is an angel food cake that is beautiful to present as a healthy dessert after a heavier meal.

Ingredients:

- 1   c. cake flour
- 1   c. plus 2 Tbs. flour
- 14   egg whites (reserve yolks for another purpose)
- 1½ tsp. cream of tartar
- 1½ tsp. vanilla extract
- ½   tsp. almond extract
- 8   fresh peaches, peeled, sliced
- 2   c. fresh strawberries, rinsed, hulled, sliced
- 1½ c. sugar
- ¼   c. peach brandy (optional)

Directions:

1. Preheat oven to 350 degrees F.
2. In large bowl, sift flours together with ½ cup of the sugar, six times.
3. In another bowl, beat egg whites until frothy; add cream of tartar, vanilla, and almond extract.
4. Continue beating until egg whites stay in the bowl when inverted.
5. Fold the remaining cup of sugar into the egg whites 2 tablespoons at a time.
6. Fold the flour mixture into the egg whites 2 tablespoons at a time, for 100 folds.
7. Spoon the batter into an ungreased tube pan.
8. Bake for 60 minutes.
9. Remove from oven; turn out of pan and cool. Place on serving dish.
10. With serrated knife, at the top of the cake ¼-inch from inner and outer side, hollow out a 3-inch depth section to form a ring around top of cake.
11. Mix sliced strawberries, sliced peaches and ½ cup of sugar together.

12. Place fruit and sugar mixture in hollowed out ring of cake and drizzle with brandy if desired.
13. Chill on serving dish until ready to serve.

Strawberry Pecan Roulade

This is a great nut roll. The ground pecans take the place of flour and make this an excellent dessert.

Ingredients:

    6   eggs, separated
    ¾   c. sugar
    1   tsp. baking powder
    1½   c. pecans, finely ground
    1½   c. heavy cream
    ⅓   c. sugar
    1   tsp. vanilla extract
         fresh strawberries, sliced, for garnish

Directions:

1. Preheat oven to 350 degrees F.
2. Grease jelly roll pan, line with paper and grease well.
3. In small bowl, beat egg yolks with ¾ cup sugar until thick.
4. In small bowl, mix baking powder with pecans; fold into egg yolks.
5. In medium bowl, whip egg whites until stiff; fold in nut and sugar mixture just until blended. Spread in prepared pan.
6. Bake 20 minutes.
7. Remove from oven; cover cake with a damp tea towel, roll and chill in refrigerator for 1 hour.
8. Remove from refrigerator, unroll onto towel and remove paper.
9. Whip heavy cream until stiff; add sugar and vanilla gradually, continuing to whip.
10. Spread onto cake; chill 1 hour.
11. When thoroughly chilled, slice and garnish each serving with fresh strawberries.

Strawberry Jelly Roll Cake

I always enjoyed making strawberry jelly roll cake as a child, and now my children are enjoying it also.

Ingredients:

- 4   eggs, separated
- 1   tsp. vanilla extract
- ¾   c. sugar
- 1   c. cake flour, sifted
- ½   tsp. baking powder
- ¼   tsp. salt
- 10   oz. strawberry jelly or jam
       powdered sugar
       sweetened whipped cream

Directions:

1. Preheat oven to 375 degrees F.
2. Lightly grease a 15 x 10-inch jelly roll pan.
3. In medium bowl, beat egg yolks until foamy.
4. Add vanilla and sugar, beat until thick and pale.
5. Sift together cake flour, baking powder, and salt, gradually adding to egg yolk mixture by folding in while sifting.
6. In another medium bowl, beat egg whites until stiff but not dry, fold into egg yolk mixture.
7. Pour into prepared pan, smooth top.
8. Bake 12 to 15 minutes, or until top springs back when pressed lightly.
9. Remove from oven and invert onto clean tea towel sprinkled with powdered sugar.
10. Quickly peel off paper and trim edges of cake.
11. Starting at short end, roll up cake with towel.
12. Cool on wire rack. When cooled, unroll cake, spread with the strawberry jelly or jam.
13. Using towel again roll up cake, removing towel as you roll.
14. Place on long platter, seam side down. Dust with powdered sugar.

Strawberry Chocolate Mousse Cake

Creamy mousse makes a great combination with fresh strawberries.

Ingredients:

1 c. chocolate wafer crumbs
3 Tbs. butter, melted
2 pt. strawberries, rinsed, hulled, halved
2 c. semi-sweet chocolate chips
½ c. water
2 Tbs. light corn syrup
2½ c. whipped cream, divided
1 Tbs. sugar

Directions:

1. In small bowl, combine wafer crumbs and butter; blend well.
2. Press mixture evenly onto bottom of 9-inch springform or cheesecake pan.
3. Stand strawberry halves, touching, side by side, pointed ends up with skin sides against side of pan; set aside.
4. Place chocolate chips in blender.
5. In small saucepan, over medium heat, mix water and corn syrup, bring to a boil, and simmer 1 minute.
6. Immediately pour hot mixture over chocolate chips; blend until smooth.
7. Cool to room temperature.
8. Meanwhile, in large mixing bowl, beat 1½ cups of cream to form stiff peaks.
9. With rubber spatula, fold cooled chocolate mixture into whipped cream to blend thoroughly.
10. Pour on top of crumb mixture and smooth.
11. Cover; refrigerate 4 to 24 hours before serving.
12. When ready to serve, whip the remaining 1½ cups of whipping cream until cream forms stiff peaks.
13. Spread on top of cake after removing from refrigerator.

Strawberry Shortcake Biscuits with Almond

This is an excellent, biscuit-style shortcake made with buttermilk just like my mom used to make, and it is delicious.

Ingredients for topping:

1½ c. whipping cream, sweetened to taste
1   tsp. vanilla extract
4   c. fresh strawberries, sliced
⅓   c. sugar

Ingredients for biscuits:

2¼ c. flour
¼   c. sugar
1½ tsp. baking soda
¼   tsp. salt
⅓   c. cold butter, cut into sm. pieces
⅔   c. buttermilk
1   lg. egg
½   tsp. vanilla extract
⅓   tsp. almond extract
⅓   c. almonds, sliced
1   Tbs. sugar

Directions for topping:

1. In small bowl, with mixer, whip cream and vanilla until peaks form.
2. Mash strawberries with sugar; set aside to blend and sweeten.

Directions for biscuits:

1. Preheat oven to 375 degrees F.
2. In blender, place flour, ¼ cup sugar, baking powder, baking soda, and salt; combine well.
3. Add butter; pulse until mixture is crumbly.
4. In small bowl, blend together buttermilk, egg yolk, and extracts.

5. With blender running, add buttermilk mixture; pulse until mixture begins to come together.
6. Transfer dough to floured work surface and knead gently 4 or 5 times.
7. Sprinkle dough with flour; gently pat out until ¾-inch-thick. Cut into six 3-inch rounds; place on ungreased baking sheet and lightly brush tops with milk.
8. Top with almonds, sprinkle with 1 tablespoon of sugar.
9. Bake 20 to 25 minutes, or until golden brown.
10. Remove from oven; place on wire rack to cool for 3 minutes.
11. Turn biscuits on side and cut in half horizontally. Place on individual plates and spoon sweetened strawberries over the biscuits and garnish with the whipped cream.

Strawberry Pound Cake

Strawberries add moisture and flavor to this traditional pound cake. Make extra because it also freezes well.

Ingredients:

1⅓ c. sugar
1 c. butter, softened
4 eggs
2 c. flour
1 tsp. vanilla extract
⅔ c. fresh strawberries, mashed
pinch of salt

Directions:

1. Preheat oven to 350 degrees F.
2. Lightly grease and flour a 9 x 5-inch loaf pan.
3. In large bowl, cream together sugar, eggs, and butter.
4. In small bowl, sift together flour and salt; add to creamed mixture and mix well.
5. Fold in strawberries and vanilla, blending thoroughly.
6. Pour into prepared pan.
7. Bake 1 hour, or until inserted toothpick comes out clean.
8. Cool 10 minutes; turn out onto wire rack.

Strawberry Chiffon Cake

My mom made us many chiffon cakes when we were growing up, and strawberry chiffon is always a favorite.

Ingredients:

2½ c. cake flour, sifted
1½ c. sugar
3 tsp. baking powder
1 tsp. salt
¾ c. water
¼ tsp. almond extract
1 tsp. vanilla extract
½ c. canola oil (not olive oil)
6 egg yolks
8 egg whites
½ tsp. cream of tartar
3 c. fresh strawberries, hulled, sliced
whipped cream, sweetened

Directions:

1. Preheat oven to 350 degrees F.
2. Sift flour before measuring, then spoon lightly into cup.
3. In large bowl, sift flour again with sugar, baking powder, and salt.
4. In small bowl, whisk together water, extracts, oil, and egg yolks; blend well.
5. Add liquid mixture to dry ingredients and beat until smooth.
6. In large bowl, beat egg whites and cream of tartar until stiff. Fold batter into beaten whites gradually, turning bowl as you fold.
7. Spoon batter into ungreased tube pan.
8. Bake 65 minutes.
9. Remove from oven; cool in pan upside down on cake rack.
10. Loosen from sides and tube with spatula.
11. Cut into slices; top with whipped cream and sliced strawberries.

Strawberry Torte Meringue Style

This is a very refreshing, tasty, and light meringue-based layer with whipped cream and strawberry topping.

Ingredients:

4	egg whites
1	tsp. vanilla extract
1	c. sugar
¼	tsp. baking powder
⅛	tsp. salt
⅛	tsp. baking soda
1½	c. nuts, chopped
10	saltines, crushed fine
1	pt. strawberries, sliced
1½	c. heavy cream, whipped, sweetened to taste

Directions:

1. Preheat oven to 300 degrees F.
2. In large bowl, beat egg whites until soft peaks form; add vanilla while beating.
3. In small bowl, sift together dry ingredients; fold into the stiff egg whites.
4. Gently fold in nuts and saltines.
5. Spread in greased 9 or 10-inch pie pan. Bake 30 minutes.
6. Remove from oven, let stand for 10 minutes and then cool completely, before cutting into squares.
7. When ready to serve, place squares on individual serving plates and top with sliced strawberries and a dollop of whipped cream.

Did You Know? . . . .

Did you know that every strawberry plant is hand-picked approximately every three days? This is the time in which it takes strawberries to complete their cycle of turning from green to white to red. There is no storage of fresh strawberries, and after they are hand-picked, they are rushed to coolers where huge fans extract the field heat.

Strawberry Torte Ladyfinger Style

Try this strawberry torte with the ladyfingers and frozen strawberries that you have prepared for the freezer during the summer.

Ingredients:

1   pkg. cream cheese, softened (11oz.)
¾   c. sugar
2   tsp. vanilla extract
1   pt. heavy whipping cream
2   pkg. ladyfinger cookies (12 oz.)
4   c. frozen strawberries, sweetened
1   Tbs. cornstarch
    fresh strawberries, rinsed, hulled

Directions:

1. In saucepan, bring cornstarch and sweetened strawberries with the juice to a gentle boil.
2. Remove from heat and let cool.
3. In small bowl, whip the cream cheese, sugar, and vanilla together.
4. In a separate bowl, beat whipping cream until peaks hold.
5. Fold into cream cheese mixture.
6. Arrange ladyfingers around sides and bottom of 8 or 9-inch springform pan, standing ladyfingers upright around side and flat on the bottom of pan.
7. Spoon half of the cream filling into lined pan.
8. Place layer of ladyfingers on top of filling, finishing with the remaining cream filling.
9. Spread the cooled strawberry sauce over cake.
10. Place whole strawberries on top.
11. Refrigerate until chilled and set.
12. When ready to serve, remove sides from pan, slip cake onto serving plate and cut into wedges.
13. Top with a dollop of whipped cream if desired.

Strawberry Shortcake

My mom used to make us strawberry shortcake, and everyone loved it. Now my family looks forward to this summer treat, which we have often.

Ingredients:

3	c. flour
3½	tsp. baking powder
1	Tbs. sugar
½	c. butter
1	c. milk
2	pt. strawberries, sliced
⅓	c. sugar
1	c. heavy cream, whipped
1	Tbs. sugar
1	tsp. vanilla extract

Directions:

1. Preheat oven to 450 degrees F.
2. In large bowl, sift together flour, baking powder, and the 1 tablespoon sugar.
3. Cut in ½ cup butter.
4. Add milk and stir until blended.
5. On floured surface, knead dough briefly and roll out to ¼-inch thick.
6. Cut into twelve 4-inch rounds and place on ungreased baking sheet.
7. Bake 20 minutes.
8. Remove shortcakes from oven.
9. Cool on wire rack.
10. In small bowl, combine the berries and ⅓ cup sugar.
11. When ready to serve, split shortcake in half and mound with sweetened strawberries.
12. Top with other half of shortcake, spooning berries on the top.
13. Top with a dollop of sweetened whipped cream.

Strawberry Angel Cake

This is a light and fluffy angel cake sweetened with strawberries and whipped cream.

Ingredients:

- 1   c. cake flour
- 1¼ c. powdered sugar
- 1½ c. egg whites
- 1½ tsp. cream of tartar
- ¼   tsp. salt
- 1½ tsp. vanilla extract
- ¼   tsp. almond extract
- 1   c. sugar
- 2   c. strawberries, sliced
  sweetened whipped cream

Directions:

1. Preheat oven to 375 degrees F.
2. In large bowl, sift flour with powdered sugar 3 times.
3. Beat egg whites with cream of tartar, salt, vanilla, and almond extract until stiff.
4. Beat in sugar, 2 tablespoons at a time; continue to beat until meringue holds stiff peaks.
5. Sift ¼ of flour mixture over meringue; lightly fold in strawberries.
6. Carefully fold in the remaining flour by fourths.
7. Pour into an ungreased 10-inch tube pan.
8. Bake 30 minutes, or until inserted toothpick comes out clean.
9. Invert pan, remove sides and cool cake thoroughly on wire rack.
10. Serve topped with sweetened whipped cream.

Did You Know? . . . .

Did you know that strawberries are grown in every state in the United States and every province of Canada?

Strawberry, Blueberry, and Raspberry Tart

This is a colorful and flavorful tart that stores easily and can be made ahead for a busy-day dessert.

Ingredients:

1	single pie crust, uncooked
6	Tbs. butter, softened
½	c. sugar
1	lg. egg
¾	c. blanched almonds, finely ground
1	tsp. almond extract
1	Tbs. amaretto flavoring
1	Tbs. flour
2	c. strawberries, rinsed, hulled
2	c. blueberries, rinsed
2	c. raspberries, rinsed
½	c. strawberry jam, melted, strained

Directions:

1. Preheat oven to 375 degrees F.
2. Fit dough into a tart pan or springform pan with removable fluted rim; chill for 1 hour.
3. Cream together butter and sugar; beat in egg, almonds, almond extract, amaretto flavoring, and flour.
4. Spread mixture evenly on the bottom of pie crust shell.
5. Bake 20 to 25 minutes, or until shell is golden.
6. Remove from oven and place on wire rack to cool.
7. Cut strawberries lengthwise into ⅛-inch thick slices, then arrange slices, overlapping decoratively, alternating with blueberries and raspberries in rows on frangipane, and then, using a pastry brush, coat all fruit gently with jam.
8. Cut into individual servings.
9. Serve with a dollop of whipped cream if desired.

Did You Know? . . . .

Did you know that California produces one billion pounds of strawberries each year?

Strawberry Upside-Down Cake

This makes a delicious upside-down cake with the sweet and colorful strawberries to top it off.

Ingredients:

½   c. butter
1½ c. sugar
1   c. milk
2¼ c. flour
2   eggs
1   tsp. vanilla extract
½   c. butter
1   c. sugar
2   c. strawberries, sliced
      sweetened whipped cream

Directions:

1. Preheat oven to 350 degrees F.
2. In large bowl, cream sugar and butter.
3. Add milk and flour alternately; blend well.
4. Add eggs and vanilla extract; set aside.
5. In a 9 x 13-inch baking pan, melt butter.
6. Sprinkle 1 cup sugar over the bottom of the pan.
7. Spread strawberries evenly in pan and pour cake batter over top.
8. Bake 30 to 40 minutes, until lightly browned.
9. Remove from oven; let stand 20 minutes.
10. Turn cake upside down onto serving plate to cool.
11. Serve with sweetened whipped cream.

Did You Know? . . . .

Did you know that after colonists tasted the great taste of the Native Americans' bread, colonists decided to create their own version, which became the American favorite that we all know and love, Strawberry Shortcake?

Strawberry Delights Cookbook

A Collection of Strawberry Recipes
Cookbook Delights Series Book 15

Candies

Table of Contents

Page

Strawberry Divinity 126

Strawberry Cream Eggs 127

Creamy Strawberry Drops 128

Chocolate Covered Strawberries 128

Strawberry Salt Water Taffy 129

Strawberry White Chocolate Pretzels 130

Chocolate Strawberry Truffles 131

Strawberry Potato Candy 132

Strawberry Pecan Balls 132

Strawberry Delight Candy 133

Strawberry Candy 134

Strawberry Taffy 134

Strawberry Caramels 135

Strawberry Peanut Butter Bites 136

Strawberry Jujubes 136

Strawberry Cream Candy 137

Strawberry Fudge 138

Strawberry Divinity

My mom used to make this divinity recipe on holidays and special occasions, and my children like making it also.

Ingredients:

2½ c. sugar
½ c. white corn syrup
½ c. water
2 egg whites, stiffly beaten
1 tsp. vanilla extract
2 drops of red food coloring
½ c. candied strawberries
½ c. nuts, chopped

Directions:

1. In heavy saucepan, mix sugar, syrup, and water.
2. Cook and stir over medium-high heat to boiling.
3. Reduce to medium heat; continue cooking for 10 to15 minutes until it reaches the hardball stage.
4. Remove from heat.
5. Gradually pour hot mixture in a thin stream over stiffly beaten egg whites while beating on high speed for 3 minutes.
6. Add vanilla and food coloring, scraping down sides of bowl.
7. Continue beating on high just until candy starts to lose its gloss.
8. When beaters are lifted, mixture should fall in a ribbon that mounds on itself. This final beating should take 5 to 6 minutes.
9. Immediately stir in fruits or nuts.
10. Quickly drop mixture by teaspoonfuls onto waxed paper.
11. If mixture flattens out, beat for another ½ to 1 minute.
12. If mixture is too stiff to spoon, beat in a few drops hot water until candy is a softer consistency.

13. You may also pour into a very lightly butter-sprayed square pan; let candy set and then cut into small squares.
14. Refrigerate to harden and then may be kept in covered container or wrapped individually.

Strawberry Cream Eggs

These are a great change of pace from the traditional chocolate candy eggs, and the flavor and color can be changed quite simply by varying the flavoring and the color of dipping chocolate. Most cake decorating stores have colored dipping chocolate readily available.

Ingredients:

¼   lb. butter, melted
2   pkg. vanilla pudding mix
½   c. milk
1   lb. powdered sugar
1   tsp. strawberry flavoring
1   tsp. almond extract
4   oz. white dipping chocolate
4   oz. pink dipping chocolate

Directions:

1. In large saucepan, combine butter, pudding mix, and milk.
2. Bring to boil; simmer 2 minutes, stirring constantly.
3. Remove from heat; cool to lukewarm and add powdered sugar and flavorings, stirring until smooth.
4. When cool enough to handle, shape into eggs and place on wax paper-lined tray.
5. Chill until firm.
6. Melt chocolate, dip cooled eggs in any variety of ways you prefer, such as half and half cream, or all one color and decorate with the other color, etc.
7. Place on wax paper.
8. Let stand until coating hardens.
9. Store in airtight container in cool temperature.

Creamy Strawberry Drops

Here is another variation of a smooth and creamy candy that will melt in your mouth. Enjoy!

Ingredients:

8	oz. cream cheese
2	Tbs. half and half cream
¼	c. butter
1	tsp. strawberry extract
1	oz. white creamy frosting
	red food coloring

Directions:

1. In heavy saucepan, combine cream cheese, half and half, and butter.
2. Stir over low heat until cream cheese and butter has melted.
3. Blend in frosting and stir until blended well.
4. Add strawberry extract and food coloring.
5. Drop by teaspoonfuls onto waxed paper, let cool until firm.
6. Store in airtight container, between sheets of waxed paper.

Chocolate Covered Strawberries

Chocolate covered strawberries are a delicious addition to any table.

Ingredients:

2	c. semi-sweet chocolate chips
2	Tbs. shortening
	fresh strawberries with stems, rinsed and air dried

Directions:

1. Cover tray with wax paper.
2. Place chocolate chips and shortening in medium microwave safe bowl.

3. Microwave on high for 1½ minutes or just until chips are melted and mixture is smooth when stirred; cool slightly.
4. Holding strawberry by top, dip ⅔ of each berry into chocolate mixture; shake gently to remove excess.
5. Place on prepared tray.
6. Refrigerate until coating is firm, about 30 minutes.
7. Keep in refrigerator covered in single layer, until ready to serve up to 3 days.
8. Note: Butter and spreads contain water, which may prevent chocolate from melting properly; oil may prevent it.

Yields: 5 dozen small strawberries.

Strawberry Salt Water Taffy

This taffy is fun to make and very tasty. Children and adults alike will enjoy making this together.

Ingredients:

⅔ c. water
1 Tbs. cornstarch
1 c. sugar
¾ c. light corn syrup
1 tsp. salt
2 tsp. butter
1 tsp. strawberry flavoring

Directions:

1. Lightly grease an 8 x 8 x 2-inch baking pan with butter.
2. In medium saucepan, mix the water and cornstarch together; blend in sugar, corn syrup, and salt.
3. Cook over medium heat, stirring occasionally until candy thermometer reads 256 degrees F.
4. Remove from heat at once.
5. Stir in strawberry flavoring and pour into prepared pan.
6. Allow candy to cool.
7. Pull taffy until it is light in color and stiff.
8. Pull into 2-inch strips, cut and wrap in waxed paper.

Strawberry White Chocolate Covered Pretzels

This is a very easy recipe to make with your children. The older ones can dip the pretzels and the younger ones can sprinkle them.

Ingredients:

- 12 oz. good quality white chocolate, finely chopped
- 2 Tbs. solid vegetable shortening
- 6-8 oz. small, salted pretzels
- 3 oz. strawberry flavored gelatin

Directions:

1. Line several baking sheets with aluminum foil, shiny side up.
2. In a medium heat-proof bowl, combine chopped chocolate and shortening.
3. Microwave on high heat 1½ minutes, or until melted and smooth.
4. Place one pretzel into the melted chocolate.
5. With a three or four tined fork, gently push the pretzel just under the surface of the chocolate to cover it completely.
6. Pick up the pretzel so that it lies flat on the fork tines, and gently shake off excess chocolate from the pretzel.
7. Carefully place the dipped pretzel on a foil lined baking sheet.
8. While chocolate is still wet, lightly sprinkle with strawberry gelatin.
9. As you're dipping, the chocolate may cool and thicken too much to enable you to dip the pretzels easily. If so, reheat the dip gently in microwave.
10. Allow dipped pretzels to stand until chocolate covering has set. After lifting from the sheet, shake the loose gelatin back into container to use again.
11. As the coating hardens it should look dull and dry, not shiny and wet, and you should be able to peel the pretzels easily from the foil lined sheet.

12. Peel pretzels from the sheet, using plastic gloves to protect the chocolate covering on the pretzels from your fingers.
13. Store the dipped pretzels in an airtight container, at a cool temperature.

Chocolate Strawberry Truffles

The beloved French truffle is fast becoming one of America's favorite candies also. This American version has a crunchy hazelnut outer coating that is delicious.

Ingredients:

¾ c. butter
1 lb. semi-sweet chocolate, finely chopped
½ c. strawberry jam
¼ c. raspberry liqueur
½ c. cocoa powder
1 tsp. powdered sugar
1 c. hazelnuts, roasted and finely chopped

Directions:

1. Cut butter into pieces; melt in top of double boiler.
2. Add chocolate, stirring occasionally until melted and smooth.
3. Remove from heat; add jam and liqueur, blending until smooth.
4. Cover; refrigerate until firm, 4 hours or overnight.
5. Combine cocoa powder, powdered sugar, and nuts in a wide, shallow pan.
6. Scoop 1 tablespoon of chocolate mixture and form into a round ball, repeat until all chocolate is in balls.
7. Roll in desired coating; and place on flat tray or dish.
8. Cover tightly with plastic wrap. Keep in refrigerator until ready to serve. Remove from refrigerator 10 minutes before serving.
9. Note: This recipe may be prepared up to 5 days ahead if truffles are covered tightly and refrigerated.
10. They may also be frozen for up to a month, double wrapped in plastic.

Strawberry Potato Candy

This is a great way to use up leftover mashed potatoes, and it is really a delicious candy.

Ingredients:

- 4 c. powdered sugar
- 4 c. coconut, flaked
- ¾ c. cold mashed potatoes, without added milk or butter
- 2 tsp. strawberry flavoring
- ½ tsp. salt
- 1 lb. white chocolate or other flavored candy coating

Directions:

1. In medium bowl, combine sugar, coconut, potatoes, strawberry flavoring, and salt, blending well.
2. Line a 9-inch pan with paper and spray with a nonstick spray or butter the paper.
3. Spread the mixture into prepared pan; cover and refrigerate overnight.
4. Remove from refrigerator and cut into rectangles.
5. Cover and freeze.
6. Melt the chocolate or candy coating; remove the bars from freezer and dip into the coating.
7. Place on waxed paper to harden.
8. Store in an airtight container or wrap individually.
9. Keep in cool place until ready to serve.

Strawberry Pecan Balls

These fruit and nut balls are an enjoyable candy and a great treat for your family and friends.

Ingredients:

- 12 oz. vanilla wafer cookies, crushed
- 1 c. powdered sugar
- ¼ c. butter, room temperature

½ c. strawberry nectar
1 tsp. strawberry extract
1 c. pecans, chopped
   additional powdered sugar and coconut

Directions:

1. In small bowl, combine crumbs with sugar; blend in butter.
2. Blend in strawberry nectar, extract, and nuts.
3. Shape mixture into bite-size balls.
4. Place in plastic bag with the additional powdered sugar and coconut.
5. Arrange balls in single layer on tray; store uncovered overnight in refrigerator for best flavor.

Strawberry Delight Candy

These make delightful candies for the whole family to enjoy as a treat.

Ingredients:

1 can sweetened condensed milk (14 oz.)
2 c. coconut, finely ground
2 tsp. almond extract
2 pkg. strawberry gelatin (3 oz. each)
   green licorice pieces
   green leaf candies

Directions:

1. In medium bowl, mix condensed milk; coconut, and almond extract. Add 1 package of gelatin; stir until thoroughly blended.
2. Chill in refrigerator for 1 hour.
3. Roll mixture into small strawberry shaped balls and then roll in the remaining package of gelatin.
4. Press a piece of green licorice into the top for a stem and press a green leaf candy into the edge next to the stem to complete the "strawberry" look.
5. Refrigerate until ready to serve.

Strawberry Candy

This is an easy-to-make treat that everyone will enjoy.

Ingredients:

- ½ c. white corn syrup
- 1 c. marshmallows
- ½ tsp. vanilla extract
- 2 c. macaroon coconut
- 2 oz. red sugar
  food coloring, if desired

Directions:

1. In large bowl, combine coconut and vanilla.
2. In small saucepan, over low heat, melt marshmallows in corn syrup.
3. Pour over coconut mixture.
4. Color as desired.
5. Shape a small amount into a "strawberry" and roll in red sugar.
6. Note: A strawberry marzipan leaf completes the reality.
7. If you want to make bonbon centers, do not color.
8. Roll into balls of desired size and dip in chocolate or a coating of various colors.

Strawberry Taffy

Taffy is such a fun candy to make with your family, and it is delicious. Try both versions to see which one you like the most.

Ingredients:

- 2 c. sugar
- 2 Tbs. butter
- ⅓ c. glucose
- 1 Tbs. vanilla extract
- ⅔ c. water
- 1 c. strawberries, rinsed, hulled, puréed

Directions:

1. Cook sugar, glucose, and water to 245 degrees F. or when tested is at hard-ball stage.
2. Add the strawberries and butter and cook to 260 degrees F.
3. Pour on oiled slab or platter, and while cooling, turn the edges continually towards the center. When cool enough, pull with hands or hook until very light colored and cold.
4. Add vanilla flavoring while pulling, adding the extract a little at a time.
5. Pull out into long strips and cut into 1-inch pieces.
6. Wrap each piece individually in small squares of waxed paper, or store several pieces without touching, between sheets of waxed paper in an airtight container.

Strawberry Caramels

Homemade caramels are delicious. Try this easy recipe, and you will want to eat only homemade caramel from that moment on.

Ingredients:

1   c. sugar
½   c. dark corn syrup
¼   c. strawberry syrup
½   c. butter
1   c. light cream
1   c. nuts, chopped
1   tsp. vanilla extract

Directions:

1. Combine sugar, syrups, butter, and ½ cup cream in saucepan.
2. Bring to boil, stirring constantly.
3. Continue stirring, add remaining ½ cup cream, and cook slowly to very hard-ball stage.
4. Add nuts and vanilla and pour into a buttered pan.
5. When firm, cut into squares of desired size.

Strawberry Peanut Butter Bites

These unique strawberry-filled creamy peanut butter and chocolate candies are delicious.

Ingredients:

- ½ c. creamy peanut butter
- 1¼ c. semi-sweet chocolate chips, divided
- 2 Tbs. whipped topping or whipped cream
- 25 lg. strawberries, rinsed and dried
- 1 tsp. butter

Directions:

1. Line a baking sheet with tin foil.
2. In microwave, melt ¼ cup of chocolate chips; cool to room temperature.
3. Slice strawberries in half diagonally.
4. In small bowl, combine chocolate, topping, and peanut butter.
5. Using a piping bag or a knife, pipe or spread a thin layer of chocolate-peanut butter mixture on one half of the cut strawberry.
6. Press the other half of the strawberry back on gently.
7. Set the berry on prepared baking sheet; repeat with remaining berries; chill 15 minutes.
8. Melt remaining 1 cup of chocolate along with 1 teaspoon butter. Dip bottom half of berries in melted chocolate and place back on the baking sheet.
9. Refrigerate 15 minutes, or until set.
10. Keep berries chilled until ready to serve.

Strawberry Jujubes

Try these chewy, fruity treats. Enjoy!

Ingredients:

- 2 oz. unflavored gelatin

1   c. sugar
2½ c. strawberry purée, strained
⅔   c. water
    superfine sugar, to coat

Directions:

1. Prepare a 6-inch square pan by wetting it lightly with water, and wetting a knife or cookie cutter.
2. In medium saucepan, stir together the gelatin and sugar.
3. Add the purée and ⅔ cup water.
4. Stir over medium heat until sugar and gelatin are dissolved.
5. Bring to a boil; cover and boil for 5 minutes.
6. Pour into prepared pan; allow to set completely.
7. Once set, turn out of the pan onto waxed paper.
8. Cut into squares or shapes with the prepared, wetted tool of your choice.
9. Roll candies in sugar.

Strawberry Cream Candy

Try this delicious candy recipe, and have fun making it, too.

Ingredients:

1   lb. sugar
1   Tbs. vinegar
10 drops strawberry flavoring
1   tsp. cream of tartar

Directions:

1. In medium saucepan, add sugar and a little water to moisten the sugar.
2. Boil until brittle.
3. Stir in flavoring.
4. Turn out quickly onto butter plates.
5. When cool, pull until white.
6. Cut into squares.

Strawberry Fudge

This is nicely flavored and very pretty candy. Mix with white fudge and chocolate fudge for a homemade gift that is sure to please.

Ingredients:

- 2   c. sugar
- ½   c. butter
- 4   oz. evaporated milk
- 4   oz. semi-sweet white chocolate
- ½   c. strawberry syrup
- 4   drops red food coloring, or more to color desired

Directions:

1. Line an 8 x10-inch shallow baking pan with buttered wax paper.
2. In heavy bottomed saucepan, over low heat, combine sugar, butter, evaporated milk, and strawberry syrup; stirring occasionally.
3. Once the sugar has dissolved, bring the mixture to a gentle boil, stirring constantly to prevent sticking and burning on the bottom of the pan.
4. Boil gently until a little of the mixture dropped into cold water forms a soft ball, about 5 minutes.
5. Remove pan from heat; stir until the bubbles subside, beat rapidly with a wooden spoon until the mixture thickens and becomes slightly granular, about 3 minutes.
6. Pour the fudge into prepared baking pan and let sit until firm.
7. Cut into squares. Store between sheets of waxed paper in an airtight container.

Did You Know?....

Did you know that Florida is the second largest strawberry producing state? Florida has approximately 5000 acres of land planted in strawberries.

Strawberry Delights Cookbook

A Collection of Strawberry Recipes
Cookbook Delights Series Book 15

Cookies

Table of Contents

Page

Glazed Strawberry Kolache Cookies 140

Creamy Strawberry Sandwich Cookies 141

Strawberry Almond Candy Kiss Cookies 142

Fruit and Oat Bars.. 143

Strawberry Heart Tarts 144

Danish Strawberry Cookies 144

Strawberry Oats and Chips Cookies 146

Strawberry French Sugar Strips... 147

Strawberry Sugar Cookies... 148

Strawberry Walnut Cookies... 149

Strawberry Fig Bars 150

Strawberry Pecan Cookies 151

Strawberry Cookies with Creamy Strawberry Frosting............... 152

Strawberry Oatmeal Cookies... 153

Strawberry Bars 154

White Chocolate Strawberry Fudgies 155

Strawberry Nut Drops.. 156

Glazed Strawberry Kolache Cookies

These cookies are very pretty when you need a cookie for a brunch or tea. They can be interchangeable with the color scheme of any celebration or event simply by changing the strawberry preserves to another of your favorite. Make sure you use preserves and not jelly!

Ingredients for cookie:

3	c. flour
1	c. butter, softened
¼	c. sugar
½	tsp. salt
¼	oz. active dry yeast
½	c. warm milk
1	lg. egg
1	tsp. vanilla or strawberry extract
½	c. strawberry preserves
1	lg. egg, well beaten

Ingredients for glaze:

⅔	c. powdered sugar
1	tsp. almond extract
2½	tsp. milk

Directions for cookies:

1. Preheat oven to 350 degrees F.
2. Line baking sheet with parchment paper.
3. In a large bowl, combine flour, butter, sugar, and salt, beating with mixer until it looks like coarse crumbs.
4. In a small bowl, dissolve yeast in milk warmed to 110 degrees F.
5. Stir in 1 egg and extract of choice.
6. Add milk mixture to flour mixture, and then beat at low speed until mixed thoroughly.
7. Divide dough into 2 portions; cover with wax paper and refrigerate for 1 hour.

8. On a lightly floured surface, roll out half of the dough at a time to ¼-inch thickness each.
9. Cut dough into 3-inch squares; top each square with 1 teaspoon of the strawberry preserves.
10. Bring up two opposite corners of each square to center and pinch tightly to seal; repeat with the other two corners.
11. Place cookies onto prepared baking sheet 2 inches apart.
12. Brush each cookie lightly with the beaten egg.
13. Bake 10 to14 minutes, or until golden brown. Cool completely before glazing.
14. For glaze: In small bowl, combine powdered sugar, almond extract, and 2½ teaspoons milk for desired glazing consistency.
15. Drizzle glaze lightly over cooled cookies and serve.

Creamy Strawberry Sandwich Cookies

These are very easy to make, and they are not baked, so you won't have to heat up the kitchen on a hot summer day.

Ingredients:

    8   oz. cream cheese, softened
    ¼   c. strawberry preserves
    ¼   c. powdered sugar
    ½   tsp. vanilla extract
    40 vanilla wafers
        milk
        powdered sugar, for garnish

Directions:

1. In a medium bowl, with a mixer, beat the cream cheese until fluffy, adding a few drops of milk as necessary.
2. Combine the strawberry preserves, powdered sugar and vanilla extract with the cream cheese, blending well.
3. Let chill in the refrigerator for 30 minutes.
4. On the flat side of one wafer, spread 2 teaspoons of mixture, then top with another wafer to make a sandwich.
5. When ready to serve, sprinkle with powdered sugar.

Strawberry Almond Candy Kiss Cookies

These are delicious cookies that also make an attractive display. Adults and children alike will enjoy this treat.

Ingredients:

2½ c. sliced almonds, toasted, cooled
½ c. sugar
1   c. dark brown sugar, firmly packed
1   c. butter, softened
2   lg. eggs
1   tsp. almond extract
½ tsp. baking powder
2¾ c. flour
2   lg. egg whites, slightly beaten
60 strawberry cream kiss candies

Directions:

1. Preheat oven to 350 degrees F.
2. Line baking sheets with parchment paper.
3. In blender, grind 1 cup almonds and sugar.
4. Scrape into a small bowl and reserve.
5. In blender, pulse or grind remaining 1½ cups almonds and the brown sugar.
6. Scrape into a large bowl; add butter, eggs, almond extract, and baking powder. With mixer on medium, beat until fluffy.
7. On low speed, gradually add flour and beat until blended.
8. Roll level tablespoonfuls of dough into balls.
9. Dip each ball into beaten egg whites and then roll in reserved almond sugar mixture.
10. Place 1-inch apart onto prepared baking sheets.
11. Press index finger one quarter of the way down into center of each cookie to make an indent.
12. Bake 9 minutes, or until light brown around edges.
13. Place sheet on wire rack; immediately place a candy kiss in each indent, so that candies will melt slightly.
14. Carefully remove cookies to wire rack and cool.

Fruit and Oat Bars

Both adults and children enjoy these bar cookies, and they also make a great lunchbox treat. You can vary the flavors by changing the combination of the preserves and nuts, and by using white chocolate instead of milk chocolate. Try raspberry preserves, macadamia nuts, and white chocolate, or apricot preserves, pecans, and white or dark chocolate, or a mixture of both! Who can resist these flavor and color combinations?

Ingredients:

- 1   c. butter, divided
- 1   c. brown sugar, firmly packed
- 1½ c. flour
- ½   tsp. baking soda
- ¼   tsp. salt
- 1½ c. oatmeal, uncooked
- 1   c. walnuts or pecans, chopped
- 2   c. strawberry preserves
- ½   c. semi-sweet chocolate chips

Directions:

1. Preheat oven to 350 degrees F.
2. Lightly grease a 9 x 13-inch baking pan.
3. In large bowl, with an electric mixer, beat together ¾ cup butter and brown sugar until light and fluffy.
4. In small bowl, combine flour, baking soda, and salt; add to butter mixture and mix well.
5. Stir in oatmeal and nuts; reserving 1½ cups crumb mixture.
6. Press remaining crumb mixture into prepared pan.
7. Spread strawberry preserves over first layer; sprinkle with reserved crumb mixture.
8. Bake 30 to 35 minutes.
9. Remove from oven, let stand 10 minutes.
10. In microwave, melt chocolate chips and ¼ cup butter together, stirring until smooth.
11. Drizzle over crumb mixture. Refrigerate 1 hour; cut into bars.

Strawberry Heart Tarts

These make a delightful treat for a homemade gift, or it can be a fun project to share with the kids any time of the year.

Ingredients:

2¼ c. flour
2 tsp. baking powder
¼ tsp. salt
½ c. butter
1 c. sugar
2 eggs, beaten
½ tsp. vanilla extract
1 Tbs. milk
strawberry preserves

Directions:

1. Preheat oven to 375 degrees F.
2. Line baking sheet with parchment paper.
3. Sift together flour, baking powder, and salt; set aside.
4. Cream together butter and sugar. Add eggs, vanilla, milk; add sifted ingredients, blending well.
5. Roll out to ½-inch thickness on floured surface. Cut out with heart shaped cookie cutters; place on baking sheet.
6. Bake for 8 to 10 minutes.
7. Remove from oven; cool on wire rack.
8. Spread strawberry preserves on one cookie and top with another cookie, repeating until all cookies are sandwiched.
9. Store in airtight container or serve as desired.

Danish Strawberry Cookies

These cookies are absolutely scrumptious, and everyone will enjoy them.

Ingredients:

2 sq. unsweetened chocolate (1 oz.)
½ c. butter

½ c. sugar
1 egg
2 c. flour
1 tsp. vanilla extract
¼ tsp. salt
1 c. milk chocolate or white chocolate chips
1 c. strawberry preserves

Directions:

1. Preheat oven to 400 degrees F.
2. Lightly grease baking sheets or line with parchment paper.
3. Melt chocolate in top of a double boiler over hot not boiling water. Remove from heat and cool.
4. Cream butter and sugar in a large bowl until light. Add egg and melted chocolate; beat until fluffy. Stir in flour, vanilla, and salt until well blended.
5. Cover; refrigerate 1 hour, until firm.
6. Divide dough into 4 equal parts and divide each part into 2 pieces (8 pieces total).
7. Roll each piece into a rope 12 inches long on a lightly floured board. The ropes should be about the thickness of a finger.
8. Place 2 inches apart on the prepared baking sheets. With your finger tip, make an indentation along the length of each rope.
9. Bake 8 minutes, or until firm.
10. Meanwhile melt the chocolate chips in a small bowl over hot water.
11. Note: If you are using both kinds of chocolate, melt separately. Stir until smooth.
12. Stir preserves and spoon them into a pastry bag fitted with a ¼-inch tip. You can use a plastic bag with a corner snipped off with scissors.
13. When you remove the cookies from the oven, place preserves down the indentation in each cookie strip. Return to the oven for 2 minutes; remove to wire racks.
14. While cookies are still warm, drizzle melted chocolate over the tops and cut into 1-inch diagonal pieces.
15. Refrigerate until the chocolate has set, then serve.

Strawberry Oats and Chips Cookies

These cookies are both chewy and crispy at the same time, and topping them with strawberries is the perfect complement to the cookie.

Ingredients:

> 1   c. butter, melted
> 1¼ c. brown sugar
> ¾   c. sugar
> 1   Tbs. honey
> 2   tsp. vanilla extract
> 2   lg. eggs
> 1½ c. flour
> ¼   tsp. baking soda
> 1   tsp. baking powder
> ¼   tsp. salt
> ¼   tsp. cinnamon
> 3   c. oatmeal, uncooked
> 1   c. semi-sweet chocolate chips
> ¾   c. pecans, chopped
> 1½ c. small, fresh, strawberries, rinsed, hulled
> ½   c. golden raisins
>   halved strawberries, as garnish
>   sugar

Directions:

1. Preheat oven to 350 degrees F.
2. Line a baking sheet with parchment paper.
3. In large bowl, with electric mixer, cream butter together with both sugars and honey.
4. Add vanilla and eggs, blending well for 3 to 4 minutes.
5. Stir in combined flour, baking soda, baking powder, salt, cinnamon, and oatmeal, blending just until moistened.
6. Fold in chocolate, nuts, and raisins. Fold in the strawberries last to avoid breaking them up.
7. Shape dough into 2-inch balls and arrange on prepared baking sheets 2 inches apart.

8. Make an indentation in center of each cookie and finish by placing a strawberry half that has been rolled in sugar, into each, cut side down.
9. Bake 12 to16 minutes, until cookies are set. (Middles are slightly dry-looking and edges have begun to brown.)
10. Remove from oven; let set 10 minutes.
11. Remove cookies to a wire rack to cool completely.

Strawberry French Sugar Strips

These are very flavorful cookies made in strip style.

Ingredients:

¾   c. butter, softened
1   Tbs. strawberry flavoring
⅔   c. sugar
2   eggs
2   c. flour, sifted
2   egg yolks
2   tsp. water
1½ c. pecans, finely chopped
     pink decorative colored sugar

Directions:

1. In large bowl, beat butter, flavoring, and sugar together until light and fluffy; add eggs and beat well.
2. Gradually add flour and mix well; chill dough several hours.
3. When dough is chilled, preheat oven to 350 degrees F.
4. Divide dough in half. Roll out each half on a baking sheet to measure 9 x 10-inches.
5. Combine the 2 egg yolks with water, and gently brush mixture on top of each half of dough.
6. Sprinkle with the nuts and colored sugar.
7. Bake 10 to 20 minutes, until done.
8. Remove from oven; while hot cut into strips 1 x 2½-inches long.
9. Place on wire rack to cool.

147

Strawberry Sugar Cookies

This is a light cookie that is nice for afternoon tea or as an afternoon snack for the children.

Ingredients:

1   c. butter, softened
¾   c. sugar
¾   c. strawberries, chopped
1   lg. egg
1   tsp. vanilla extract
2¾ c. flour
1   tsp. baking soda
1   tsp. cream of tartar
¾   c. strawberries, chopped
    decorating sugar or colored sprinkles, for garnish

Directions:

1. In large bowl, mix butter and sugar together until fluffy; mix in strawberries.
2. Add egg and beat well; mix in vanilla.
3. In separate bowl, combine flour, baking soda, and cream of tartar.
4. Add flour mixture to butter mixture, blend thoroughly.
5. Divide dough into two equal portions, and flatten each into a disk.
6. Cover each portion in plastic wrap; refrigerate for 2 to 3 hours, or until the dough is firm enough to work with. If it becomes too firm, soften at room temperature for 5 minutes.
7. Preheat oven to 350 degrees F.
8. On a lightly floured board roll out one portion of dough, until it is ⅓-inch thick.
9. Cut out cookies with cookie cutter.
10. Using a spatula, carefully move the cookies onto a baking sheet, spacing them 2 inches apart.

11. Sprinkle cookies with decorating sugar, or colored sprinkles. Continue with other portion of dough in same order.
12. Bake 8 to 11 minutes, or until golden along the edges.
13. Remove from oven and place on wire racks to cool before serving.

Strawberry Walnut Cookies

These cookies are healthy, delicious, and loaded with fiber.

Ingredients:

½	c. walnuts, ground
1	c. rolled oats, ground
1	c. whole wheat flour
1	pinch salt
2	lg. eggs, beaten
⅔	c. corn syrup
2	Tbs. canola oil
¾	c. strawberry jam
1	tsp. almond extract
1	tsp. vanilla or strawberry extract

Directions:

1. Preheat oven to 350 degrees F.
2. Lightly spray a baking sheet with oil.
3. Grind the walnuts in a blender; measure after grinding.
4. Grind rolled oats the same way; measure after grinding.
5. Mix together walnuts, oats, flour, and salt in a bowl.
6. In a separate bowl, mix corn syrup, corn oil, eggs, jam, and extracts.
7. Pour liquid ingredients into dry ingredients; mix well until just moistened.
8. Drop by tablespoons of batter onto baking sheet.
9. Bake 20 minutes.
10. Cool on wire rack.

Strawberry Fig Bars

My oldest daughter loves figs, and these make an enjoyable treat.

Ingredients for dough:

- 1   c. butter
- 2   c. brown sugar, packed
- 3   eggs
- 1   tsp. vanilla extract
- 1   Tbs. lemon juice
- 4   c. flour
- 1   tsp. baking soda
- 1   tsp. baking powder

Ingredients for fig filling:

- 1¼ c. ground figs
- 1   c. frozen strawberries, thawed, drained
- 1   c. water
- ¾   c. sugar
- 3   Tbs. flour
- ½   c. nuts, chopped
- 1   Tbs. orange juice

Directions for filling:

1. In medium saucepan, boil figs and strawberries in water 5 minutes.
2. Blend sugar and flour, stir into fig mixture.
3. Cook over low heat until thick.
4. Remove from heat; stir in nuts and juice; set aside.

Directions for dough:

1. In large bowl, cream together butter and sugar.
2. Add eggs, vanilla, and juice, beat well.
3. In small bowl, sift flour, baking soda, and baking powder together.
4. Blend into creamed mixture.

5. Divide dough in half; on a floured pastry cloth, roll into a rectangle 12 inches wide and ⅛-inch thick.
6. Cut into four 3-inch wide strips.
7. Put cooled filling down center of strips.
8. Using spatula fold each side of the dough over the filling.
9. Place seam side down on ungreased baking sheet.
10. Bake 15 minutes.
11. Remove from oven, let stand 5 minutes.
12. Cut each strip into 2-inch lengths.
13. Cool on wire rack.

Strawberry Pecan Cookies

Here is a simple drop cookie that is easy to stir up and bake for a quick treat.

Ingredients:

1 c. butter
1½ c. sugar
2 lg. eggs
¾ c. strawberry purée
3 c. flour
1 tsp. salt
½ tsp. baking soda
¾ c. pecans, chopped

Directions:

1. Preheat oven to 350 degrees F.
2. Lightly grease baking sheets.
3. In a mixing bowl, cream butter and sugar. Add eggs, one at a time, beating well after each addition.
4. Beat in puréed strawberries with mixer, just until blended.
5. Combine together flour, salt, and baking soda; gradually add to creamed mixture; fold in pecans.
6. Drop by tablespoonfuls onto prepared baking sheets.
7. Bake 12 to 15 minutes, or until edges are lightly browned.
8. Remove from oven and lift to wire rack to cool.

Strawberry Cookies with Creamy Strawberry Frosting

These are delicious cookies with a creamy, buttery frosting.

Ingredients for cookies:

1½ c. powdered sugar
1   c. butter, softened
1   egg
1   tsp. strawberry flavoring
½   tsp. almond extract
3   c. flour
1   tsp. baking soda
1   tsp. cream of tartar

Ingredients for frosting:

¼   c. butter, softened
2   c. powdered sugar
2   tsp. strawberry flavoring
2   Tbs. milk, as needed
3   drops red food coloring

Directions for cookies:

1. Preheat oven to 350 degrees F.
2. In large bowl, cream together powdered sugar, butter, egg, flavoring, and extract.
3. Sift together flour, baking soda, and cream of tartar; add to the creamed mixture and blend well to form dough.
4. Roll dough out ¼-inch thick; use a cookie cutter or top of a jar lid to cut out into a shape.
5. Bake 8 minutes, or just until edges turn light brown.
6. Remove from oven and lift onto wire rack to cool.

Directions for frosting:

1. In medium bowl, combine butter, powdered sugar, red food coloring, and flavoring; mix well.

2. Add the milk, a little at a time, until proper consistency.
3. Spread on top of the cooled cookies.

Strawberry Oatmeal Cookies

This makes a nice twist to the basic oatmeal cookie, and it is a great way to add fruit, vitamins, and fiber to your diet.

Ingredients:

1   c. butter
2   c. brown sugar
3   lg. eggs
1   c. sour milk or buttermilk
2   tsp. vanilla extract
3   c. flour
1   tsp. baking powder
1   tsp. baking soda
½   tsp. salt
1½ tsp. ground cinnamon
2   c. oatmeal, uncooked
1   c. pecans, chopped
½   c. raisins
1   c. strawberries, chopped

Directions:

1. Preheat oven to 350 degrees F.
2. In large bowl, cream together butter and sugar until light and fluffy.
3. Add eggs one at time, beating well with each addition; stir in vanilla and sour milk.
4. In medium bowl, combine flour, baking powder, baking soda, salt, and cinnamon; gradually stir into the creamed mixture.
5. Stir in pecans, raisins, and oatmeal.
6. Gently fold in chopped strawberries.
7. Drop by rounded spoonfuls onto baking sheets.
8. Bake 12 to 15 minutes.
9. Cool 5 minutes before removing to a wire rack.

Strawberry Bars

These are delicious bars that will make great snacks or lunchbox treats, so you might want to double the recipe to have extras on hand.

Ingredients for crust:

1½ c. flour
½   c. cold butter
5   Tbs. powdered sugar
3   Tbs. cold water

Ingredients for filling:

3   eggs
½   c. sugar
1   c. brown sugar
1   tsp. baking powder
½   c. flour
3   c. strawberries, rinsed, hulled, halved

Directions:

1. Preheat oven to 350 degrees F.
2. In large bowl, mix flour and powdered sugar together; cut in butter until mealy appearance.
3. Add water a tablespoon at a time, and only enough to make dough stick together. Refrigerate at least 1 hour, so dough handles easier.
4. Press into a 9 × 13-inch pan on bottom and ¾ of an inch up sides.
5. Bake for 15 minutes; cool on wire rack.
6. Beat eggs and both sugars together until frothy.
7. Add flour and baking powder; blend well.
8. Stir in the strawberries and then pour mixture onto the partially baked crust.
9. Return pan to oven at the same temperature for another 45 minutes.
10. Remove from oven; cool and serve either warm or completely cooled.

White Chocolate Strawberry Fudgies

These are absolutely decadent, and best of all, they can be made using frozen fruit, which makes them just as easily made out of season as in.

Ingredients:

- ⅔ c. butter, softened
- 1 c. sugar
- 1 lg. egg
- 1 tsp. strawberry extract
- ½ c. buttermilk
- ½ c. frozen sweetened strawberries, puréed
- 2 c. flour
- ½ c. unsweetened baking cocoa
- ¾ tsp. baking soda
- ½ tsp. salt
- 1½ c. white chocolate chips

Directions:

1. Preheat oven to 350 degrees F.
2. Lightly grease baking sheets.
3. In large bowl, combine butter, sugar, egg, and strawberry extract.
4. Beat mixture until well blended.
5. Beat in buttermilk and strawberry purée.
6. In medium bowl, combine flour, cocoa, baking soda, and salt.
7. Mix into creamed mixture until blended.
8. Fold in white chocolate chips.
9. Drop by rounded tablespoonfuls 2 inches apart onto prepared baking sheets.
10. Bake 10 to12 minutes, or until tops spring back when touched lightly.
11. Remove from oven.
12. Immediately lift cookies from baking sheets to wire racks.
13. Cool completely.

Strawberry Nut Drops

These are easy-to-make and very good. They are best when iced and eaten warm.

Ingredients:

    1   c. sugar
    ½   c. butter
    1   tsp. almond extract
    1   egg
    2   c. flour
    1   tsp. baking powder
    ½   tsp. baking soda
    1¼   c. strawberries, rinsed, hulled, crushed, divided
    ½   c. walnuts, chopped
    ¾   c. powdered sugar

Directions:

1. Preheat oven to 375 degrees F.
2. Lightly spray a baking sheet with cooking spray.
3. In large bowl, cream sugar, butter, and almond extract until creamy.
4. Beat in egg until well blended.
5. Mix flour with baking powder and soda.
6. Add to creamed mixture alternately with 1 cup of the crushed strawberries, reserving the remainder.
7. Fold in walnuts.
8. Drop by tablespoons onto prepared baking sheet.
9. Bake 12 to 14 minutes.
10. Remove from oven.
11. In small bowl, stir together the reserved berries with ¾ cup powdered sugar to make a thin glaze.
12. Spread glaze over warm cookies and serve.

Did You Know? . . . .

Did you know that there is a strawberry research center in Dover, Florida?

Strawberry Delights Cookbook

A Collection of Strawberry Recipes
Cookbook Delights Series Book 15

Desserts

Table of Contents

Page

Strawberry Hazelnut Flan 158
Philadelphia Style Strawberry Ice Cream 159
Strawberry Flan 160
Strawberry and Chocolate Tortilla 161
Baked Meringues with Strawberries 162
Strawberry Pineapple Ice Box Dessert 164
Strawberries in Chocolate Cream Fruit Dip 165
Strawberry Fool 165
Bakewell Strawberry Tart 166
Strawberry Dessert Soup 166
Strawberry Yogurt Freeze 167
Strawberry Rhubarb Cobbler 168
Strawberry Cobbler 169
Strawberry Pudding 170
Strawberry Dessert 171
Strawberry Jam Bread Pudding 172
Strawberry Torte 173
Cheesecake Tart with Strawberries 174
Strawberry Ice Cream 175
Dark Chocolate Pavé with Strawberry Sauce 176
Summer Strawberry Orange Cups 178
Strawberries in Balsamic Vinegar 178
Strawberry Crêpes 179
Strawberry Filling for Boston Cream Pie 180
Berry Parfait 180
Strawberries and Cream 181
Strawberry and Raspberry Tart 182

Strawberry Hazelnut Flan

This strawberry hazelnut flan is time consuming to make, but well worth the effort.

Ingredients for crust:

½   c. hazelnuts, toasted
3   Tbs. sugar
1¼ c. flour
½   tsp. salt
6   Tbs. butter, chilled and cut into sm. pieces
1   lg. egg, beaten
2   oz. semi-sweet chocolate
1   tsp. canola oil
   dried beans

Ingredients for filling:

¼   c. strawberry jelly
½   tsp. lemon zest, grated
½   tsp. lemon juice
2   c. strawberries, sliced
6   c. small, whole strawberries
2   oz. semi-sweet chocolate
1   tsp. canola oil
   powdered sugar

Directions:

1. Preheat oven to 350 degrees F. To toast hazelnuts, spread nuts on baking sheet; bake 8 to 10 minutes, or until golden.
2. Transfer nuts to towel; rub vigorously to remove skins.
3. In blender, process hazelnuts and sugar until nuts are finely ground. Add flour and salt, process until well combined; transfer to large bowl.
4. Using fingertips, work butter into dry ingredients until mixture resembles coarse crumbs. Stir in egg with fork.
5. Do not overwork; mixture should be crumbly.

6. Press evenly into 10-inch flan pan; refrigerate 30 minutes.
7. Using fork, prick bottom and sides of pastry.
8. Line pastry with foil and fill with dried beans.
9. Bake for 15 minutes.
10. Remove foil and beans, and bake an additional 10 minutes or until golden.
11. Place on rack to cool completely.
12. Melt chocolate and oil together; brush over bottom and about a third of the way up sides of crust.
13. Refrigerate until set.
14. In small saucepan, combine strawberry jelly, lemon zest and juice. Place over low heat and stir constantly until jelly melts.
15. Place sliced berries evenly over chocolate coated crust.
16. Arrange whole berries on top; brush with currant jelly mixture.
17. Melt chocolate and oil together; drizzle over strawberries.
18. Refrigerate until chocolate sets, or up to 2 hours.
19. When ready to serve, dust with powdered sugar.

Philadelphia Style Strawberry Ice Cream

This is a rich, creamy ice cream, and you can change the flavor easily by changing the extracts and fruits.

Ingredients:

    1   c. heavy cream
    2   c. half and half cream
    ½   c. sugar
    1   c. fresh strawberries, rinsed, hulled, crushed
    1   Tbs. strawberry extract

Instructions:

1. In blender, combine cream, and half and half.
2. Add sugar, strawberries, and extract; blend well.
3. Pour into ice cream freezer; process according to manufacturer's directions.
4. Place in seal tight container and freeze until ready to serve.

Strawberry Flan

This is a variation of a traditional flan, and it is one which we are sure you will enjoy.

Ingredients for crust:

- ½ c. butter, room temperature
- 2 Tbs. sugar
- ¼ c. cold water
- 1 tsp. lemon zest, grated
- 1⅓ c. flour

Ingredients for filling:

- 1 c. Mascarpone cheese
- 3 Tbs. powdered sugar
- 2 tsp. lemon zest, grated
- ¼ tsp. vanilla extract
- ¼ c. whipping cream
- 2 c. small strawberries, halved

Ingredients for glaze:

- ¼ c. strawberry jelly
- 1 Tbs. lemon juice

Directions for crust:

1. Preheat oven to 400 degrees F.
2. In large bowl, using a pastry cutter or two knives, cut together butter, sugar, lemon zest, and flour.
3. Add ¼ cup cold water and mix just until mixture starts to cling together.
4. Turn onto floured surface and gently knead until mixture forms ball.
5. With floured fingertips, press dough into a 9-inch flan pan.
6. Place in freezer for 20 minutes.
7. Bake for 12 minutes, or until golden.
8. Let cool completely on rack.

Directions for filling:

1. In medium bowl, beat together Mascarpone cheese, powdered sugar, lemon zest, and vanilla.
2. Add whipping cream and beat until blended.
3. Spread cheese mixture onto cooled crust.
4. Top with strawberries, arranging berries in concentric circles.
5. To make glaze: Heat jelly and lemon juice until jelly melts.
6. Brush over strawberries.
7. Refrigerate until ready to serve.

Yields: 6 to 8 servings.

Strawberry and Chocolate Tortilla

If you need a quick, sweet treat, this is easy to make and satisfying. If you roll the tortillas up tightly, you can slice each burrito-style tortilla in 1-inch slices and serve them as an appetizer.

Ingredients:

2   sm. flour tortillas
4   Tbs. Belgian chocolate, chopped
1   c. fresh strawberries, sliced
    powdered sugar

Directions:

1. Sprinkle each tortilla with 2 tablespoons chopped chocolate.
2. Place on paper towel in microwave.
3. Heat on high for 30 seconds.
4. Place the strawberries in center of tortilla and roll it up.
5. To serve, place on individual plates with edge down.
6. Sprinkle lightly with powdered sugar.

Baked Meringues with Strawberries

Our family really enjoys meringue desserts with the flavor of strawberries and a thin layer of bittersweet chocolate.

Ingredients for meringue:

5   lg. egg whites, room temperature
½   tsp. cream of tartar
½   c. plus 2 Tbs. sugar
½   c. powdered sugar
½   tsp. almond extract

Ingredients for strawberry sauce:

10   oz. frozen strawberries in syrup, thawed

Ingredients for filling:

1   pt. frozen strawberry yogurt, softened
12   oz. whole frozen strawberries, partially thawed
7   oz. bittersweet chocolate (optional)
¼   c. pistachio nuts, shelled, chopped

Directions for meringue:

1. Place oven racks in lower and middle positions; preheat oven to 225 degrees F.
2. Lightly butter tart molds, or nonstick baking sheets.
3. Lightly grease waxed or parchment paper with cooking spray.
4. Fit large pastry bag with ⅜-inch plain tip. Set aside.
5. Place egg whites in large mixing bowl; beat on low speed until foamy and white.
6. Sprinkle cream of tartar over surface and continue beating.
7. Sprinkle 2 tablespoons sugar over egg whites; increase mixer speed to medium, whipping until soft peaks form.
8. Gradually add remaining ½ cup sugar, 2 tablespoons at a time, beating after each addition until sugar is

dissolved, and meringue feels smooth. If meringue feels grainy, continue beating.

9. When meringue is smooth and stands up in stiff, glossy peaks, beat in almond extract.

10. Sift powdered sugar over meringue, and fold in just until incorporated.

11. Fill pastry bag with meringue, and starting at outside edge, trace circle shape eight times.

12. Each time, continue to inside without lifting tip, they need not be perfect.

13. With remaining meringue, pipe at least two small mounds about 1½-inch in diameter amid hearts on each baking sheet. These will be used to test meringues toward the end of baking time.

14. Bake 1 to 1¼ hours, rearranging baking sheets after 30 minutes, so that the lower sheet is in middle position, and middle sheet in lower position.

15. Meringues should be checked after 1 hour, and are done when test meringues are easily removed from baking sheet and breaks crisply after cooling for 5 minutes.

16. Remove baking sheets from oven; leave on waxed or parchment paper for approximately 30 minutes, until cool.

17. At this point, if wrapped in plastic freezer bags and stored in airtight containers, meringues will keep for months.

18. Melt chocolate in double boiler over low heat.

19. Dip 4 rounds so that half of round is covered in chocolate, or with a spoon, drizzle chocolate over top.

20. Replace on the waxed or parchment paper to harden.

21. When chocolate has hardened, place in airtight containers until ready to serve.

Directions for sauce:

1. In blender or food processor, purée strawberries and syrup until smooth.

2. Strain to remove seeds.

3. Can be prepared 1 day ahead.

4. Cover and refrigerate.

Directions for filling:

1. When ready to serve, spread softened frozen yogurt or whipped topping over 4 plain meringue rounds.
2. Spoon strawberry sauce over this filling, adding partially thawed strawberries. Top each with chocolate covered round.
3. Set meringues on dessert plates decoratively; finish with strawberry sauce. Garnish with pistachio nuts.

Strawberry Pineapple Ice Box Dessert

This is a great dessert to make ahead of time because it freezes well. You may as well double the recipe and keep one on hand for an instantly ready treat.

Ingredients:

2	eggs
¼	lb. butter
3	c. powdered sugar
1	box vanilla wafers, crushed
1	sm. can crushed pineapple, well drained
1	c. fresh strawberries, washed, hulled, chopped
1	c. ground nuts
½	pint cream, whipped, sweetened

Directions:

1. In medium bowl, cream together butter, eggs, and powdered sugar.
2. Add crushed wafers, mixing until crumbly.
3. Press half of the crumb mixture in the bottom of an 8 x 12-inch baking pan.
4. Combine pineapple, strawberries, and half the nuts, and whipped cream; blend well.
5. Spoon this mixture into the crumb lined pan.
6. Sprinkle top with remaining crumbs and nuts.
7. Refrigerate overnight to serve, or freeze until ready to serve.
8. Remove from freezer 15 minutes before serving.

Strawberries in Chocolate Cream Fruit Dip

This dip is a nice change of pace from the traditional vegetable dip trays. Try it when you want to have a light, refreshing dessert.

Ingredients:

8   oz. cream cheese, softened
¼   c. chocolate syrup
1   jar marshmallow crème
    fresh strawberries

Directions:

1. In small mixing bowl, beat cream cheese and chocolate syrup; fold in marshmallow crème.
2. Cover and refrigerate until serving time.
3. Serve with fresh strawberries.

Strawberry Fool

This simple dish is delicious, and it is a real time saver when you have had a busy day.

Ingredients:

½   c. whipping cream
¾   c. dairy sour cream or crème fraîche
4   c. fresh strawberries, reserving 4 whole strawberries
½   c. sugar, or to taste

Directions:

1. In small bowl, whip cream.
2. Stir in sour cream or crème fraîche.
3. In blender, purée strawberries with sugar to taste.
4. Fold sour cream or crème fraîche into fruit purée.
5. Spoon mixture into individual dessert dishes; chill.

Bakewell Strawberry Tart

This is an English style tart that is absolutely delicious.

Ingredients:

- 1   9-inch baked pastry shell, cooled
- ¼   lb. butter
- ¼   c. almonds, ground
- ½   tsp. almond extract
- ½   tsp. vanilla extract
- ¼   c. sugar
- 2   lg. eggs
- 2   c. strawberries, rinsed, hulled

Directions:

1. Preheat oven to 400 degrees F.
2. In small saucepan, over low heat, barely melt butter.
3. Remove from heat; add sugar; stir in almonds, almond extract, and eggs in that order. (called bakewell)
4. Place berries into pie shell, spreading them evenly, and then pour the almond mixture over the fruit.
5. Bake 35 to 40 minutes, until the bakewell topping is golden and puffy.

Strawberry Dessert Soup

This is a wonderful dessert soup with a great aroma and even better taste.

Ingredients:

- 4   c. fresh strawberries, washed, hulled
- 12   oz. frozen whipped topping, thawed
- ⅛   tsp. ground nutmeg
- ¼   tsp. vanilla extract
- 1   c. white sugar
- ¼   c. sour cream
- 12   oz. prepared pound cake, cubed
- 12   sprigs fresh mint

12 fresh strawberries, washed, hulled

Directions:

1. In a large bowl, combine strawberries, whipped topping, nutmeg, cinnamon, vanilla, and sugar.
2. With an electric mixer, mix at low speed 5 to 7 minutes, or until sugar has dissolved completely, and mixture is smooth.
3. Add sour cream and blend 1 minute.
4. Place in refrigerator to chill.
5. Toast pound cake cubes under broiler for approximately 6 minutes, turning once to brown both sides.
6. Serve soup in chilled bowls, and garnish with whole strawberries, pound cake croutons, and fresh mint sprigs.

Strawberry Yogurt Freeze

This freeze is a delicious and refreshing dessert that is perfect for refreshment on a hot summer day.

Ingredients:

16 oz. strawberry yogurt
1 pt. fresh strawberries, rinsed, hulled
1 tsp. orange peel, grated

Directions:

1. Mix strawberry yogurt if not premixed.
2. Spoon into ice cube tray and freeze until completely frozen, 3 to 4 hours.
3. Remove cubes from tray.
4. Place in bowl of electric food processor; process until finely chopped.
5. Add strawberries and orange peel.
6. Process until smooth.
7. Place in freezer until ready to serve if not serving immediately.

Strawberry Rhubarb Cobbler

This is a delicious comfort dessert, very popular in the spring. You can also use frozen fruit, thawed before using.

Ingredients for filling:

1¼ c. sugar
3 Tbs. flour
1½ tsp. cinnamon
6 c. fresh rhubarb, coarsely chopped
3 c. fresh strawberries, rinsed, hulled, sliced

Ingredients for topping:

1½ c. flour
3 Tbs. sugar
1½ tsp. baking powder
½ tsp. baking soda
¼ tsp. salt
3 Tbs. butter
1 c. buttermilk

Directions for filling:

1. Preheat oven to 400 degrees F.
2. Lightly butter a 9 x 13-inch baking dish.
3. In large bowl, combine sugar, flour, and cinnamon.
4. Add rhubarb and strawberries; toss to coat.
5. Spread mixture into prepared dish.
6. Bake 10 minutes; remove from oven and add cobbler topping.

Directions for topping:

1. In medium bowl, combine flour, sugar, baking powder, baking soda, and salt.
2. Cut in butter until mixture resembles small peas.
3. With fork, stir in buttermilk to form soft dough.
4. Drop dough by tablespoonfuls over hot filling, making 12 mounds equally spaced apart.

5. Bake 25 minutes, until topping is golden brown and has risen.
6. Remove from oven.
7. Cool on wire rack before serving.

Strawberry Cobbler

My family loves strawberry cobbler, and this one is delicious.

Ingredients:

4	c. strawberries, sliced
1	Tbs. lemon juice
¾	c. plus 3 Tbs. sugar
1	Tbs. cornstarch
2	c. buttermilk biscuit mix
3	Tbs. butter, melted
½	c. milk
1	tsp. vanilla extract
½	Tbs. sugar
⅛	tsp. ground cardamom

Directions:

1. Preheat oven to 400 degrees F.
2. In small saucepan, combine strawberries, lemon juice, sugar, and cornstarch.
3. Heat and stir until boiling and thickened.
4. Pour into an 8-inch square baking dish.
5. In small bowl, combine biscuit mix, butter, milk, vanilla and 3 tablespoons of sugar for dumpling batter.
6. Stir until well mixed; drop by tablespoonfuls onto strawberry mixture.
7. Combine ½ tablespoonful sugar with cardamom; sprinkle over top of dumplings.
8. Bake 25 minutes, or until dumplings are done.
9. Remove from oven; cool on wire rack.
10. May be served warm or cold; try it with some vanilla ice cream on the side or sweetened whipped cream.

Strawberry Pudding

This is a fun dessert to make and delicious for all to enjoy.

Ingredients:

1	pt. fresh strawberries, rinsed, hulled, sliced
½	bottle red wine
⅛	c. honey
½	tsp. lemon zest, grated
¼	c. sugar
16	slices stale potato bread
1	Tbs. butter, room temperature
4	empty vegetable cans (15 oz.)
1	c. whipping cream, sweetened to taste

Directions:

1. In bowl, combine strawberries, red wine, honey, lemon zest, and sugar.
2. Refrigerate 2 hours to blend flavors.
3. Remove both ends from empty cans; save 4 of the ends.
4. Using one of the cans with the ends removed, cut the potato bread into 16 rounds.
5. To avoid tearing the edges of the bread, press straight down without twisting.
6. Let bread sit for 2 hours to dry out.
7. Lightly butter the inside of the vegetable cans, and place the cans on a baking sheet lined with parchment paper.
8. Butter one side of 4 of the bread rounds.
9. Place buttered bread rounds, buttered side up, in each can.
10. Spoon 2 tablespoons strawberries, with liquid, to cover each round inside the cans.
11. Dredge one side of 4 bread rounds in strawberry liquid and place over strawberries, one to each can.
12. Repeat steps 8 through 11, layering strawberries and dredged bread rounds until you have 3 layers of strawberries and 4 layers of bread.
13. Place reserved ends of soup cans on top of final round and weight with full cans of soda.

14. Refrigerate for 8 hours.
15. Just before serving, whip cream, sweetening to taste.
16. Remove cans, placing each pudding on individual serving plates.
17. Top each with whipped cream.

Strawberry Dessert

This is an elegant dessert and also a picnic favorite, since it can be made ahead and chilled.

Ingredients:

1½ c. graham cracker crumbs
¼ c. sugar
¼ c. butter, melted
1 Tbs. strawberry gelatin powder
1 c. water, boiling
¾ c. frozen strawberries, partially thawed
20 lg. marshmallows
½ c. milk
1 c. whipping cream, whipped

Directions:

1. In small bowl, mix cracker crumbs, sugar, and butter.
2. Reserve ¼ cup of crumb mixture.
3. Press the rest in bottom of a 9 x 13-inch pan.
4. Mix gelatin powder and boiling water.
5. Chill until slightly set.
6. Stir in strawberries.
7. Pour over crumb crust.
8. In medium saucepan, over low heat, melt marshmallows with milk; let cool.
9. Fold in whipped cream.
10. Spread mixture over strawberry layer.
11. Garnish with reserved crumb mixture.
12. Refrigerate several hours, or overnight.

Strawberry Jam Bread Pudding

This is an easy-to-make dessert that is colorful and nicely flavored. For a change of pace, substitute the meringue topping with sweetened whipped cream, and sprinkle with toasted almonds.

Ingredients:

3	c. toasted bread cubes
4	lg. eggs, divided
4	c. milk, scalded
1	c. sugar, divided
1	tsp. vanilla extract
½	c. butter, melted
¾	c. strawberry jam

Directions:

1. Preheat oven to 350 degrees F.
2. Place bread cubes in a buttered 2-quart casserole.
3. Beat two whole eggs plus two egg yolks, reserving two egg whites for the meringue.
4. Gradually beat the cooled, scalded milk into eggs.
5. Beat in ½ cup of the sugar, vanilla, and butter.
6. Pour milk mixture over bread cubes.
7. Bake 25 minutes, or until inserted toothpick comes out clean.
8. Remove from oven; set on wire rack to cool to lukewarm.
9. While pudding is cooling, beat the egg whites until stiff but not dry.
10. Continue beating whites while adding sugar, one tablespoon at a time until meringue is stiff and glossy.
11. Spread the jam evenly over top of the warm pudding. (If substituting whipped cream, omit the rest of directions).
12. Pile meringue over the jam, making sure to spread the meringue clear onto the edge of the dish.
13. Bake 15 minutes, until meringue is set or golden brown.
14. Remove from oven, let stand for 10 minutes.
15. Serve warm or cold with or without ice cream.

Strawberry Torte

Try this delicious version of strawberry torte. This is a great winter season dessert, and you can use frozen strawberries.

Ingredients for cake:

- ½ c. butter
- ½ c. sugar
- 4 egg yolks, beaten
- 4 Tbs. milk
- ½ c. flour, plus 2 Tbs.
- 1 tsp. baking powder

Ingredients for topping:

- 4 egg whites
- 1 c. sugar
- ⅛ tsp. cream of tartar
- 2 c. strawberries, sliced
- 2 c. whipped cream, sweetened to taste
  pinch of salt

Directions:

1. Preheat oven to 350 degrees F.
2. Lightly grease two 8-inch round baking pans.
3. In large bowl, with electric mixer, cream butter and sugar.
4. Blend in egg yolks, milk, flour, and baking powder.
5. Spread in bottom of prepared pans.
6. In small bowl, beat egg whites until stiff peaks form.
7. Add sugar, cream of tartar, and salt; beat until thick and glassy.
8. Spread over cake layers.
9. Bake 20 to 25 minutes.
10. Cool 5 minutes; remove to plates.
11. When completely cool, arrange strawberries over the egg-white topping side of one layer.
12. Top with second layer, with the egg-white topping side down.
13. Spread whipped cream on top.

Cheesecake Tart with Strawberries

This is a delicious little tart that is actually made in two steps, so it is easily made a day or two ahead. The finishing touch is added when you are ready to serve it.

Ingredients for crust:

    2   c. graham crackers
    3   Tbs. sugar
    3   Tbs. butter, melted

Ingredients for filling:

    1½ c. Mascarpone cheese, room temperature
    ½   c. sugar
    2   lg. eggs (adding one at a time)
    1   Tbs. lemon juice
    2   tsp. lemon zest
    1   tsp. vanilla extract
    ¼   tsp. almond extract
    3   Tbs. flour
    2   qt. fresh strawberries, rinsed, hulled, sliced

Directions for crust:

1. Preheat oven to 350 degrees F.
2. Crush graham crackers; add sugar; cut in butter.
3. Press crust into bottom of the springform pan and about ¾ of the way up the sides.
4. Bake 10 to15 minutes until crisp.
5. Cool completely.

Directions for filling:

1. Combine cheese, sugar and eggs, beating until smooth; add lemon juice, zest, extracts, and flour, blending well.
2. Scrape the filling into cooled crust.
3. Bake 30 to 35 minutes until golden color.

4. Remove from oven; cool completely in pan.
5. Place on serving plate and chill tart overnight in the refrigerator.
6. When ready to serve; toss the strawberries with about 4 tablespoons of sugar in bowl.
7. Let stand a few minutes to let the sugar dissolve.
8. Pile the berries on the tart, remove the springform pan, and serve immediately.

Strawberry Ice Cream

It seems that nothing is more refreshing on a hot day than cold strawberry ice cream.

Ingredients:

5   c. milk
4   lg. eggs
1½ c. sugar
½   tsp. salt
1   can evaporated milk
1   can sweetened condensed milk
2   Tbs. vanilla extract
1½ pt. strawberries, crushed, sweetened with 3 Tbs. sugar

Directions:

1. Bring 5 cups of milk gently to a boil, stirring often, to prevent scorching.
2. In large bowl, beat eggs.
3. Add sugar and salt to eggs, beating until completely blended.
4. Slowly add boiled milk in a thin stream to egg mixture, beating constantly.
5. Add evaporated milk, condensed milk, and vanilla.
6. Add crushed fruit with its juice.
7. Let mixture cool in refrigerator or freezer.
8. Pour into a 4-quart ice cream container and freeze according to manufacturer's directions.

Dark Chocolate Pavé with Strawberry Sauce

This memorable combination of dark chocolate, orange, and strawberries is perfect for the fanciest of dinner parties. In spite of all the steps, it is easy to prepare and can be made ahead of time.

Ingredients for pavé:

2	c. milk
6	oz. quality bitter-sweet chocolate
1	c. sugar
½	c. butter
1	c. cocoa
1	tsp. orange extract or 2 drops orange oil
2	tsp. unflavored gelatin
1	c. heavy whipping cream

Ingredients for strawberry sauce

3	pkg. frozen strawberries in syrup, thawed
½	c. sugar, to taste
1½	Tbs. cornstarch
	juice of ½ orange
	orange zest, for garnish
	frozen whole strawberries, for garnish

Directions for pavé:

1. Prepare an 8½ x 4½-inch loaf pan by lining bottom and long sides with a double layer of wax paper which extends over each edge of pan. Set aside.
2. In a small heavy saucepan, over medium-low heat, bring milk to simmering.
3. Add bitter-sweet chocolate; stir occasionally until chocolate is melted, and mixture is smooth.
4. Add sugar, butter, and cocoa; whisk until completely dissolved. Do not allow mixture to boil.
5. When mixture looks smooth, strain into medium bowl, add orange flavoring, and set aside to cool.

6. In a small microwaveable cup, sprinkle gelatin over 3 tablespoons cold water, and allow this mixture to soften for 2 to 3 minutes.
7. Microwave on high for 20 seconds and allow to stand 2 minutes, or until granules are completely dissolved.
8. Blend into chocolate mixture; set aside.
9. Beat heavy cream in a chilled bowl with chilled beaters until nearly stiff and peaks hold their shape.
10. Cool chocolate mixture to room temperature and fold in whipped cream.
11. Pour into prepared loaf pan and freeze 6 hours or overnight.

Directions for strawberry sauce:

1. In processor, add undrained strawberries and orange juice; blend until smooth. Strain.
2. In a small saucepan, blend sugar, cornstarch and strained strawberries.
3. Place over medium heat and bring to a simmer, stirring frequently.
4. Reduce heat and continue stirring until sauce thickens.
5. Remove from heat and allow cooling.

Directions for serving:

1. Remove pavé from freezer 20 minutes before serving time.
2. Place 2 to 3 tablespoons strawberry sauce on each dessert plate.
3. Slice pavé with a clean knife dipped in warm water and place a slice on each plate.
4. Garnish with thin slices of orange zest and partially frozen whole strawberries.
5. Pass any extra strawberry sauce around the table.

Did You Know?....

Did you know that Wepion, Belgium is known as the strawberry capital of the world? In Wepion, strawberries are topped with lemon juice and white pepper and served fresh.

Summer Strawberry Orange Cups

Try these different cups. The combination of strawberry and orange flavors is delicious.

Ingredients:

1	pt. fresh strawberries, washed, hulled
1	envelope unflavored gelatin
2	Tbs. cool water
2	Tbs. boiling water
½	c. frozen orange juice concentrate, thawed
1½	c. milk
1	tsp. vanilla extract
1	Tbs. sugar

Directions:

1. Cut half the berries into thin slices; place in bottoms of six 8-ounce custard cups, dividing equally; reserve remainder.
2. Soften gelatin in cool water for 5 minutes.
3. Add boiling water to softened gelatin; stir until completely dissolved.
4. Combine orange juice concentrate, milk, vanilla, and sugar; blending well.
5. Stir in dissolved gelatin and pour mixture over sliced strawberries in custard cups.
6. Place in refrigerator for about 2 hours, or until completely jelled.
7. When ready to serve, divide remaining strawberries equally to put on top of each cup.

Strawberries in Balsamic Vinegar

This is an unusual but delicious dessert.

Ingredients:

4	c. fresh strawberries, washed, hulled, quartered
3	Tbs. balsamic vinegar

3   Tbs. sugar
    pepper, freshly ground

Directions:

1. In large bowl, sprinkle berries with balsamic vinegar and sugar; combine well. Marinate 30 minutes, up to 4 hours.
2. Divide strawberries among 4 dessert dishes.
3. Just before serving, sprinkle with freshly ground pepper.

Strawberry Crêpes

Try these delicious crepes. They are definitely a family favorite.

Ingredients:

3   eggs
½   c. flour
½   c. milk
¼   tsp. salt
2   Tbs. butter, melted
2   Tbs. sugar
2   Tbs. almonds, sliced
2   Tbs. powdered sugar
1   Tbs. butter, melted
1   Tbs. lemon juice
3½   c. strawberries, sliced, sweetened with ¼ c. sugar
1   c. heavy cream, whipped

Directions:

1. Preheat oven to 450 degrees F.
2. Lightly grease a 9-inch quiche dish.
3. In large bowl, beat eggs; slowly add flour beating constantly.
4. Stir in milk, salt, butter, and sugar until well blended.
5. Pour into prepared dish.
6. Bake 12 minutes, or until golden brown and fluffy.
7. Sprinkle with almonds and powdered sugar.
8. Drizzle with mixture of butter and lemon juice.
9. Top with berries and whipped cream.

Strawberry Filling for Boston Cream Pie

This is a delicious change of pace from the regular vanilla flavored filling for this cream pie.

Ingredients:

- 1½ c. light cream
- ½ c. sugar
- 2 Tbs. strawberry flavoring
- 2 Tbs. cornstarch
- 1 Tbs. butter
- 1 tsp. vanilla extract

Directions:

1. In medium saucepan, stir together sugar and cornstarch; gradually stir in light cream.
2. Cook over medium heat, stirring constantly, until mixture thickens and begins to boil.
3. Boil 1 minute, stirring constantly; remove from heat. Stir in butter, strawberry and vanilla flavorings.
4. Press plastic wrap directly onto surface.
5. Cool completely.

Berry Parfait

This makes a red, white, and blue dessert that is great to serve at a Fourth of July celebration, or any other festive occasion.

Ingredients:

- 8 oz. cream cheese, at room temperature
- 6 Tbs. powdered sugar
- 1 c. whipping cream
- 2 tsp. fresh lemon juice, to taste
- 1 pt. fresh huckleberries lightly sprinkled with sugar
- 1 pt. fresh strawberries, lightly sprinkled with sugar
  fresh mint leaves, or lemon zest for garnish

Directions:

1. With electric mixer, whip cream cheese and powdered sugar until fluffy; add lemon juice to taste.
2. Slowly add whipping cream, until incorporated and mixture is light and fluffy.
3. To assemble, use parfait glasses, tall wine glasses, or champagne flutes.
4. Spoon 1 inch of huckleberries into glass, top with a dollop of cream mixture, then spoon 1 inch of strawberries on top, followed by another dollop of cream mixture.
5. Spoon another layer of huckleberries, another dollop of cream mixture and top the parfait with a spoonful of strawberries; garnish with mint or lemon zest.
6. You may prepare ahead and refrigerate up to 3 hours.

Strawberries and Cream

Fresh strawberries and this cream topping make an elegant dessert for a dinner party. It is wonderful with Amaretto liqueur, but you may use orange juice in place of liqueur if you prefer.

Ingredients:

1   c. whipping cream
2   Tbs. sugar
½   c. sour cream
1   Tbs. Grand Marnier or Amaretto liqueur
2   pt. fresh strawberries, rinsed, hulled
6   strawberries, for garnish

Directions:

1. In large mixing bowl, with mixer, whip cream and sugar until thick but not stiff.
2. Add sour cream; beat until thoroughly combined.
3. Continue to beat while gradually adding liqueur.
4. Divide strawberries into 6 dessert dishes.
5. Pour cream over berries; top with reserved strawberries.

Strawberry and Raspberry Tart

This is a very colorful and flavorful tart that can be served immediately or can be made ahead and stored for a busy day dessert.

Ingredients:

1	unbaked pie crust
6	Tbs. butter, softened
½	c. sugar
1	lg. egg
¾	c. blanched almonds, finely ground
1	tsp. almond extract
1	Tbs. amaretto flavoring
1	Tbs. flour
2	c. fresh, firm strawberries, rinsed, hulled
2	c. fresh, firm raspberries, picked over, rinsed
¼	c. strawberry jam or jelly, melted, strained

Directions:

1. Preheat oven to 375 degrees F.
2. Roll dough ¼-inch thick on lightly floured surface.
3. Fit into an 8 x 11-inch rectangular or 11-inch round tart pan with removable fluted rim.
4. Chill the shell in refrigerator.
5. In a small bowl, cream together butter and sugar.
6. Beat in egg, almonds, almond extract, and amaretto flavoring; stir in flour.
7. Spread frangipane evenly on the bottom of pie shell.
8. Bake tart in the middle of the oven for 20 to 25 minutes, or until the exposed part of shell is pale golden.
9. Remove from oven; cool.
10. Cut strawberries lengthwise into ⅛-inch thick slices.
11. Arrange the slices, overlapping, decoratively, alternating with the raspberries in rows on the frangipane.
12. Brush gently with melted jam.
13. Let set for 30 minutes hour before serving.

Strawberry Delights Cookbook

A Collection of Strawberry Recipes
Cookbook Delights Series Book 15

Dressings, Sauces, and Condiments

Table of Contents

Page

Strawberry Vinegar.. 184
Sweet-Hot Strawberry Barbecue Sauce 184
Strawberry Grand Marnier Sauce 185
Strawberry Poppy Seed Dressing.. 186
Strawberry Sweetened Whipped Cream...................................... 186
Warm Double Strawberry Sauce... 187
Strawberry Butter 188
Strawberry Rhubarb Sauce 188
Strawberry Orange Sauce 189
Strawberry Raspberry Sauce 189
Strawberry Chutney 190
Strawberry Orange Chutney... 190
Cranberry and Strawberry Relish.. 191
Strawberry Sauce 192
Strawberry Blueberry Sauce... 192

Strawberry Vinegar

This is a wonderful dressing. Serve over your favorite tossed greens, or substitute this versatile dressing in your favorite salad.

Ingredients:

> 5   c. fresh strawberries, rinsed, hulled
> 1   qt. white wine vinegar
> ¼   c. sugar
> 3   pint jars

Directions:

1. After preparing berries, reserve 1 cup whole berries and crush remaining berries.
2. Add vinegar and sugar; and stir well.
3. Cover and refrigerate for 2 days.
4. Place a jelly bag or sieve lined with cheesecloth over bowl and strain berry mixture; do not squeeze. Discard pulp.
5. Place juice in large saucepan and bring just to boil.
6. Place ⅓ cup reserved berries in each jar or bottle.
7. Add very hot juice to within ¼ inch of top; cap or cork.
8. Store in dark cool place for 3 weeks before using.
9. After opening, refrigerate remaining vinegar.

Sweet-Hot Strawberry Barbeque Sauce

This makes a wonderful sauce to put on top of your chicken or pork chops.

Ingredients:

> 2   c. fresh strawberries, hulled, sliced
> ⅓   c. strawberry preserves
> 1   lg. garlic clove, minced
> ⅓   c. ketchup
> 2   Tbs. soy sauce
> 2   Tbs. fresh squeezed lemon juice

1 tsp. fresh ginger, chopped
½ tsp. cayenne powder
½ tsp. fresh grated lemon zest
1 scallion, white part and 1 inch of green, minced
2 Tbs. fresh cilantro, chopped

Directions:

1. In blender container, place strawberries, preserves, garlic, and ketchup; purée until smooth.
2. Add soy sauce, ginger, cayenne, and lemon juice; purée until smooth.
3. Stir in scallion, lemon zest, and cilantro; blend to combine flavors.
4. Refrigerate until ready to serve.

Yields: 2 cups.

Strawberry Grand Marnier Sauce

Grand Marnier makes an excellent combination with strawberries. This sauce is simple yet elegant.

Ingredients:

½ c. sugar
1½ Tbs. cornstarch
1 c. orange juice
¼ c. Grand Marnier liqueur
6 c. fresh strawberries, hulled, sliced

Directions:

1. In 3-quart saucepan, stir together sugar, cornstarch, orange juice, and liqueur until smooth.
2. Bring to boil over medium-high heat, stirring until clear and thickened.
3. Stir in strawberries until well combined.
4. Let cool and serve over good quality vanilla ice cream.

Strawberry Poppy Seed Dressing

This is a very tasty dressing to serve over your favorite salads.

Ingredients:

- ¾ c. sugar
- 1 c. fresh strawberries, hulled
- ½ Tbs. Dijon mustard
- ⅛ tsp. salt
- ¼ red onion, sliced
- ⅔ c. red wine vinegar
- 2 c. canola oil
- 2 Tbs. poppy seeds

Directions:

1. Combine sugar, strawberries, Dijon mustard, salt, onion, and vinegar in blender.
2. Blend ingredients until smooth; lightly stir in the oil and poppy seeds.
3. Keep in refrigerator until ready to serve.

Strawberry Sweetened Whipped Cream

This makes a wonderful topping for cakes and pies.

Ingredients:

- 1½ c. heavy cream, chilled
- 1½ Tbs. sugar
- ½ tsp. vanilla extract
- 3 Tbs. strawberries, mashed

Directions:

1. Chill deep bowl and beaters of electric mixer in freezer for at least 20 minutes.
2. Remove bowl and beaters from freezer; add cream, sugar, and vanilla to chilled bowl.

3. Beat on low speed until small bubbles form, about 30 seconds.
4. Increase speed to medium; continue beating until beaters leave trail in beaten mixture, about 30 seconds.
5. Increase speed to high, continue beating until cream is smooth, thick, and nearly doubled in volume, about 20 seconds for soft peaks, or about 30 seconds for stiff peaks.
6. Fold in strawberries and use immediately.

Warm Double Strawberry Sauce

This is a sweet sauce that can be enjoyed over your favorite angel food or pound cake. This sauce is also great on waffles and crêpes.

Ingredients:

½   c. sugar
¼   c. water
3   Tbs. strawberry jam
2   Tbs. lemon juice
1   Tbs. cornstarch
2   c. fresh strawberries, hulled, halved

Directions:

1. In medium saucepan, combine sugar, water, and jam; stir over medium heat until sugar is dissolved and mixture comes just to boil.
2. Meanwhile, mix juice with cornstarch; stir into sugar mixture.
3. Cook until slightly thickened.
4. Mix in strawberries; heat through but do not cook.
5. Cool slightly and serve.

Did You Know? . . . .

Did you know that if you are expecting a baby, you will be very interested in some of the new discoveries about folic acid? In fact, eight strawberries have 20 percent of the folic acid you need every day.

Strawberry Butter

This butter mixture is delicious on your favorite toast, English muffin, crumpet, or bagel.

Ingredients:

    1   pt. fresh or frozen strawberries, thawed and drained
    ½   lb. butter, softened
    1   c. powdered sugar (use ½ c. if using frozen berries)

Directions:

1. In blender container, place strawberries, butter, and powdered sugar. Process until smooth and creamy.
2. Place in small containers and refrigerate until ready to use.

Yields: 2 cups.

Strawberry Rhubarb Sauce

This is a classic spring sauce to be enjoyed by gardeners and shared with friends.

Ingredients:

    ½   c. sugar
    ⅓   c. water
    1   lb. rhubarb stalks, cleaned, diced
    1   qt. strawberries, cleaned, hulled, halved
    ½   Tbs. lemon juice

Directions:

1. In heavy saucepan, over medium heat, combine sugar and water, stirring until sugar is dissolved.
2. Add rhubarb; simmer 15 minutes, or until tender.
3. Add strawberries and lemon juice; simmer 10 minutes more.
4. Cool and refrigerate until ready to serve, up to 2 or 3 days.

Strawberry Orange Sauce

This is a fresh sauce that can be used over ice cream, cake or even used as a dressing for salad.

Ingredients:

- 2   c. fresh strawberries, washed, hulled
- 4   Tbs. sugar
- 1   Tbs. orange juice concentrate

Directions:

1. In food processor, crush berries.
2. Add sugar and orange juice.
3. Cover.
4. Chill until ready to serve.

Strawberry Raspberry Sauce

Kirsch has a wonderful flavor when added to this strawberry recipe combination.

Ingredients:

- 2   c. fresh strawberries, rinsed, hulled
- 10 oz. frozen raspberries, thawed, drained
- 1   Tbs. Kirsch liquor

Directions:

1. In blender, combine strawberries, raspberries, and liquor.
2. Purée until smooth.
3. Refrigerate in covered container until ready to serve.
4. Serve over ice cream or fresh fruit sorbet.
5. Note: This may be kept in the refrigerator for up to three days.

Strawberry Chutney

This chutney is delicious with your favorite cheese and crackers.

Ingredients:

- ¼   c. raisins
- ¼   c. brown sugar, firmly packed
- ¼   c. fresh lemon juice
- ¼   c. raspberry vinegar
- 2   Tbs. honey
- 2   c. fresh strawberries

Directions:

1. In medium saucepan, combine first 5 ingredients.
2. Bring to a boil.
3. Reduce heat to medium; cook 15 minutes or until slightly thick.
4. Stir in strawberries.
5. Reduce heat to low; simmer 10 minutes or until thick, stirring occasionally.

Strawberry Orange Chutney

This is another version of chutney. It is delicious served with cream cheese and gingersnaps.

Ingredients:

- ½   c. golden raisins
- ½   c. dark brown sugar, firmly packed
- ½   c. strawberry preserves
- ½   c. strawberry wine vinegar
- ½   c. fresh orange juice
- 2   tsp. gingerroot, minced, peeled
- ½   tsp. curry powder
- 1   med. navel orange

4   c. whole strawberries, hulled, diced
½   c. almonds, sliced
     strawberry fans, for garnish (optional)

Directions:

1. Combine the first 8 ingredients in a large nonreactive saucepan; bring to boil.
2. Cook, uncovered, over medium heat for 15 minutes or until slightly thickened and syrupy, stirring frequently.
3. Add strawberries; reduce heat; simmer, uncovered, 10 minutes, or until thickened, stirring occasionally.
4. Remove from heat.
5. Stir in almonds.
6. Spoon into a bowl; cover and chill.
7. Serve with cream cheese and gingersnaps.
8. Garnish with strawberry fans, if desired.

Cranberry and Strawberry Relish

Try this delicious combination in a relish. Serve on or with anything you like.

Ingredients:

1   pkg. frozen strawberries, thawed (10 oz.)
½   c. sugar
3   c. cranberries

Directions:

1. Drain frozen strawberries, reserving the liquid and adding water to make 1 cup.
2. In a saucepan, heat the liquid, sugar, and cranberries.
3. Bring to a boil, reduce heat; simmer uncovered for 10 minutes.
4. Stir strawberries into the mixture, cover, and refrigerate until served.

Strawberry Sauce

This is a whipped cream type of sauce that is delicious served over warm pound cake or with hot scones, biscuits, pancakes, crêpes, or waffles.

Ingredients:

5   Tbs. butter, softened
1   c. powdered sugar
⅔   c. fresh strawberries, hulled, crushed
½   c. whipping cream

Directions:

1. Cream butter; slowly add sugar until well blended.
2. Gradually add strawberries, beating until smooth.
3. Add whipping cream and beat until sauce is light and barely holds soft peaks.
4. Cover and chill until ready to serve, up to 4 days.

Strawberry Blueberry Sauce

Try this rich, tart sauce on your favorite pancakes or bagels.

Ingredients:

1   c. water
2   Tbs. lemon juice
2   Tbs. cornstarch
2   c. blueberries
2   c. strawberries
¼   c. sugar

Directions:

1. In small saucepan, combine first 3 ingredients; mix well.
2. Add blueberries and strawberries; bring to a boil.
3. Reduce heat; simmer 2 minutes; stirring constantly until clear and thickened.
4. Remove from heat; add sugar and mix well.

Strawberry Delights Cookbook

A Collection of Strawberry Recipes
Cookbook Delights Series Book 15

Jams, Jellies, and Syrups

Table of Contents

Page

A Basic Guide for Canning Jams, Jellies, and Syrups 194
Citrus Strawberry Preserves 195
Strawberry Preserves 196
Strawberry Hedgerow Jam 196
Strawberry Gooseberry Jam 197
Freezer Strawberry Jam 198
Strawberry Syrup 198
Strawberry Kiwi Jam 199
Strawberry Guava Jam 200
Strawberry Huckleberry Jam 200
Mango Strawberry Jam with Kiwifruit 201
Strawberry Raspberry Jam 202
Strawberry Blueberry Jam 202
Strawberry Drink Mix Jelly 203
Strawberry Peach Jam 204
Rhubarb Strawberry Jam 204
Strawberry Apple Jelly 205
Strawberry Orange Jam 206

A Basic Guide for Canning Jams, Jellies, and Syrups

1. Wash jars in hot, soapy water inside and out with brush or soft cloth.
2. Run your finger around rim of each jar, discarding any with cracks or chips.
3. Rinse well in clean, clear, hot water, using tongs to avoid burns to hands or fingers.
4. Place upside down on clean cloth to drain well.
5. Place lids in boiling water for 2 minutes to sterilize and keep hot until placing on rim of jar.
6. Immediately prior to filling each jar with hot food, immerse in hot water for 1 minute to heat jars. Heating jars avoids breakage.
7. Fill each jar to within ⅛ inch of top of rim or to level recommended in recipe.
8. Wipe rims of jars with clean, damp cloth to remove any particles of food, and check again for any chips or cracks.
9. Using tongs, place lids from hot bath directly onto jars.
10. Place rings over lids, and using cloth, gloves, or holders, tighten down firmly while hanging onto jars.
11. Do not tighten lids down too hard as air may become trapped in jars and prevent them from sealing.
12. Place on protected surface to cool, taking care to not disturb lid and ring. Lids will show slight indentation when sealed.
13. Leave overnight until thoroughly cooled.
14. When cooled, wipe jars with damp cloth, and then label and date each.
15. Store upright on shelf in cool, dark place.

Did You Know? . . . .

Did you know that strawberries were named in the 19th century? English children picked strawberries and strung them on grass straws and sold them as "Straws of berries?"

Citrus Strawberry Preserves

These strawberry preserves have just a hint of lemon, lime, and orange flavor added with the pieces of peel, and are absolutely delicious.

Ingredients:

5	c. strawberries, rinsed, hulled, chopped small
1	sm. lemon
1	sm. lime
1	sm. orange
5	c. sugar
1	pkg. liquid fruit pectin

Directions:

1. Place strawberries in large pot.
2. Remove skins in quarters from lemon, lime, and orange; lay skins flat. Shave off and discard half of the inside white membranes; with a sharp knife or scissors, slice remaining rind very fine.
3. Add to strawberries.
4. Add sugar to berries and mix well, let stand for 10 minutes.
5. Bring to a full rolling boil; stirring constantly, boil hard for 5 minutes. Remove from heat.
6. Immediately stir in liquid fruit pectin.
7. Stir and skim foam for 7 minutes to prevent floating fruit.
8. Process following a basic guide for canning found in the front of this section.

Did You Know? . . . .

Did you know the strawberry is not classified by botanists as a true berry? True berries have seeds inside; the strawberry however, has dry, yellow "seeds" on the outside, each of which is actually considered a separate fruit.

Strawberry Preserves

We like the pieces of fruit that come in preserves, and this one is chock full of berry pieces.

Ingredients:

    5   c. strawberries, washed, hulled
    6   c. sugar
        juice of ½ orange

Directions:

1. Stir ingredients together and let stand for 2 hours.
2. Bring to rolling boil; boil for 7 minutes.
3. Remove from heat and skim off foam.
4. Process following a basic guide for canning found in the front of this section.

Strawberry Hedgerow Jam

I haven't figured out where the title comes from in this recipe, but I can definitely tell you that the taste is delicious.

Ingredients:

    1   lb. cooking apples, peeled, cored, chopped
    2   lb. strawberries, rinsed, hulled
    1   lb. blueberries, cleaned, and loose stems removed
    1   orange rind, finely grated
    ½   cinnamon stick
    2   lb. sugar
    1¾ c. water
         juice from 1 orange

Directions:

1. In large pot, stew apples with 1¾ cup water for 15 minutes, until soft.

2. Add strawberries, blueberries, orange rind, orange juice, and cinnamon; cook for 10 minutes until berries start to break up.
3. Add sugar, stirring over low heat until dissolved.
4. Remove cinnamon stick and boil rapidly for 15 to 20 minutes or until good set is obtained.
5. Good set can be tested by placing a spoon of jam onto a flat plate to test if it holds its shape rather than running across plate. No liquid should be noted when testing.
6. Process following a basic guide for canning found in the front of this section.

Strawberry Gooseberry Jam

This jam is a recipe that comes from a time when people grew strawberries and gooseberries in abundance in the garden.

Ingredients:

6   c. gooseberries
3   c. strawberries, hulled, mashed
1½ c. water
4   c. sugar

Directions:

1. Rinse, stem and hull berries. Place in saucepan with sugar and water; bring to boil.
2. Reduce heat; simmer until gooseberries and strawberries are soft, approximately 15 minutes.
3. Process following a basic guide for canning found in the front of this section.

Did You Know? . . . .

Did you know the scientific classification for strawberry was derived from the old Latin word for fragrant?

Freezer Strawberry Jam

This is an easy-to-make strawberry jam, and, because it is frozen, it is always handy.

Ingredients:

- 2   c. strawberries, finely crushed
- 3   c. sugar
- 1   pkg. powdered fruit pectin
- 1   c. water

Directions:

1. In large bowl, combine fruit and sugar; let stand 20 minutes, stirring occasionally.
2. Boil pectin and water rapidly for 1 minute, stirring constantly; remove from heat.
3. Add strawberries and stir 2 minutes.
4. Spoon into freezer containers, wipe clean and place lids on with date.

Strawberry Syrup

This syrup makes a wonderful gift. Strawberry syrup is great served over pancakes, waffles, or your favorite crêpes.

Ingredients:

- 8   c. strawberries, washed, hulled, crushed
- ¼   c. lemon juice
- 3   c. sugar
- 1   c. corn syrup
- 3   pint jars, sterilized

Directions:

1. Place strawberries in 4 to 6-quart pot; bring to boil over medium heat, stirring occasionally.

2. Pour berries into damp jelly bag set over a bowl covered with double thickness of cheesecloth. (To keep cheesecloth from slipping, fasten with clip clothespins to rim of bowl.)
3. Let juice drip for 2 hours; there will be 3 to 4 cups of juice.
4. Return juice to pot; combine with remaining ingredients.
5. Stir constantly; bring to rolling boil over high heat; boil 1 minute.
6. Pour syrup into 3 hot, sterilized pint jars, leaving 1 inch headspace. Wipe rim of jar with damp cloth and attach lid.
7. Note: Recipe can be halved and refrigerated without processing when used within a few weeks.

Strawberry Kiwi Jam

With the addition of kiwis, this strawberry jam has a refreshingly tropical flavor.

Ingredients:

2¾ c. strawberries, rinsed, hulled, crushed
1¼ c. kiwi fruit, peeled, chopped
3¼ c. sugar, divided
1   pkg. pectin, powdered

Directions:

1. Measure prepared fruits into large bowl.
2. Measure sugar and set aside.
3. Combine pectin with ¼ cup of measured sugar.
4. Gradually add to fruit, stirring well; let stand 30 minutes stirring occasionally.
5. Stir in remaining sugar.
6. Continue to stir for 3 minutes until most of sugar is dissolved.
7. Spoon into freezer containers.
8. Wipe clean and place lid on container with date and name of jam.
9. Place in freezer until ready to use.

Strawberry Guava Jam

This makes a delicious and different-tasting jam. Guavas are hard to find but worth the effort.

Ingredients:

2   lb. ripe guavas, firm to the touch
1   lb. strawberries
6   c. water
5   c. sugar

Directions:

1. Rinse guavas and cut into quarters.
2. Rinse, hull, and quarter strawberries.
3. Boil strawberries and guavas uncovered, in a big pot on medium heat, for 45 minutes.
4. Drain using colander; reserve liquid.
5. Use 5 cups of the reserved liquid and combine with boiled fruit and sugar, then return mixture to a boil.
6. Cook at medium-high, uncovered, for 35 minutes until thick or 226 degrees F. on a candy thermometer and fruit is disintegrated.
7. Process following a basic guide for canning found in the front of this section.

Strawberry Huckleberry Jam

This jam is even more special with the addition of the elusive huckleberry!

Ingredients:

6   c. strawberries, rinsed, hulled, crushed
1   c. water
7   c. sugar
1   c. huckleberries
½   c. bottled liquid pectin

Directions:

1. In a large kettle, combine strawberries with water.
2. Cover, bring to a boil; reduce heat and simmer 5 minutes.
3. Measure fruit mixture, adding water to make 3 cups of strawberry pulp.
4. Combine pulp, huckleberries, and sugar in large kettle, mixing well.
5. Heat to full rolling boil and boil hard 1 minute, stirring constantly.
6. Remove from heat, stir in pectin, and skim off foam.
7. Process following a basic guide for canning found in the front of this section.

Mango Strawberry Jam with Kiwifruit

This mango strawberry jam with kiwifruit is a great change of pace. The mangoes and kiwifruit add a tropical touch of flavor and make this an excellent jam for use as a glaze on pork or grilled chicken.

Ingredients:

2   c. mango, diced
1¾   c. strawberries, mashed
¾   c. kiwi, diced
¼   c. lemon juice
1   tsp. citric acid
7½   c. sugar
2   pouches fruit pectin

Directions:

1. In large heavy kettle or saucepan, combine fruits, citric acid, lemon juice, and sugar; bring to boil.
2. Stir in fruit pectin and return to hard boil; boil 1 minute before placing in jars.
3. Process following a basic guide for canning found in the front of this section.
4. Freeze until ready to use.

Strawberry Raspberry Jam

This jam is reminiscent of hot summer days spent on the old fashioned swing on the back porch where we laid for hours smelling the raspberries as they ripened on their canes.

Ingredients:

> 3   c. sugar
> 1⅔ c. strawberries, rinsed, hulled, finely chopped
> 1½ c. fresh or frozen raspberries, crushed
> 1½ tsp. lemon juice

Directions:

1. In large kettle, combine all ingredients.
2. Over low heat, cook 10 minutes, stirring occasionally, until sugar is dissolved and mixture is bubbly.
3. Bring to rolling boil, cooking for 15 minutes, stirring constantly; remove from heat.
4. Skim foam from top of jam before processing.
5. Process following a basic guide for canning found in the front of this section.

Strawberry Blueberry Jam

Strawberries and blueberries are great together and also make delicious jam.

Ingredients:

> 3   c. fresh strawberries
> 1   c. fresh blueberries
> 3¼ c. sugar, divided
> 1   pkg. fruit pectin

Directions:

1. Rinse, hull, and stem fruit thoroughly.
2. Crush in a large bowl.
3. Measure sugar into a separate bowl.

4. In small bowl, combine ¼ cup sugar and fruit pectin.
5. Stir fruit pectin mixture into berries gradually.
6. Let stand 30 minutes, stirring occasionally.
7. Stir remaining sugar gradually into berry mixture.
8. Stir constantly until sugar completely dissolves, about 3 minutes.
9. Process following a basic guide for canning found in the front of this section.

Yields: 6 cups.

Strawberry Drink Mix Jelly

This is a jelly that is made with fruit, and its flavor is enhanced even more with the addition of unsweetened powdered drink mix.

Ingredients:

2   c. fresh strawberries, mashed
2   c. water
1   pkg. unsweetened, fruit-flavored drink mix (0.13 oz.)
1   pkg. dry pectin (2 oz.)
5   c. sugar

Directions:

1. In large saucepan, over medium-high heat, mix together strawberries, water, drink mix, and pectin powder.
2. Bring to a full rolling boil; stir in sugar.
3. Boil 3 minutes more.
4. Transfer to sterile jars, leaving ½ inch space at the top.
5. Process following a basic guide for canning found in the front of this section.
6. Store in the refrigerator.

Did You Know? . . . .

Did you know that there is a centuries old myth that says if someone breaks a double strawberry in half and shares it with someone else, they will fall in love?

Strawberry Peach Jam

Try this delicious fruit combination on your favorite muffin, toast, or bagel.

Ingredients:

    1¾ c. prepared fruit (1 pt. strawberries, ¾ lb. ripe peaches)
    4   c. sugar
    1   Tbs. lemon juice
    ¾   c. water
    1   box powdered fruit pectin

Directions:

1. Thoroughly crush 1 pint of fully ripe strawberries.
2. Measure 1 cup into a large bowl or pan.
3. Peel, pit, and finely chop peaches.
4. Measure ¾ cup and combine with strawberries.
5. Measure sugar and lemon juice, add to fruits; mix well and let stand.
6. Mix water and powdered fruit pectin in a small saucepan.
7. Bring to a boil and boil 1 minute, stirring constantly.
8. Stir into fruit mixture; continue stirring 3 minutes.
9. Ladle quickly into glasses. Cover at once with tight lids.
10. When jam is set, store in freezer.
11. If jam will be used within 2 or 3 weeks, it may be stored in the refrigerator.

Rhubarb Strawberry Jam

This is a traditional way to make rhubarb jam, and the strawberry gelatin really does add quite a bit of flavor to the recipe.

Ingredients:

    5   c. fresh rhubarb, chopped
    3   c. sugar
    1   pkg. strawberry flavored gelatin (3 oz.)

Directions:

1. In large saucepan or stockpot, stir together the rhubarb and sugar; cover and let stand overnight.
2. Over medium heat, bring rhubarb and sugar to boil.
3. On low heat; boil, stirring constantly, 12 minutes.
4. Remove from heat.
5. Stir in dry gelatin mix.
6. Transfer to sterile jars and refrigerate.

Strawberry Apple Jelly

Try this jelly on your favorite toast, bagel, or muffin.

Ingredients:

1½ c. unsweetened apple juice
1   pt. fully ripe strawberries
3½ c. sugar
1   pouch liquid fruit pectin

Directions:

1. Pour apple juice into a preserving kettle or large saucepan.
2. Thoroughly crush strawberries.
3. Measure ½ cup prepared berries; add to apple juice.
4. Add sugar.
5. Place pan over high heat; bring to boil, stirring continuously.
6. Stir in liquid fruit pectin; bring to a full rolling boil.
7. Boil hard for 1 minute, stirring continuously.
8. Remove kettle from heat.
9. Skim off foam with a metal spoon.
10. Pour quickly into hot sterilized jars leaving ½ inch head space.
11. Seal with melted paraffin wax. Cover with clean lids.
12. Store in a cool, dark, dry place.
13. Note: Bottled strawberry cocktail can be substituted for the fresh strawberry juice, giving a slightly sweeter product.

Strawberry Orange Jam

This recipe is a good choice to make for novice jam makers.

Ingredients:

    10 c. whole strawberries, semi-crushed
    1   lg. thin-skinned orange
    7   c. sugar

Directions:

1. Lightly spray pot on bottom and sides with cooking spray.
2. Wash and hull berries.
3. Remove all small berries and set aside.
4. Crush or mash remaining berries coarsely in a food processor or by hand (hand method is messier but best).
5. Wash orange, cut, seed, and grind in a food processor until it is a fine paste.
6. Combine reserved whole berries with crushed berries and puréed orange and mix well.
7. Place fruit and sugar in pot; stir over low-medium heat.
8. As sugar dissolves, increase heat to medium-high and simmer jam until foam forms.
9. Boil gently until jam tests done.
10. Ladle into sterilized jars.
11. Process following a basic guide for canning found in the front of this section.

Yields: 7 to 9 half pint jars.

Did You Know?....

Did you know that Ancient Romans used strawberries as medicine? They believed the fruit could cure fever, bad breath, gout, sore throats, depression, fainting, and diseases of the blood.

Strawberry Delights Cookbook

**A Collection of Strawberry Recipes
Cookbook Delights Series Book 15**

Main Dishes

Table of Contents

Page

Grilled Shrimp with Strawberry Salsa 208
Chicken Strawberry Sauce Bake 209
Pork Chops with Strawberry Mustard Glaze 210
Grilled Tuna Steaks with Fresh Fruit.. 210
Strawberry Lemon Sole 212
Prawns, Peas, and Strawberries 213
Chicken with Strawberry Sauce.. 214
Sea Bass with Spicy Strawberry Sauce 214
Spiced Glazed Pork Tenderloin... 216
Strawberry Glazed Ham 217
Quesadillas with Strawberry Salsa... 218
Stir-Fried Scallops with Strawberries... 219
Almond Dusted Strawberry Balsamic Chicken 220

Grilled Shrimp with Strawberry Salsa

This dish is flavorful and a bit spicy, so serve with a salad and a mild side dish such as white rice or fettuccine alfredo to complete the meal.

Ingredients:

    1½ lb. fresh or frozen shrimp in shells
    1   Tbs. butter, melted
    ¼   tsp. salt
    ¼   tsp. ground cumin
    ¼   tsp. white pepper
    ¼   tsp. ground red pepper or cayenne pepper

Ingredients for the salsa:

    1   fresh serrano pepper
    2   c. strawberries, rinsed, hulled, sliced
    ⅓   c. jicama, chopped, peeled
    2   Tbs. pineapple juice or orange juice
    1   Tbs. fresh cilantro, snipped
    ⅓   c. red sweet pepper, chopped

Directions:

1. Thaw shrimp, if frozen, peel and devein, leaving tails intact, if desired.
2. In small bowl, stir together melted butter, salt, cumin, white pepper, and ground red pepper.
3. Drizzle over shrimp, tossing to coat.
4. For salsa, wear plastic gloves to halve serrano pepper, remove seeds, stem, and veins; finely chop.
5. In a bowl, toss together serrano pepper, cilantro or parsley, strawberries, sweet pepper, jicama, pineapple or orange juice, and set aside.
6. Spray a grill basket with nonstick coating.
7. Arrange shrimp in basket and close, or thread shrimp on 8 metal skewers, leaving ¼ inch between pieces.

8. Place basket or skewers on rack or uncovered grill directly over medium coals. Grill 10 to 12 minutes, or until shrimp turn opaque, turning once halfway through grilling.
9. Remove shrimp from basket or skewers.
10. Serve shrimp with salsa.

Yields: 6 servings.

Chicken Strawberry Sauce Bake

This is a fruity sauce reminiscent of barbecue sauce, and is an excellent use for summer strawberries.

Ingredients:

4   chicken breasts
½   c. onion, chopped
2   tsp. canola oil
1½ c. ketchup
¾   c. brown sugar, packed
½   tsp. orange peel, grated
1½ c. strawberries, rinsed, hulled, puréed
      parsley sprigs, for garnish

Directions:

1. Preheat oven to 400 degrees F.
2. Lightly grease a 9 x 13-inch baking dish.
3. Place chicken breast halves in prepared dish.
4. Bake 25 minutes.
5. Heat oil in a medium skillet, over medium heat. Cook and stir onion until tender.
6. Add ketchup, brown sugar, and orange peel; stir until all is dissolved. Stir in strawberries.
7. Spoon mixture over partially baked chicken breast.
8. Bake an additional 20 minutes, or until chicken is tender.
9. Serve immediately with sauce spooned over chicken breasts and garnish with a sprig of parsley.

Pork Chops with Strawberry Mustard Glaze

This is a fantastic glaze for pork, with a hint of sweet, and a hint of sour. This glaze is also great on ribs, chicken, or ham.

Ingredients for pork chops:

4　loin pork chops, ½-inch thick, trimmed of fat
½　tsp. garlic salt

Ingredients for glaze:

¼　c. strawberry preserves
2　Tbs. coarse mustard or Dijon mustard

Directions:

1.　Heat grill; rub both sides of pork chops with garlic salt.
2.　In a small bowl, combine glaze ingredients, mixing well.
3.　When grill is hot, place pork chops on gas grill over medium heat, or on charcoal grill 4 to 6 inches away from medium coals.
4.　Cook 8 to 11 minutes, or until tender and no longer pink, turning once.
5.　Brush with glaze during the last 5 minutes of cooking time.
6.　Serve immediately.

Grilled Tuna Steaks with Fresh Fruit

These tuna steaks are wonderfully seasoned and then topped with warm tropical fruit to make the most enticing dish. Try this recipe the next time you have company coming for dinner, and you will be sure to impress your guests.

Ingredients:

¼　c. fresh basil leaves
⅔　c. mild olive oil
2　Tbs. balsamic vinegar

210

1   Tbs. soy sauce
½   Tbs. fresh ground black pepper
¼   tsp. sugar
¼   tsp. salt
2   Tbs. hot water
4   whole tuna steaks
½   c. banana, sliced
½   c. strawberries, diced
½   c. mango, peeled, pitted, diced
½   c. papaya, peeled, seeded, diced
2   Tbs. fresh cilantro leaves, snipped
2   Tbs. butter
2   Tbs. lemon juice
1   Tbs. sugar

Directions:

1. In blender, place basil leaves, olive oil, vinegar, soy sauce, pepper, sugar, salt, and 2 tablespoons hot water; purée for the marinade.
2. Arrange tuna steaks in a baking dish large enough to hold them in a single layer. Pour marinade over the fish.
3. Cover; marinate 3 to 4 hours in refrigerator, turning the steaks occasionally.
4. Prepare coals for grilling, or preheat the broiler.
5. Drain the tuna steaks; grill over medium-hot coals, or broil 4 to 5 inches from heat for 3 minutes, or until charred on the outside but still pink in the center, turning once. Do not over cook.
6. Remove from heat; place steaks on warmed dinner plates.
7. In large skillet, over medium heat, melt 2 tablespoons butter.
8. Add banana, strawberries, mango, papaya, fresh cilantro leaves, lemon juice, and sugar.
9. Sauté, just until the mixture is heated through, about 30 seconds. Do not overcook.
10. Season to taste with salt and freshly ground black pepper.
11. Spoon the sautéed fruit mixture over the tuna and serve immediately.

Strawberry Lemon Sole

This is an easy-to-make dish with a strawberry dipping sauce that both adults and children will love.

Ingredients for fish fillets:

1	egg
1	Tbs. water
½	c. corn flakes crumbs
¼	tsp. salt
¼	tsp. paprika
⅛	tsp. pepper
4	fillets of sole or flounder, sliced lengthwise in half

Ingredients for strawberry sauce:

⅔	c. strawberry preserves
1	Tbs. lemon juice
1	tsp. prepared mustard
½	tsp. grated lemon peel
⅛	tsp. salt

Directions for fish fillets:

1. Preheat oven to 425 degrees F.
2. Coat baking sheet with nonstick cooking spray.
3. In pie plate, combine egg and water.
4. In plastic bag, combine crumbs, salt, paprika, and pepper.
5. Dip each fish fillet into egg mixture, drop into bag and shake to coat with crumbs. Arrange fish in single layer on baking sheet.
6. Bake 10 minutes, or until fish flakes easily with a fork. Do not turn fish.

Directions for strawberry sauce:

1. In small saucepan, combine preserves, lemon juice, mustard, grated lemon peel, and salt.
2. Heat together until mixture just comes to boil.
3. Remove from heat; cool slightly. Serve with the fish.

Prawns, Peas, and Strawberries

The strawberries add just the right contrast of flavors to the dish. Try this dish for a change of pace when cooking prawns.

Ingredients:

32	med. size prawns
3	bay leaves, broken in half
½	tsp. fennel seeds
2	tsp. salt
4	Tbs. extra virgin olive oil
1	lg. onion, peeled, finely chopped
2	lg. garlic cloves, peeled, finely chopped
2	c. shelled fresh or frozen peas
⅓	c. pesto
1	lb. strawberries, rinsed, hulled, sliced

Directions:

1. Remove shells from prawns; cut them lengthwise halfway through from the top so that they look like butterflies.
2. Remove the alimentary tract.
3. Wash prawns in cold water, drain them, and set aside.
4. Put 2 quarts of water in a saucepan; add bay leaves, fennel seeds, salt, and 1 tablespoon olive oil.
5. Bring the water to a simmer.
6. Meanwhile, sauté onion in 2 tablespoons of olive oil until it is transparent.
7. Add garlic and sauté 2 minutes more.
8. Add peas and stir well.
9. Cook peas for 3 minutes, or until they are just done.
10. Put the prawns in the simmering water; let them cook for 2 minutes. Remove from water and mix in with the peas, tossing well.
11. Add pesto; toss again, remove from heat.
12. Cool; serve at room temperature, garnished with sliced strawberries.

Chicken with Strawberry Sauce

Our family loves chicken, and with the added flavor of strawberries, this makes a unique dish.

Ingredients:

- ½   c. dry red wine
- ¼   c. canola oil
- 4   chicken breasts, boneless, skinless
- ¼   c. water
- 1   tsp. lime juice
- ¼   tsp. caraway seeds, crushed
- ½   c. strawberry preserves
- ¾   tsp. pepper, divided
- 1   tsp. prepared mustard
- 1   Tbs. steak sauce
- ½   c. soy sauce, divided

Directions:

1. In shallow dish, place chicken.
2. In small bowl, combine ¼ cup soy sauce, oil, and ¼ teaspoon ground pepper, stirring well; pour over chicken.
3. Cover; refrigerate 2 hours, turning occasionally.
4. In small saucepan, combine strawberry preserves, water, mustard, lime juice, ¼ cup soy sauce, ½ teaspoon pepper, caraway seeds, and steak sauce.
5. Cook over low heat until thoroughly hot.
6. Place chicken on broiler; broil 5 inches from heat, 15 to 20 minutes; slice thin and serve with sauce.

Sea Bass with Spicy Strawberry Sauce

Try this spicy dish the next time you are serving bass, and enjoy the compliments you will receive about your cooking.

Ingredients:

- 4   sea bass fillets
- 1   Tbs. hot sauce

2   Tbs. olive oil
    salt and pepper, to taste

Ingredients for the sauce:

¾   Tbs. hot sauce
6   Tbs. strawberry preserves
3   Tbs. red wine vinegar
½   Tbs. soy sauce
2   Tbs. seafood cocktail sauce
¼   tsp. garlic powder
    salt, to taste
    fresh strawberries, rinsed, hulled, sliced, for garnish

Directions:

1. In a plastic zipper bag, combine sea bass fillets, salt and pepper to taste, and hot sauce.
2. Refrigerate 4 hours, or overnight.
3. In a small saucepan, combine hot sauce, strawberry preserves, vinegar, soy sauce, cocktail sauce, and garlic powder.
4. Over low heat, simmer, stirring occasionally.
5. Correct seasoning with salt to taste.
6. Sauté the marinated sea bass fillets in olive oil, until fish is lightly browned and flakes easily but is not dry, about 5 to 6 minutes per side.
7. Serve immediately.
8. Drizzle with strawberry sauce.
9. Garnish with strawberry slices.

Did You Know? . . . .

Did you know if all the strawberries produced in California this year were laid berry to berry, they would wrap around the world 15 times?

Spiced Glazed Pork Tenderloin

This is an aromatic and flavorful way of preparing roast pork. Try this with new strawberries in the spring for a mouth watering delight.

Ingredients:

1	Tbs. sugar
1	tsp. kosher salt
1	tsp. black pepper, coarsely ground
½	tsp. ground coriander
¼	tsp. ground cloves
2	lbs. pork tenderloins, fat trimmed
1	tsp. olive oil
2	c. maple syrup, divided
1	lb. strawberries, puréed

Directions:

1. In a large, zippered plastic bag, combine sugar, salt, pepper, coriander, and cloves.
2. Place tenderloins in bag; shake bag to coat with spice mixture.
3. Add ¾ cup of maple syrup and strawberries to the bag; massage into the tenderloins.
4. Refrigerate for 6 hours.
5. Preheat the oven to 375 degrees F.
6. Place tenderloins on a rack in a roasting pan; tuck the thin tail end of the tenderloin under itself to form a roast of even thickness. Brush each loin with olive oil; roast 20 minutes.
7. Brush loins with more maple syrup; roast 25 to 30 minutes longer, basting twice more with maple syrup, until a meat thermometer inserted in the center reads 155 degrees F.
8. Remove from oven; let rest for 5 to 10 minutes.
9. Brush meat with pan juices, or more maple syrup and sauté strawberry halves in the remaining juice.
10. Move to serving platter, slice, and spoon the sauté over the meat.

Strawberry Glazed Ham

Try your next ham with this fruity, delicious glaze, and you just may choose to bake your ham this way from now on.

Ingredients:

    5-7 lb. smoked ham, fully cooked
    1½ c. strawberry preserves
    ⅓ c. prepared mustard
    ¼ c. lemon juice
        cloves, to stud ham with

Directions:

1. Preheat oven to 325 degrees F.
2. With a sharp knife, score fat surface, making uniform diagonal cuts about ⅛-inch deep and ¾ inches apart.
3. Place ham fat side up, on rack in a shallow roasting pan.
4. Bake 1½ hours.
5. In small saucepan, combine preserves, mustard, and lemon juice.
6. Cook over low heat, stirring until blended.
7. Stud ham with cloves.
8. Brush ham with ½ cup glaze.
9. Return to oven for another 45 minutes.
10. Remove from oven and place on serving platter.
11. Slice.
12. Serve warm with remaining glaze as accompaniment.

Did You Know? . . . .

Did you know that strawberry juice combined with honey will reduce inflammation or sunburn? Rub the mixture thoroughly into the skin before rinsing off with warm water and lemon juice.

Did you know that strawberries can also play a part in helping to reduce the risk of cancer or heart disease?

Quesadillas with Strawberry Salsa

Quesadillas make a great main dish. Try these for a light meal that is satisfying.

Ingredients:

3	c. mixed Monterey jack and Cheddar cheese, shredded
4	lg. tortillas, 9 or 10-inch
8	oz. deli roast beef, chicken, turkey, or ham, thin sliced

Ingredients for salsa:

½	c. onion, chopped
2	c. fresh strawberries, rinsed, hulled, chopped
3	Tbs. cilantro leaves, chopped
2	Tbs. jalapeno peppers, chopped fine
	salt
	fresh lime juice

Directions:

1. In medium bowl, combine salsa ingredients.
2. Add salt and lime juice to taste.
3. Cover and refrigerate until serving time.
4. Sprinkle ¼ of the cheese on one tortilla.
5. Top with ½ of the meat evenly.
6. Sprinkle with another ¼ of the cheese.
7. Top with another tortilla.
8. On a grill, over medium heat, place quesadilla.
9. Grill for 4 to 5 minutes, or until golden brown.
10. Repeat with the remaining ingredients.
11. Cut into wedges; serve with strawberry salsa.
12. Note: You can also do the quesadilla in a large frying pan over medium heat.

Did You Know? . . . .

Did you know that there is a species of bird called the Strawberry Finch?

Stir-Fried Scallops with Strawberries

Be sure to prepare all ingredients before you start cooking as it will be cooked quickly. Enjoy!

Ingredients:

1¼ lb. bay scallops
¼   tsp. salt
1   tsp. sugar
1   Tbs. rice vinegar or white wine vinegar
1   tsp. sesame oil
1   tsp. cornstarch
1   egg white
1   pt. strawberries, hulled, cut into 6 wedges
⅓   lb. sugar snap peas, strings removed
1   Tbs. sesame oil
     juice of 1 lime
1   tsp. minced fresh gingerroot
     dash white pepper

Directions:

1. Wash scallops; dry with paper towels.
2. Cut in half if they are very large.
3. In medium bowl, combine salt, sugar, vinegar, sesame oil, cornstarch, and egg white.
4. Beat well; add scallops and stir gently to coat well.
5. Chill 1 hour; drain and pat dry with paper towels.
6. Blanch snap peas in boiling water for 10 seconds.
7. Immediately drain under cold water.
8. Pat with paper towels to dry.
9. In wok or large skillet, heat oil and add scallops.
10. Stir-fry over medium-high heat for 3 to 5 minutes, or until just opaque.
11. Add remaining ingredients; cook 1 minute longer just to heat through, stirring gently but constantly.
12. Serve immediately.

Almond Strawberry Balsamic Chicken Breast

This is a delicious chicken dish that is so aromatic, everyone will be asking, "What's for dinner"? Serve with white rice and a fruit dessert and you have a delicious company dinner.

Ingredients:

- 4   boneless, skinless chicken breast halves
- ⅓   c. unblanched almonds, very finely chopped
- ¼   c. shallots or green onions, minced
- ⅓   c. chicken broth
- ⅓   c. strawberry preserves
- 3   Tbs. balsamic vinegar
- 1   Tbs. fresh rosemary, minced
- 10   oz. fresh spinach, cooked tender and kept warm
- 2   Tbs. extra light olive oil
-     salt and pepper, to taste

Directions:

1. Coat a large nonstick skillet with olive oil, heat over medium heat.
2. Sprinkle chicken with salt and pepper; dredge in almonds.
3. Place chicken in skillet; sauté 4 minutes on each side, turning once.
4. Remove from pan and keep warm.
5. Reduce heat to low.
6. Add green onions to skillet, sauté 1 minute.
7. Add chicken broth, strawberry preserves, vinegar, and rosemary. Simmer until slightly thickened, 2 to 3 minutes.
8. Place spinach on warm serving platter.
9. Top with chicken and pour sauce over top.
10. Serve immediately.

Did You Know? . . . .

Did you know that the fresh juice from sieved strawberry pulp has a cooling effect on feverish patients?

Strawberry Delights Cookbook

A Collection of Strawberry Recipes
Cookbook Delights Series Book 15

Pies

Table of Contents

Page

A Basic Recipe for Pie Crust.. 222
A Basic Cookie or Graham Cracker Crust 223
Strawberry Cream Pie.. 224
Strawberry Custard Pie... 225
Strawberry Ice Cream Pie 226
Strawberry Rhubarb Pie 227
Amish Sour Cream Apple Strawberry Pie 228
Strawberry Kiwi Pie.. 229
Strawberry Glazed Pie 230
Strawberry Cream Cheesecake Pie.. 230
Strawberry Filling for Boston Cream Pie 231
Fresh Banana Strawberry Pie 232
Strawberry Cream Cheese Pie.. 233
Frosty Strawberry Cream Pie 234

A Basic Recipe for Pie Crust

This is a very good recipe for a delicious, flaky crust.

Ingredients for single crust:

1½ c. sifted all-purpose flour
½   tsp. salt
½   c. shortening
4-5 Tbs. ice water

Ingredients for double crust:

2   c. sifted all-purpose flour
1   tsp. salt
⅔   c. shortening
5-7 Tbs. ice water

Directions for single crust:

1. In large bowl stir together flour and salt.
2. Cut in shortening with pastry blender or mix with fingertips until pieces are size of coarse crumbs.
3. Sprinkle 2 tablespoons ice water over flour mixture, tossing with fork.
4. Add just enough remaining water 1 tablespoon at a time to moisten dough, tossing so dough holds together.
5. Roll pastry into 11-inch circle, and wrap in plastic wrap; refrigerate for 1 hour.
6. Preheat oven to 425 degrees F.
7. Remove plastic wrap from pastry, and fit pastry into a 9-inch pie plate.
8. Fold edge under and then crimp between thumb and forefinger to make fluted crust.
9. For filled pie with an instant or cooked filling (cream-filled, custard-filled, etc.), prick crust all over with fork then bake 15 to 20 minutes until done.
10. If preparing pie with uncooked filling (such as pumpkin), do not prick crust; pour filling into unbaked pastry shell, and then bake as directed.

Directions for double crust:

1. Turn desired filling into pastry-lined pie plate; trim overhanging edge of pastry ½ inch from rim of plate.
2. Cut slits with knife in top crust for steam vents.
3. Place over filling; trim overhanging edge of pastry 1 inch from rim of plate.
4. Fold and roll top edge under lower edge, pressing on rim to seal; flute.
5. Cover fluted edge with 2- to 3-inch-wide strip of aluminum foil to prevent excessive browning.
6. Remove foil during last 15 minutes of baking.

Yields: 1 pie crust (9-inch single or double).

A Basic Cookie or Graham Cracker Crust

This is a great crust for use with cream pies or for an unbaked pie. Use your favorite flavor of cookie to complement your filling, or use graham crackers.

Ingredients:

2   c. cookie or graham cracker crumbs, finely crushed
⅓   c. sugar
½   c. butter, melted

Directions:

1. Combine crumbs, sugar, and butter.
2. Press mixture firmly against bottom and up sides of 9-inch pie plate.
3. Baking is not necessary, but if preferred crust may be baked at 400 degrees F. for 10 minutes.

Yields: 1 pie crust (9-inch).

Strawberry Cream Pie

This pie tastes like a bite of heaven! Serve it chilled, and make sure there is plenty to go around!

Ingredients:

 3 Tbs. cornstarch
 ½ tsp. salt
 ½ c. sugar
 3 Tbs. flour
 2 c. milk
 1 egg, slightly beaten
 1 c. whipping cream, whipped
 1 tsp. vanilla extract
 2½ c. fresh strawberries, rinsed, hulled, halved
 ½ c. water
 2 tsp. cornstarch
 ¼ c. sugar
 1 baked 9-inch pie crust
   almonds, slivered, toasted

Directions:

1. In medium saucepan, combine cornstarch, salt, sugar, and flour; gradually stir in milk.
2. On medium heat, stirring constantly, bring to a boil.
3. Reduce heat; cook and stir until mixture starts to thicken.
4. Spoon a small amount of hot mixture into egg while stirring; return to remaining hot mixture.
5. Bring just to boiling, stirring constantly.
6. Cool and chill.
7. When thoroughly chilled, beat cream filling well.
8. Whip ½ cup of the whipping cream and fold into the cream filling; fold in vanilla. Chill.
9. Toast almonds until lightly browned, and then sprinkle over the bottom of the cooled pie crust.
10. Fill crust with chilled cream filling.

11. Place 2 cups of the strawberries over the filling.
12. Crush the remaining ½ cup berries, add water, and cook 2 minutes and then sieve.
13. Mix sugar and cornstarch; gradually stir into berry juice.
14. Cook and stir until thick and clear.
15. Cool slightly; pour over halved strawberries on cream filling.
16. Keep refrigerated until serving time.
17. Sweeten the remaining ½ cup of whipping cream with 1 tablespoon sugar and whip.
18. Serve pie with dollops of sweetened whipped cream.

Strawberry Custard Pie

This is an old fashioned custard pie, like grandma used to make. It is simple, yet delicious.

Ingredients:

1	9-inch pastry shell, unbaked
2	c. fresh strawberries, rinsed, hulled
¾	c. sugar
3	Tbs. flour
2	eggs
½	c. cream

Directions:

1. Preheat oven to 425 degrees F.
2. Cut strawberries in half.
3. Blend sugar and flour, toss lightly with strawberries in a bowl.
4. Place strawberries in unbaked pastry lined pie pan.
5. Spread evenly to smooth layer.
6. In small bowl, beat eggs slightly.
7. Add cream, pour over strawberry layer in pastry shell.
8. Bake 10 minutes; reduce heat to 350 degrees F.
9. Continue baking 25 to 30 minutes, or until custard is set.
10. Cool to room temperature; chill until ready to serve.

Strawberry Ice Cream Pie

What a delightful treat on a hot summer day! This pie also makes a great substitute for a birthday cake.

Ingredients:

- 10 oz. shortbread cookies
- ⅓ c. butter, melted
- ¼ tsp. ground cinnamon
- ¼ tsp. ground ginger
- 2 qt. strawberry ice cream, softened
- ¼ c. fudge topping

Directions:

1. In a food processor or blender, process cookies to fine crumbs.
2. Add butter, cinnamon and ginger, process or mix well.
3. Turn crumb mixture into a 9-inch pie plate. Pat into place, and place crust in freezer 10 minutes.
4. Scoop ice cream into balls, mound in prepared crust. Cover with plastic wrap.
5. Place pie in freezer until ready to serve, up to 2 days.
6. When ready to serve pie, place fudge topping in small bowl and heat in the microwave for 20 seconds until just warm.
7. Drizzle the topping from tip of spoon onto pie in a random pattern.
8. Slice and serve.

Did You Know? . . . .

Did you know that in a recent survey, strawberries were picked as the number one fruit with children and were a favorite of people of all ages?

Did you know that native forms of strawberries adapt to various climates? Strawberries are indigenous to every major continent except Africa, Australia, and New Zealand.

Strawberry Rhubarb Pie

This classic dessert is delicious, especially with a scoop of vanilla ice cream!

Ingredients:

4   c. fresh or frozen rhubarb, chopped
2   c. strawberries, sliced
1⅓ c. sugar
¼   c. cornstarch
1   Tbs. lemon juice
¼   tsp. cinnamon
1   egg, beaten
    pastry for a two-crust 9-inch pie

Directions:

1. Preheat oven to 425 degrees F.
2. Roll out half the pastry and line a 9-inch pie plate.
3. Trim, leaving ½ inch over the pie plate.
4. Combine rhubarb, strawberries, sugar, cornstarch, lemon juice, and cinnamon, mixing well.
5. Spoon mixture into the pie shell.
6. Roll out remaining pastry and cut into 1-inch strips.
7. Make a lattice top crust on the pie by crisscrossing the strips over the filling.
8. Trim the strips even with the pie plate.
9. Fold the ½ inch of the bottom crust over the ends of the strips.
10. Seal and flute the edges.
11. Brush lattice with beaten egg.
12. Place on a baking sheet, or tin foil, in the oven.
13. Bake for 15 minutes, until the crust starts to brown.
14. Reduce heat to 375 degrees F.
15. Bake 50 to 60 minutes, or until crust is golden, rhubarb is tender, and filling is thickened.
16. Cool to lukewarm and serve.

Amish Sour Cream Apple Strawberry Pie

My husband and I lived in Iowa City for four years, and it was always a treat to go to visit the Amish colonies! They served an Amish apple strawberry pie that we still like to bake and enjoy at home.

Ingredients for pie:

1	c. sour cream
1	egg
½	c. sugar
2	Tbs. flour
2	c. apples, diced, peeled
2	c. strawberries, rinsed, hulled
1	unbaked 9-inch pie shell

Ingredients for crumb topping:

½	c. brown sugar
⅓	c. flour
⅓	c. butter
1	tsp. cinnamon

Directions for pie:

1. Preheat oven to 400 degrees F.
2. In large bowl, beat together sour cream and egg; add flour, sugar, and vanilla, blending well.
3. Fold in apples and strawberries.
4. Pour into the unbaked pie shell.
5. Bake 25 minutes; place on wire rack.

Directions for crumb topping:

1. In small bowl, combine brown sugar, flour, and cinnamon; cut in butter until crumbly.
2. Sprinkle over top of pie; return to oven and bake 20 minutes more.
3. Remove from oven and cool before serving.

Strawberry Kiwi Pie

This is a delicious summer dessert and looks beautiful with the contrast of fresh slices of kiwi and strawberries on the top.

Ingredients:

⅓   c. sugar
¼   c. cornstarch
¼   tsp. salt
2⅔ c. milk
2   Tbs. butter
1   tsp. vanilla extract
¼   c. nuts, finely chopped
1   baked pie shell
4   med. kiwis, peeled, sliced
2   c. fresh strawberries, rinsed, hulled, sliced
    whipped cream, sweetened

Directions:

1. In medium saucepan, mix sugar, cornstarch, and salt.
2. Gradually stir in milk until blended.
3. Over medium heat, stir until mixture comes to a boil.
4. Boil 1 minute; remove from heat.
5. Stir in butter, vanilla, and chopped nuts.
6. Fill a baked pie shell, refrigerate until cooled completely.
7. Remove from refrigerator, and starting from outer edge of pie, add kiwi slices, alternating with strawberry slices in a circle, until surface is completely covered.
8. Refrigerate; when ready to serve, top with whipped cream if desired.

Did You Know? . . . .

Did you know that the Norwegian municipalities of Norddal and Kvæfjord have strawberries in their coat of arms?

Strawberry Glazed Pie

This is another simple, yet attractive pie that is easy to make, and makes a beautiful presentation for company.

Ingredients:

- 1   9-inch pie shell, baked
- 6   c. fresh strawberries, rinsed, hulled
- ½   c. water
- 1   c. sugar
- 3   Tbs. cornstarch
- 2   Tbs. butter
  - red food coloring
  - sweetened whipped cream

Directions:

1. Place 4 cups of berries in baked pastry shell.
2. Crush remaining berries and combine with water, sugar, and cornstarch in a saucepan.
3. Boil 2 minutes or until clear. Add butter and enough food coloring to get a bright red color; cool to lukewarm.
4. Spoon glaze evenly over berries in pie shell.
5. Cool; cover with whipped cream before serving.

Strawberry Cream Cheesecake Pie

Try this excellent strawberry cream pie. It is a delicious change of pace and a wonderful treat.

Ingredients:

- 1   graham cracker crust, chilled
- 8   oz. cream cheese
- 4   eggs, at room temperature
- ¾   c. sugar
- ½   c. Irish cream
- 1½ c. fresh strawberries, washed, hulled, halved

½   c. sugar
1   c. sweetened cream

Directions:

1. Preheat oven to 325 degrees F.
2. In medium bowl, blend cheese and sugar until smooth.
3. Blend in 1 egg and Irish cream; add remaining eggs, one at a time. Pour into chilled crust.
4. Bake 45 minutes, or until inserted toothpick comes out clean.
5. Cool to room temperature. Cover with plastic wrap and refrigerate for 2 days.
6. When ready to serve, toss the strawberries with ½ cup sugar and spoon over the top of pie.
7. Whip the sweetened cream and place on top of pie.

Strawberry Filling for Boston Cream Pie

This is a delicious change of pace from the regular vanilla-flavored filling.

Ingredients:

1½ c. light cream, chilled
½   c. sugar
2   Tbs. strawberry flavoring
2   Tbs. cornstarch
1   Tbs. butter
1   tsp. vanilla extract

Directions:

1. In medium saucepan, stir together sugar and cornstarch; gradually stir in cream.
2. Cook over medium heat, stirring constantly, until mixture thickens and begins to boil.
3. Boil 1 minute, stirring constantly; remove from heat. Stir in butter, strawberry flavoring, and vanilla extract.
4. Pour into bowl, press plastic wrap directly onto surface.
5. Cool completely before using.

Fresh Banana Strawberry Pie

Fresh bananas and strawberries make a great tasty pie, and with the addition of ice cream on top of warm or cooled pie, it is a delicious treat.

Ingredients:

> 3   c. fresh strawberries, rinsed, hulled, sliced
> 3   c. bananas, peeled, sliced
> 1   c. sugar
> 1   Tbs. cornstarch
> ¼   c. orange juice
> ¼   tsp. cinnamon
> 1   tsp. nutmeg
> 1   Tbs. butter
> 1   9-inch unbaked double pie crust
>   vanilla ice cream

Directions:

1. Preheat oven to 450 degrees F.
2. In large bowl, combine strawberries, bananas, sugar, cornstarch, orange juice, and spices, tossing gently to incorporate flavors and juices.
3. Spoon into unbaked pie crust and dot with butter.
4. Place crust on top and make several slit vents in top crust.
5. Bake 15 minutes.
6. Reduce oven temperature to 350 degrees F.
7. Bake for 20 more minutes, or until browned.
8. Remove from oven.
9. Place on wire rack to cool.
10. Serve cool or warm.
11. Top with ice cream if desired.

Did You Know? . . . .

Did you know that a survey also found that non-strawberry lovers are said to be weird, boring, fussy, picky eaters who avoid healthy foods?

Strawberry Cream Cheese Pie

Cream cheese is an excellent combination with strawberries. Enjoy this refreshing pie.

Ingredients for pie crust:

1   9-inch pastry shell, unbaked
8   oz. cream cheese, softened
½   c. powdered sugar

Ingredients for strawberry filling:

3   c. fresh strawberries
¼   c. water
⅔   c. sugar
4   tsp. cornstarch
    whipped cream
    grated coconut, for garnish

Directions:

1. Preheat oven to 425 degrees F.
2. Bake pie shell for 10 minutes; cool.
3. In small bowl, blend cream cheese and powdered sugar.
4. Spread in bottom of pastry shell.
5. Rinse berries, hull and sort, reserving largest and best berries.
6. Crush enough remaining berries to make 1 cup.
7. In small saucepan, mix water, sugar, and cornstarch.
8. Add crushed berries and bring to a boil.
9. Cook 2 minutes until thick and clear.
10. Cool.
11. Press whole berries, tips up, into cream cheese.
12. Spoon cooled strawberry mixture evenly over berries.
13. Sprinkle with coconut.
14. Chill.
15. To serve, top pie with whipped cream or serve cream alongside.

Frosty Strawberry Cream Pie

This is a tasty strawberry pie, and it is great served frozen on a warm summer day.

Ingredients:

- ½ c. butter
- 2 Tbs. sugar
- 1 c. flour
- 2 c. strawberries
- ½ c. sugar
- 2 tsp. lemon juice
- 1 c. sweetened whipping cream, to taste

Directions:

1. Preheat oven to 375 degrees F.
2. In small bowl, cream butter with 2 tablespoons sugar. Add flour and blend well.
3. Place ¼ cup of mixture aside and press remaining mixture into a 9-inch pie pan.
4. Bake pie crust, and at the same time the remaining ¼ cup crumbs in a separate dish, for 12 to15 minutes. Cool.
5. In mixing bowl, combine strawberries, sugar, and lemon juice. Beat at high speed until thick and creamy, 5 to 8 minutes. (Frozen strawberries that are half thawed out work best.)
6. In small bowl, beat whipping cream until thick. Fold gently but thoroughly into strawberry mixture by hand.
7. Spoon lightly into pie shell; sprinkle with reserved crumbs.
8. Place in freezer until ready to serve; serve frozen.

Did You Know?....

Did you know that Madame Tallien, a prominent figure at the court of the Emperor Napoleon, was famous for bathing in the juice of fresh strawberries? She used 22 pounds per basin; needless to say, she did not bathe daily.

Strawberry Delights Cookbook

A Collection of Strawberry Recipes
Cookbook Delights Series Book 15

Preserving

Table of Contents

Page

A Basic Guide for Canning, Dehydrating, and Freezing 236

Strawberry and Banana Fruit Leather 239

Frozen Strawberries 239

Canned Strawberries... 240

Strawberry and Apple Fruit Leather... 240

Strawberry and Plum Rollups.. 241

Strawberry Rhubarb Rollup.. 242

Strawberry Raspberry Fruit Leather... 242

Strawberry Fruit Rollup.. 243

Strawberry Margarita Preserves... 244

Strawberry Honey 244

Surprise Strawberry Apple Butter 245

Strawberry and Blueberry Fruit Leather..................................... 246

Dried Strawberries.. 246

A Basic Guide for Canning, Dehydrating, and Freezing

1. Wash jars in hot, soapy water inside and out with brush or soft cloth.
2. Run your finger around rim of each jar, discarding any with cracks or chips.
3. Rinse well in clean, clear, hot water, using tongs to avoid burns to hands or fingers.
4. Place upside down on clean cloth to drain well.
5. Place lids in boiling water for 2 minutes to sterilize and keep hot until placing on rim of jar.
6. Immediately prior to filling jars with hot food, immerse in hot bath for 1 minute to heat jars. Heating jars avoids breakage.
7. If filling with room-temperature food, you need not immerse immediately prior to filling.
8. Fill jars with food to within ½ inch of neck of jars.
9. When ladling liquid over food, fill jars to 1 inch from rim. This leaves air allowance for sealing purposes.
10. Wipe rims of jars with clean, damp cloth to remove any particles of food, and check again for any chips or cracks.
11. Using tongs, place lids from hot bath directly onto jars.
12. Place rings over the lids, and using a cloth, gloves, or holders, tighten down firmly while hanging onto jars.
13. Do not tighten lids down too hard as air may become trapped in jars and prevent them from sealing.
14. For fruits, tomatoes, and pickled vegetables, place jars into water bath canning kettle so water covers jars by at least 1 inch.
15. For vegetables, process in pressure canner according to manufacturer's directions.
16. Follow time recommended for food being canned.
17. Do not mix jars of food in same canning kettle as times may vary for each kind of food.
18. At end of time recommended for canning, gently lift each jar out of bath with tongs, and place on protected surface.
19. Turn lids gently to be sure they are firmly tight.
20. Place filled, ringed jars on cloth to cool gradually.
21. Do not disturb rings, lids, or jars until sealed. Lids will show slight indentation when sealed.
22. Leave overnight until thoroughly cooled.

23. When cooled, wipe jars with damp cloth, and then label and date each jar.
24. Store upright on shelf in cool, dark place.

Dehydrating

1. Always begin with fresh, good quality food that is clean and inspected for damage.
2. Pretreatment before drying is not necessary, but food that is blanched will keep its color and flavor better. Use same blanching times as you would for freezing. Fruit, especially, responds well to pretreatment.
3. Doing some research on pretreatments may help you decide what procedure you would like to use.
4. You can marinate, salt, sweeten, or spice foods before you dehydrate them.
5. Jerky is meat that has been marinated and/or flavored by rubbing spices into it; avoid oil or grease of any kind as it will turn rancid as the food dries.
6. Vegetables and fruit can be treated the same way.
7. Slice or dice food thin and uniform so that it will dehydrate evenly. Uneven thicknesses may cause food to spoil because thicker parts did not dry as thoroughly as thinner parts.
8. Space food on dehydrator tray so that air can move around each piece.
9. Try not to let any piece touch another.
10. Fill trays with all the same type of food as different foods take different amounts of time to dry.
11. You can, of course, dry different types of food at the same time, but you will have to remember to watch and remove the food that dehydrates more quickly. You can mix different foods in the same dehydrator batch, but do not mix strong vegetables like onions and garlic as other foods will absorb their taste while they are dehydrating.
12. The smaller the pieces, the faster a food will dehydrate. Thin leaves of spinach, celery, etc., will dry fastest. Remove them from the stalks before drying them or they will be overdone, losing flavor and quality. In very warm areas, they might even scorch. If they do, they will taste just like burned food when you rehydrate them.

13. Dense food like carrots will feel very hard when they are ready. Others will be crispy. Usually, a food that is high in fructose (sugar) will be leathery when it is finished dehydrating.
14. Remember that food smells when it is in the process of drying, so outdoors or in the garage is an excellent place to dry a big batch of those onions!
15. Always test each batch to make sure it is "done."
16. Finished food may be pasteurized by putting it in a slow oven (150 degrees F.) for a few minutes.
17. Let food cool before storing.
18. Store in airtight containers to guard against moisture. Jars saved from other food work well as long as they have lids that will keep moisture out.
19. Zip-closure food storage bags work well.
20. Jars of dehydrated carrots, celery, beets, etc., may look cheerful on your countertop, but the color and flavor will fade. Dehydrated food keeps its color and flavor best if stored in a dark, cool place.
21. Dehydrating food takes time, so do not rush it. When you are all done, you will have a dried food stash to be proud of!

Freezing

1. Wash all containers and lids in hot, soapy water using soft cloth.
2. Rinse well in clear, clean, hot water.
3. Cool and drain well.
4. Place food into container to within 1 inch of rim. This allows for expansion of food during freezing.
5. Wipe rim of container with clean, damp cloth, checking for chips or breaks.
6. Be certain cover fits the container snugly to avoid leaks. Burp air from container.
7. If food is hot when placed in container, cool prior to placing in freezer.
8. Label and date each container.
9. Store upright in freezer until frozen solid.

Did You Know? . . . .

Did you know that strawberries have long been associated with love? The strawberry was a symbol for the Love Goddess, Venice.

Strawberry and Banana Fruit Leather

This fruit leather is full of vitamins without added chemicals or dyes. It makes a great treat.

Ingredients:

1   banana, peeled
2   c. strawberries

Directions:

1. In a blender container, purée banana and strawberries.
2. Line a 9 x 13-inch tray with plastic; spread puréed fruit on the tray, making edges thicker than the middle.
3. Microwave 5 minutes on medium; let sit 2 hours, or until dry.
4. Fruit leather may be rolled up when dry and wrapped in plastic wrap for storing.

Frozen Strawberries

It is always great to have some frozen strawberries in your freezer to pull out for treats.

Ingredients:

1   qt. strawberries, rinsed, hulled
3   lb. dry ice

Directions:

1. Cover strawberries with paper towel. Refrigerate 4 hours.
2. Break dry ice into small pieces.
3. Toss berries in a large bowl.
4. Place into a container and cover with a towel.
5. Place in a cooler for 25 to 30 minutes.
6. Remove berries; put into sealable bags and store in the freezer.

Canned Strawberries

It is always helpful to have homemade canned strawberries on the shelf to use for desserts or your favorite recipe.

Ingredients:

4   qt. strawberries, rinsed, hulled, sliced, or whole
4   pt. sugar
10 Tbs. water

Directions:

1. In large saucepan, let sugar and water dissolve.
2. Add fruit; bring to boil.
3. Remove from heat; skim if necessary.
4. Process following a basic guide for canning, dehydrating, and freezing found in the front of this section.

Strawberry and Apple Fruit Leather

Kids love fruit leathers and it is much better when it is homemade. They are easy to make and children, as well as adults, will gobble them up.

Ingredients:

2   c. fresh strawberry purée
1   Tbs. lemon juice
1   c. applesauce
¼   c. sugar

Directions:

1. In medium bowl, combine puréed berries and applesauce with lemon juice and sugar.
2. Line a 10 x 15-inch jelly roll pan with plastic wrap.
3. Pour fruit into pan and spread over surface leaving edges slightly thicker than center.

4. Bake 5 hours at 200 degrees F., or until leather pulls away from wrap.
5. Flip leather onto counter, peel away plastic, and remove any mixture that has not set.
6. Cut into slices and wrap each in plastic.

Strawberry and Plum Rollups

Strawberries and plums mix together for a great fruit roll up flavor.

Ingredients:

3   c. plums, pitted, sliced, not peeled
2   c. strawberries, hulled, sliced
½ c. sugar
½ tsp. nutmeg
¼ tsp. cloves

Directions:

1. Preheat oven to 150 degrees F.
2. In saucepan, combine plums, sugar, and spices; bring to a boil stirring to dissolve sugar.
3. Boil for 3 to 4 minutes until fruit begins to soften.
4. Cool 10 minutes.
5. Pour mixture into a blender.
6. Purée until smooth, and cool.
7. Spread heavy plastic wrap on two baking sheets 10 x 13-inch or a 14 x 16-inch sheet.
8. Pour evenly, spreading purée to fill bare spots.
9. Purée should be ¼-inch thick and slightly thicker on outside edges.
10. Place baking sheets in upper part of oven.
11. Leave oven door ajar.
12. Dry for 6 to 10 hours.
13. Fruit is ready when it can be peeled off plastic wrap.
14. Cut into slices and serve.
15. Roll up and wrap in plastic wrap to store.

Strawberry Rhubarb Rollup

This is a healthy treat and a great way to use your spring fruits.

Ingredients:

    1½ c. fresh strawberries, sliced and hulled
    ½   c. fresh rhubarb, cut into sm. pieces

Directions:

1. In saucepan, boil rhubarb pieces just until soft; drain.
2. Put strawberries and rhubarb in blender and purée well.
3. In saucepan, over medium heat, add purée; cook 5 minutes.
4. Lay out clear plastic wrap on a baking sheet.
5. Use various small pieces.
6. Spoon mixture onto the wrap, staying away from the edges.
7. Spread as thin as possible.
8. Spread another piece of plastic wrap over the mixture, and press to make evenly thin.
9. Remove top sheet of plastic before drying.
10. Repeat until you've used up all your fruit.
11. Preheat oven to 150 degrees.
12. Place the tray in the oven and leave overnight 6 to 8 hours.
13. If the fruit is dry by morning, remove from oven and roll up.
14. You may eat it right away, or save for later.
15. Note: Rollups will last several months stored in airtight containers and refrigerated.

Strawberry Raspberry Fruit Leather

This fruit leather is full of vitamins without added chemicals or dyes. It makes a great treat.

Ingredients:

    1   c. raspberries, washed
    2   c. strawberries, washed, hulled

Directions:

1. In blender, add raspberries and strawberries; purée.
2. Line a 9 x 13-inch tray with plastic.
3. Spread the puréed fruit on the tray, making the edges thicker than the middle.
4. Microwave on medium heat for 5 minutes.
5. Let sit 2 hours, or until dry.
6. Note: Fruit leather may be rolled up when dry and wrapped in plastic wrap for storing.

Strawberry Fruit Rollup

There is nothing like fresh strawberries. My children love making these.

Ingredients:

2   c. fresh strawberries, sliced and hulled

Directions:

1. Preheat oven to 150 degrees F.
2. Put strawberries in blender to purée.
3. In saucepan, over medium heat, cook for 5 minutes.
4. Lay out clear plastic wrap on a baking sheet.
5. Use various small pieces.
6. Spoon mixture onto the wrap.
7. Staying away from the edges, spread as thin as possible.
8. Spread another piece of plastic wrap over the mixture.
9. Press to make evenly thin.
10. Remove top sheet of plastic before drying.
11. Repeat until you have used up all your fruit.
12. Place the tray in the oven. Leave in oven for 6 to 8 hours.
13. Note: When it is dry, remove from oven and roll up.
14. This will keep several months stored in airtight containers and refrigerated.
15. I always make this at night and by morning it is dried.

Strawberry Margarita Preserves

Try this unique strawberry margarita preserve recipe. Enjoy!

Ingredients:

    2   qt. strawberries, cleaned, hulled, halved
    2   c. tart apples, pared
    ¼   c. lemon juice
    4   c. sugar
    ½   c. tequila
    7   Tbs. triple sec
    2   Tbs. strawberry schnapps

Directions:

1. Measure 6 cups of prepared strawberries.
2. Measure 2 cups of prepared apples.
3. In large stainless steel or enamel saucepan, combine strawberries, apples, and lemon juice.
4. Bring to a full boil stirring constantly.
5. Add sugar to boiling fruit and stir until dissolved.
6. Boil gently, uncovered, 30 to 40 minutes, stirring frequently until mixture reaches gel stage.
7. Prepare six ½-pint jars for filling.
8. Remove mixture from heat; stir in tequila, triple sec, and schnapps.
9. Return to heat and boil for 5 minutes.
10. Ladle into hot jars, leaving ¼ inch headspace.
11. Remove bubbles. Put lids on and secure.

Strawberry Honey

Try this delicious strawberry honey on your favorite toast, muffin, or bagel.

Ingredients:

    2½ c. strawberries, crushed
    1⅓ c. water

6   c. sugar
1   tsp. powdered alum

Directions:

1. In large saucepan, cook water and sugar together for 7 minutes.
2. Add strawberries; boil 5 minutes; add alum.
3. Remove from heat.
4. Pour into jars and seal with paraffin wax.

Surprise Strawberry Apple Butter

This recipe makes a unique butter to enjoy on your favorite breads. It can be stored for 2 months in the refrigerator.

Ingredients:

1   can frozen apple juice concentrate (6 oz.)
¼   c. sweet red wine
6   c. strawberries, cut in half
6   c. cooking apples, peeled, cored, cut into quarters
¾   c. brown sugar, packed
½   c. strawberry schnapps
½   tsp. ground cinnamon
½   tsp. ground ginger
     pinch of ground cloves

Directions:

1. In Dutch oven, heat concentrate, wine, and fruit to boiling.
2. Reduce heat; simmer, uncovered, for 1 hour, stirring occasionally until fruit is very soft.
3. Put mixture into food processor to remove all lumps.
4. Stir in remaining ingredients; heat to boiling; reduce heat.
5. Simmer, uncovered, for 2 hours, stirring occasionally until no liquid separates from pulp.
6. Pour mixture into hot sterilized jars leaving ½ inch headspace; wipe rims of jars and seal. Cool on rack 1 hour.

Strawberry and Blueberry Fruit Leather

Strawberries and blueberries make delicious fruit leather with the added flavor of citrus juices.

Ingredients:

- 2   c. strawberries
- 2   c. blueberries
- 2   Tbs. frozen orange juice concentrate
- 2   Tbs. honey
- 1   tsp. lemon juice

Directions:

1. Preheat oven to 140 degrees F.
2. Line a baking sheet with plastic.
3. Blend berries and concentrate until very smooth; stir in honey and lemon juice.
4. Pour purée onto sheet; smoothing with a spatula, making edges thicker than the middle.
5. Bake 4 to 6 hours, keeping the oven door slightly open.
6. Leather will be done when it is no longer too sticky and begins to shrink away from sides of pan.
7. Cool; roll longwise, and cut into desirable sizes.
8. Wrap each piece individually for storage.

Dried Strawberries

These dried strawberries are great for adding to recipes or for snacks.

Ingredients:

strawberries, washed, hulled

Directions:

1. Arrange on dehydrator tray, without touching.
2. Dry at 120 degrees F. for 12 to 24 hours; rotating tray after 10 hours.
3. When the berries break easily, they are dried.
4. For storage, vacuum seal and store in the freezer, or place in jars and screw lids on tightly.

Strawberry Delights Cookbook

A Collection of Strawberry Recipes
Cookbook Delights Series Book 15

Salads

Table of Contents

Page

Fruit Salad with Poppy Seed Dressing 248
Strawberry and Avocado Salad 249
Chicken and Strawberry Salad.. 250
Spinach, Asparagus, and Strawberry Salad 251
Strawberry Fruit Salad.. 252
Double Strawberry Salad 252
Strawberry Blueberry Salad... 253
Strawberry Frog-Eye Salad 254
Strawberry Chicken Salad.. 255
Strawberry Kiwi Salad 256
Strawberry Ambrosia Salad... 256
Tropical Compote 257
Strawberry and Brown Rice Salad... 258
Strawberry Salad with Crystallized Almonds............................ 259
Molded Strawberry Cran-Orange Salad.................................... 260
Gouda and Strawberry Salad 260
Strawberry and Spinach Salad... 261
Strawberry Salad.. 262

Fruit Salad with Poppy Seed Dressing

This makes a very attractive and colorful salad. Any fruits available may be used in place of fruits not in season, including exotic fruits such as kiwi, pineapple, and mangos.

Ingredients for poppy seed dressing:

1¼ c. honey
1   Tbs. dry mustard
1   tsp. salt
¾   c. red wine vinegar
¼   c. onion, grated
1   pt. safflower oil
4   Tbs. poppy seeds, heaping
½   tsp. coriander, ground

Ingredients for salad:

1   lemon
1   c. water
1-2 bananas, peeled, sliced into ¼-inch rounds
1   apple, partially peeled, cored, sliced
1   c. fresh green grapes
1   c. seedless purple grapes
8   plums, pitted, quartered
1   pt. fresh strawberries, stems removed
2   pears, peeled, cored, sliced
1   cantaloupe or other melon, cut from rind into chunks
2   peaches, peeled, sliced

Directions for poppy seed dressing:

1. Place honey, dry mustard, salt, red wine vinegar, and grated onion into a mixing bowl and stir together.
2. With an electric mixer, on medium speed, slowly add oil.
3. Mix until thickened.
4. Add coriander and poppy seeds; beat a few minutes longer.
5. Pour into jars and refrigerate. Stir before using.

Directions for salad:

1. Use the freshest fruit possible.
2. Make a solution of the juice of 1 lemon and 1 cup water.
3. Soak bananas, apples, and pears in this liquid to prevent discoloring.
4. Place all fruit in a large glass bowl lined with curly lettuce leaves, and pour poppy seed dressing over the salad.
5. If served individually, place fruit on top of a curly lettuce leaf centered on a salad plate and pour dressing over it.

Strawberry and Avocado Salad

This salad is refreshing and easy to make.

Ingredients:

1   ripe avocado
1   head lettuce, washed, drained
1   c. alfalfa sprouts
1   pt. strawberries, halved
½   c. macadamia nuts, roasted

Directions:

1. Peel and slice avocado.
2. Arrange on a plate with lettuce leaves.
3. Cover with alfalfa sprouts and strawberries.
4. Sprinkle the macadamia nuts over top.
5. Serve immediately with your favorite vinaigrette or dressing.

Did You Know?....

Did you know that Arizona and California both have cities named Strawberry?

Chicken and Strawberry Salad

This is a savory chicken and strawberry salad that will impress your guests.

Ingredients:

4	Tbs. orange juice
1	Tbs. olive or canola oil
1	Tbs. lemon juice
2	tsp. sugar
¼	c. soy sauce
¼	c. green onions, thinly sliced
1	garlic clove, minced
12	oz. skinless, boneless chicken breasts
4	c. spinach leaves
1	can mandarin oranges, drained (11 oz.)
1	c. strawberries, sliced

Directions:

1. In a screw top jar, combine 2 tablespoons of orange juice, oil, lemon juice, and sugar.
2. Cover and shake well. Chill until serving time.
3. In small bowl, combine soy sauce, green onions, remaining orange juice, and garlic.
4. Place chicken in a plastic bag set into a shallow dish.
5. Add marinade and seal bag. Turn chicken to coat well.
6. Chill 2 hours, or up to 24 hours, turning chicken occasionally.
7. Remove chicken from bag, reserving marinade.
8. Grill chicken on an uncovered grill directly over medium coals for 5 minutes.
9. Brush chicken with marinade; turn chicken and brush with marinade.
10. Grill 7 to 10 minutes more, or until chicken is tender and no longer pink.
11. Cool slightly and slice chicken breasts.
12. Line 4 individual salad plates with spinach leaves.

13. Arrange oranges, strawberries, and chicken breast slices on spinach-lined plates.
14. Shake dressing and drizzle over salad.

Spinach, Asparagus, and Strawberry Salad

This is another delicious strawberry salad. The combination of strawberries, asparagus, and toasted walnuts is particularly delicious.

Ingredients:

3   Tbs. olive oil
1   lb. asparagus, rinsed, ends trimmed, cut into 1-inch pieces
2   Tbs. raspberry vinegar or balsamic vinegar
8   oz. spinach leaves, rinsed
8   oz. strawberries, rinsed, hulled, sliced
½   c. walnuts, chopped, toasted
    salt and pepper, to taste

Directions:

1. Preheat oven to 350 degrees F.
2. To toast walnuts, place in baking pan.
3. Bake 10 minutes, or until golden.
4. Increase oven temperature to 400 degrees F.
5. Pour 1 tablespoon of olive oil into a 12 x 15-inch baking pan.
6. Add asparagus; sprinkle with salt, and mix to coat.
7. Spread in a single layer.
8. Bake 15 to 20 minutes, stirring often, until tender when pierced.
9. Cool 15 minutes.
10. In large bowl, mix vinegar and remaining 2 tablespoons of olive oil.
11. Add spinach, strawberries, toasted walnuts, and cooled asparagus; mix to coat.
12. Add more salt and pepper to taste; serve.

Strawberry Fruit Salad

This is an excellent frozen salad that is versatile enough to be served as a salad or dessert.

Ingredients:

- 8 oz. cream cheese, at room temperature
- ¾ c. sugar
- 20 oz. crushed pineapple
- 10 oz. frozen strawberries
- 3 bananas, sliced
- frozen dessert topping, thawed

Directions:

1. In medium bowl, soften cream cheese with fork; add sugar and blend well.
2. Stir in pineapple, strawberries, and topping; mix well.
3. Fold in bananas last to maintain shape.
4. Spoon into a 9 x 13-inch pan and freeze 6 to 8 hours.
5. Keep frozen until ready to serve then cut into squares.

Double Strawberry Salad

This recipe is easy to make and delicious.

Ingredients:

- 1 pkg. strawberry gelatin
- 1 c. boiling water
- 10 oz. frozen strawberries, thawed
- 1 can whole berry cranberry sauce
- ½ c. whipping cream
- 2 Tbs. sugar

Directions:

1. Dissolve gelatin in boiling water.
2. Mix in strawberries and cranberry sauce.

3. Chill until firm.
4. In small bowl, whip cream with 2 tablespoons sugar.
5. Serve with a dollop of whipped cream.

Strawberry Blueberry Salad

This salad is delightfully fresh and may be made in any season with the fruits either fresh or frozen.

Ingredients for salad:

    12 oz. spinach leaves
    ¼   red onion, chopped
    1   c. strawberries, rinsed, hulled, chopped
    ½   c. blueberries
    ½   c. walnuts, chopped
        salt and pepper, to taste

Ingredients for dressing:

    2   Tbs. olive oil
    1   Tbs. orange concentrate
    2   Tbs. balsamic vinegar
    1   Tbs. honey
    1   tsp. curry powder

Directions:

1. In large bowl, mix spinach leaves with salt and pepper.
2. Add strawberries, blueberries, and onions.
3. Toss with spinach, reserving a few slices of strawberries and some blueberries for decoration.
4. Just before serving, whisk together all ingredients for dressing.
5. Toss salad with the dressing to coat.
6. Place tossed salad onto salad plates.
7. Decorate with remaining strawberries and blueberries.
8. Top with walnuts.
9. Serve immediately.

Strawberry Frog-Eye Salad

Strawberries add a delightful surprise to this traditional salad. The frog-eye is a type of pasta known by the name of Acini de Pepe or spezziello.

Ingredients:

1	c. sugar
2	Tbs. flour
2½	tsp. salt
1¾	c. pineapple juice
2	eggs, beaten
1	Tbs. lemon juice
3	qt. water
1	Tbs. canola oil
1	pkg. pasta, Acini de Pepe or spezziello (16 oz.)
3	cans mandarin oranges, drained
1	can pineapple chunks, drained
2	c. fresh strawberries, rinsed, hulled, chopped
1	can crushed pineapple, drained
1	c. whipped cream
1	c. miniature marshmallows
1	c. coconut

Directions:

1. In small bowl, combine sugar, flour and ½ tsp. of the salt.
2. Gradually stir in pineapple juice and eggs.
3. Cook over moderate heat, stirring, until thickened.
4. Remove from heat; stir in lemon juice.
5. Cool mixture to room temperature.
6. Bring water, remaining 2 teaspoons of salt, and oil to boil.
7. Stir in pasta.
8. Cook at a rolling boil until done.
9. Drain pasta, rinse with water, drain again, and cool to room temperature.
10. Combine egg mixture and pasta.
11. Mix lightly, but thoroughly.

12. Add mandarin oranges, pineapple chunks, crushed pineapple, strawberries, whipped cream, marshmallows, and coconut; mix thoroughly.
13. Refrigerate until chilled in airtight container.
14. When ready to serve, place in serving bowl.

Yields: 25 servings.

Strawberry Chicken Salad

This is a lovely salad for a special brunch or luncheon. Serve it on a bed of fresh spring greens for a beautiful presentation.

Ingredients:

¾   c. sweet onion, chopped
¼   c. canola oil
¼   c. honey
1   Tbs. red wine vinegar
1   c. chicken breast, cooked, cubed
1   c. strawberries, rinsed, hulled, sliced
½   c. seedless grapes
½   c. pecans, chopped
2   Tbs. fresh parsley, chopped
¼   tsp. pepper
⅛   tsp. salt

Directions:

1. In saucepan, combine onion, oil, honey, and wine.
2. Bring to a boil.
3. Set aside to cool.
4. In large bowl, toss together the chicken, strawberries, grapes, pecans, and parsley.
5. Season to taste with salt and pepper.
6. Pour cooled sauce mixture over chicken and fruit mixture.
7. Cover and chill for 12 hours, or overnight to blend flavors.
8. When ready to serve, spoon over lettuce leaves on 4 individual serving dishes.

Strawberry Kiwi Salad

The addition of mint makes this a truly refreshing strawberry kiwi salad.

Ingredients:

- 2   Tbs. fresh lime juice
- 2   Tbs. honey
- 2   Tbs. mint, freshly chopped
- 1   lb. fresh strawberries, hulled, quartered
- 4   kiwis, peeled, halved, sliced
- ½   c. hazelnuts, chopped
      romaine lettuce leaves

Directions:

1. In large bowl, stir lime juice, honey, and mint until well blended.
2. Add strawberries and kiwis and toss gently to combine.
3. Let stand 30 minutes to allow flavors to blend.
4. Serve slightly chilled on a luscious bed of romaine leaves.

Strawberry Ambrosia Salad

Many people have tried different versions of ambrosia. Try this version with colorful strawberries.

Ingredients:

- 1   lg. can pineapple chunks, drained
- 1   lg. can sliced peaches, drained
- 2   sm. cans mandarin oranges, drained
- 3   c. whipped cream
- 1   c. coconut, shredded
- ½   c. walnuts, chopped
- 2   c. strawberries, rinsed, hulled, sliced
- ¼   c. sugar

Directions:

1. In large bowl, combine pineapple, peaches, and mandarin oranges with whipped cream.
2. Gently fold in the walnuts and coconut.
3. Toss strawberries with sugar; fold into the salad.
4. Place in refrigerator and chill until ready to serve.

Yields: 8 to10 portions.

Tropical Compote

This is a delicious, combination fruit dish, and may be served as a salad or dessert.

Ingredients:

1½ c. strawberries, rinsed, hulled, halved
2   kiwis, peeled, sliced
1   banana, peeled, sliced
1   papaya, peeled, seeded, sliced
½   c. sweetened flaked coconut, toasted

Ingredients for honey lime dressing:

¾   c. plain yogurt
2   Tbs. lime juice
¼   c. honey, to taste
¼   tsp. lime peel, grated

Directions for salad:

1. In large bowl, combine the fruits and toss lightly.
2. Sprinkle with coconut, and serve with honey lime dressing.

Directions for dressing:

1. In small bowl, combine yogurt, lime juice, and lime peel; blend well.
2. Add the honey a little at a time, and stir well.
3. Serve with the fruit salad.

Strawberry and Brown Rice Salad

This is a satisfying and unique salad that is great as a main dish for a luncheon or brunch, or even for a light supper.

Ingredients:

- 2   c. chicken or vegetable stock
- 1   c. whole grain brown rice
- ⅓   c. pecans, coarsely chopped
- ⅓   c. sunflower seeds
- ⅓   c. pumpkin seeds
- ¼   c. cider vinegar
- ¼   c. canola oil
- 1   Tbs. honey
- 1   tsp. ground or cracked pepper
- 3   c. strawberries, rinsed, hulled, quartered
- 3   green onions, sliced
- ½   c. fresh basil, torn
- ⅓   c. dried apricots, slivered
      lettuce leaves, fanned strawberries, and basil leaves, for garnish

Directions:

1. In large saucepan, on medium-high heat, bring stock and rice to a boil; cover. Reduce heat to medium-low and cook 20 to 25 minutes, or just until tender.
2. Drain off any liquid and let cool.
3. In medium skillet, toast pecans, sunflower seeds, and pumpkin seeds for 2 to 3 minutes; let cool.
4. In small bowl, mix together vinegar, oil, honey, and pepper.
5. Pour dressing over berries; toss to coat 5 to 10 minutes before serving.
6. Add toasted nuts, seeds, green onions, and basil to rice; stir in strawberry mixture and apricots.
7. Serve at room temperature on lettuce lined plates.
8. Garnish with fanned strawberries and basil leaves if desired.

Strawberry Salad with Crystallized Almonds

The crystallized almonds make this salad a delicious side dish.

Ingredients salad:

- 1 lg. bunch mixed greens
- 2 stalks celery, chopped
- 2½ c. strawberries, sliced
- 1 can mandarin oranges, drained
- ½ c. sliced almonds
- 3 Tbs. sugar

Ingredients for dressing:

- ½ c. olive oil
- 4 Tbs. sugar
- 4 Tbs. purple basil vinegar
- ½ tsp. salt
- ½ tsp. black pepper, ground
- ¼ tsp. red pepper flakes

Directions for salad, dressing, and almonds:

1. Mix oil, sugar, vinegar, salt, black, and red pepper flakes in a small shaker jar, and blend well.
2. In small skillet, over low heat, cook almonds and sugar, stirring constantly until sugar is melted and almonds are coated.
3. Sprinkle almonds onto a sheet of waxed paper and let cool, then break almonds apart.
4. Toss the greens, celery, strawberries, and mandarin oranges together; chill.
5. To serve, drizzle dressing and sprinkle bits of almond over the entire creation.

Did You Know? . . . .

Did you know that the ideal temperature for growing strawberries is 78 degrees and no lower than 55 degrees F.?

Molded Strawberry Cran-Orange Salad

This is a flavorful gelatin salad with a dollop of sweetened whipped cream for a crowning touch. If you are not fond of nuts, omit them, and it will still be just as tasty.

Ingredients:

- 1½ c. cranberry juice cocktail
- 2 c. strawberry nectar
- 1 pkg. strawberry flavor gelatin (6 oz.)
- ½ c. frozen or fresh cranberries, chopped
- ½ c. walnuts, chopped
- 1 can mandarin orange segments, drained (11 oz.)

Directions:

1. In small saucepan, bring cocktail to a boil; stir in gelatin.
2. Continue stirring until dissolved.
3. Stir in 2 cups strawberry nectar.
4. Refrigerate 1 hour, until thickened but not set.
5. Stir cranberries, walnuts, and orange segments into thickened gelatin.
6. Spoon into 6-cup ring or other mold, lightly sprayed with nonstick coating.
7. Refrigerate until firm, about 4 hours.
8. Unmold gelatin onto serving plate.

Gouda and Strawberry Salad

This makes a great side for any chicken or beef dish.

Ingredients for salad:

- 6 c. romaine, spinach, or radicchio greens
- 8 oz. Gouda cheese, sliced in wedges
- 1½ c. strawberries, sliced
- ½ c. pecans, coarsely chopped, toasted strawberry vinaigrette (see next page)

Ingredients for strawberry vinaigrette:

- ¼ c. seedless strawberry jam or strawberry preserves
- ¾ c. extra virgin olive oil
- ¾ c. red wine, strawberry, or raspberry vinegar
   salt and pepper, to taste

Directions for salad:

1. Arrange greens, cheese, and strawberries on 4 salad plates, using 2 ounces cheese and ½ cup strawberries per plate.
2. Divide dressing equally between plates; garnish with 2 tablespoons toasted pecans on top of salads.

Directions for strawberry vinaigrette:

1. In small bowl, combine jam, oil, wine, salt, and pepper.
2. Place in jar with lid and chill; shake when ready to use.

Strawberry and Spinach Salad

The wonderful taste of strawberries, poppy seeds, and spinach all come together in this lovely salad.

Ingredients:

- 2 bunches spinach, rinsed and torn into bite-size pieces
- 4 c. strawberries, sliced
- ½ c. canola oil
- ¼ c. white wine vinegar
- ½ c. sugar
- ¼ tsp. paprika
- 2 Tbs. sesame seeds
- 1 Tbs. poppy seeds

Directions:

1. In large bowl, toss together spinach and strawberries.
2. In medium bowl, combine oil, vinegar, sugar, paprika, sesame seeds, and poppy seeds.
3. Pour over the spinach and strawberries; toss to coat.

Strawberry Salad

This strawberry salad is very flavorful and packed with fruit.

Ingredients for dressing:

1   pt. strawberries, rinsed, hulled, sliced
1   tsp. mint, finely chopped
½   tsp. honey
½   c. sour cream

Ingredients for salad:

2   c. assorted fresh blueberries, peaches, plums, kiwi, oranges
    romaine lettuce leaves

Directions for dressing:

1. In blender, purée ½ cup of strawberries to make ¼ cup purée; reserve the rest of the strawberries.
2. In small bowl, stir purée, mint, sour cream, and honey; blend thoroughly.

Directions for the salad:

1. Line individual salad plates with lettuce leaves.
2. Arrange reserved strawberries with other fruit on romaine lettuce; top with the strawberry dressing.
3. Place a strawberry half on top of creamy dressing for garnishment.

Did You Know? . . . .

Did you know that eight medium strawberries contain 140 percent of the RDA of Vitamin C and are a good source of folic acid, potassium, fiber, and are fat-free?

Did you know that you can make a cool and purifying drink by crushing or chopping some strawberries and adding a little water?

Strawberry Delights Cookbook

A Collection of Strawberry Recipes
Cookbook Delights Series Book 15

Side Dishes

Table of Contents

Page

Hot Spiced Strawberries 264
Strawberry Fruit Stuffing 264
Strawberry Ginger Carrots 265
Strawberry Nut Rice 266
Hot Fruit Casserole 267
Patriotic Layered Gelatin Mold 268
Strawberry Kiwi Sorbet 269
Creamed Strawberry Rice 270
Asparagus with Strawberry Vinaigrette 270
Strawberry Pecan Stuffing 271
Strawberry Rhubarb Applesauce 272
Strawberry Ginger Slaw 272

Hot Spiced Strawberries

This is a great side dish when serving pork roast, chicken, or ham.

Ingredients:

- 1¼ c. apple juice
- 1   Tbs. cornstarch
- ½   c. sugar
- ¼   tsp. ground cloves
- ¼   tsp. ground nutmeg
- ¼   tsp. ground cinnamon
- 1   Tbs. butter
- 4   c. strawberries, hulled

Directions:

1. Preheat oven to 350 degrees F.
2. In medium saucepan, heat apple juice, cornstarch, and sugar until thickened.
3. Add cloves, nutmeg, cinnamon, and butter, mixing well.
4. Place strawberries in buttered casserole dish.
5. Pour apple juice mixture over strawberries.
6. Bake for 30 minutes, or until bubbling hot.
7. Remove from oven.
8. Place on wire rack for 20 minutes to cool.

Strawberry Fruit Stuffing

This is a delicious side dish and an alternative to classic stuffing.

Ingredients:

- 3   Tbs. canola oil
- 1   med. onion, chopped
- 1   stalk celery, chopped
- 1   garlic clove, minced

2   Tbs. water
¼   c. strawberry preserves
2½   c. breadcrumbs or croutons
¾   c. mixed dried fruit, chopped
2   Tbs. fresh parsley, chopped

Directions:

1. Preheat oven to 350 degrees F.
2. Lightly butter a casserole dish.
3. Heat oil in a large skillet over medium heat.
4. Add onion, celery, and garlic; sauté until soft.
5. Add water and preserves.
6. Remove from heat; stir in bread crumbs, fruit, and parsley.
7. Bake 30 to 45 minutes.
8. Cool 10 minutes on wire rack before serving.

Strawberry Ginger Carrots

This is a new twist on an old favorite vegetable, and a delightful one at that!

Ingredients:

1   lb. fresh carrot slices
2   Tbs. strawberry jelly
1½   tsp. butter
¼   tsp. ground ginger
¼   tsp. white pepper
     salt, to taste

Directions:

1. In small saucepan, cook carrot slices until tender but still crisp; drain.
2. In large skillet, heat strawberry jelly, until bubbling and foaming, stirring well.
3. Add butter and ginger, stirring until butter is melted and ginger is well blended.
4. Lightly toss the carrots in the glaze.
5. Season with pepper and salt before serving.

Strawberry Nut Rice

This is an old fashioned recipe that has been around for ages, and for a good reason – it tastes great!

Ingredients:

1½ c. celery, chopped
1½ c. onions, chopped
2 Tbs. butter
6 c. long grain white rice, cooked
½ c. raisins
¼ c. honey
2 Tbs. fresh lemon juice
1½ tsp. salt
½ tsp. ground cinnamon
½ tsp. black pepper
⅛ tsp. cayenne pepper
½ c. fresh strawberries, chopped
⅔ c. walnuts or pecans, chopped
¼ c. parsley, chopped

Directions:

1. Preheat oven to 325 degrees F.
2. Lightly butter a baking dish with a cover.
3. In large heavy pot, add butter; cook celery and onions for 5 minutes, or until soft.
4. Add rice and raisins, blending well; let set 15 minutes.
5. Add honey, lemon juice, salt, cinnamon, pepper, and cayenne, blending completely.
6. Lightly fold in strawberries and pecans together.
7. Spoon into prepared dish; cover.
8. Bake 30 minutes.
9. Sprinkle the top with parsley and serve immediately.

Did You Know? . . . .

Did you know that Strawberry Mountain can be found in Oregon State?

Hot Fruit Casserole

This dish is wonderful as a side dish to serve with roasted meats.

Ingredients:

1	can sliced pineapples, drained
1	can apricot halves, drained
1	lb. frozen whole strawberries, thawed, drained
1	can peach halves in syrup, drained
⅓	c. butter
2	tsp. curry powder
1	c. brown sugar
2	Tbs. cornstarch

Directions:

1. Preheat oven to 350 degrees F.
2. Lightly butter a casserole dish.
3. Drain all fruits well, reserving 2 tablespoons pineapple juice.
4. Combine all fruits in prepared dish.
5. Mix cornstarch with pineapple juice until cornstarch is dissolved.
6. In small saucepan, melt butter and curry powder together until bubbly.
7. Add brown sugar, while stirring continuously; add cornstarch mixture; cook until thick and bubbly.
8. Drizzle evenly over the drained fruit.
9. Cover; bake for 45 minutes.
10. Remove from oven place on wire rack; let stand for 20 minutes.
11. Serve warm or hot with your meal.

Did You Know? . . . .

Did you know that Strawberry Point, Iowa, is home of the world's largest strawberry?

Patriotic Layered Gelatin Mold

Any patriotic holiday is made extra special with this colorful layered gelatin mold.

Ingredients:

 6   c. boiling water, divided
 1   pkg. strawberry-flavored gelatin (6 oz.)
 1   pkg. frozen strawberries (16 oz.)
 1   pkg. lemon-flavored gelatin (3 oz.)
 2   pkg. cream cheese, softened (3 oz. ea.)
 ¼   c. mayonnaise
 1   c. whipping cream, divided
 1   pkg. blueberry-flavored gelatin (6 oz.)
 1   pkg. frozen blueberries (12 oz.)
     fresh raspberries and/or blueberries (optional)
     11-cup star mold or other decorative mold
     pastry bag and medium star tip
     large serving plate

Directions:

1. Spray mold with nonstick cooking spray; set aside.
2. In medium bowl, add strawberry gelatin; pour in 2½ cups boiling water stirring until gelatin dissolves.
3. Refrigerate 15 minutes, or until slightly thickened.
4. Add frozen strawberries; stir until berries are thawed.
5. Spoon into prepared mold; refrigerate 30 minutes, or until firm.
6. In small bowl, add lemon gelatin.
7. Pour in 1 cup boiling water stirring until gelatin dissolves.
8. Refrigerate 15 minutes, until thickened, but not firm.
9. In medium bowl, beat cream cheese and mayonnaise until well blended.
10. Add ½ cup cream and chilled lemon gelatin; beat until light colored and foamy.
11. Spoon over gelatin layer in pan.
12. Refrigerate about 30 minutes or until firm.
13. In medium bowl, add blueberry gelatin.

14. Pour in 2½ cups boiling water stirring until gelatin is dissolved.
15. Refrigerate 15 minutes, or until slightly thickened.
16. Add frozen blueberries; stir until blueberries are thawed.
17. Spoon over lemon gelatin layer in mold.
18. Refrigerate 8 hours until set, or overnight.
19. To unmold, pull gelatin mixture from edge of mold with moistened fingers. Or, run small metal spatula or pointed knife around edge of mold.
20. Dip bottom of mold briefly into warm water.
21. Place serving plate on top of mold.
22. Invert mold and plate; shake to loosen gelatin. Gently remove mold.
23. Just before serving, beat remaining ½ cup of cream in medium bowl until stiff peaks form.
24. Spoon into pastry bag fitted with star tip; decorate as you wish.
25. Top with fresh berries if desired.

Yields: 14 to 16 servings.

Strawberry Kiwi Sorbet

This fruit combination makes a very delicious sorbet.

Ingredients:

   2   containers of fresh strawberries, cleaned
   6   fresh kiwi fruit, peeled, diced
   1   c. sugar
   ¾   c. water

Directions:

1. In small saucepan, bring sugar and water to boil; refrigerate 1 hour.
2. In blender, purée fruit; add to sugar mixture; mix well.
3. Place in a deep dish container; freeze for several hours.
4. Note: Every hour, using a fork, rake the sorbet and put back in the freezer.

Creamed Strawberry Rice

Try this different flavor combination of rice with your favorite meal.

Ingredients:

> 1 c. strawberries
> 2 c. white rice
> 2 c. hot water
> 2 c. milk
> ⅓ c. sugar

Directions:

1. Mash half the strawberries with a fork, reserve remaining strawberries for decorating.
2. Wash rice, drain well.
3. Place rice in shallow dish with water and milk.
4. In microwave, on high heat, cook 20 minutes, or until all liquid is absorbed, stirring occasionally during cooking.
5. Add sugar and strawberries; reheat on high for 2 minutes.
6. Serve hot or cold with cream and reserved strawberries.

Asparagus with Strawberry Vinaigrette

Here is another flavor combination that will make a nice side dish.

Ingredients:

> 2½ lb. asparagus
> 2 c. strawberries, washed, hulled, cut in half
> ¼ c. strawberry vinegar

Ingredients for dressing:

> 1 Tbs. walnut oil
> ½ c. peanut oil
> 1½ tsp. honey

Directions:

1. Trim asparagus and cut each stalk into thirds.
2. Steam until tender, but still crisp.
3. Plunge in ice water; drain.
4. In large bowl, combine strawberries and asparagus.
5. In small bowl, combine dressing ingredients.
6. Toss asparagus and strawberries gently with dressing.
7. Chill well before serving.

Strawberry Pecan Stuffing

Try this unique stuffing with its sweet strawberry flavor and pecan-packed crunch. This dish is perfect with pork or poultry.

Ingredients:

4	slices day-old bread, cubed
½	c. pecans, chopped, toasted
½	c. green onions, chopped
1	egg, beaten
2	Tbs. butter, melted
1	tsp. cider vinegar
	salt and pepper, to taste
1	c. fresh strawberries

Directions:

1. Preheat oven to 350 degrees F.
2. Lightly grease a 1-quart baking dish.
3. In large bowl, place bread cubes, pecans, and onions.
4. In small bowl, combine egg, butter, vinegar, salt, and pepper.
5. Pour over bread mixture; toss to combine.
6. Gently fold in strawberries; transfer to prepared dish.
7. Cover; bake 20 to 25 minutes, or until inserted toothpick comes out clean.

Strawberry Rhubarb Applesauce

This is a great side dish, and it may be served hot or chilled.

Ingredients:

- 2   apples, peeled, chopped
- 1   c. rhubarb, chopped
- ½   c. strawberries, hulled, sliced
- ½   c. white sugar
- 2   tsp. grated orange rind
- ⅓   c. orange juice

Directions:

1. Place apples in a saucepan along with 1 tablespoon cold water.
2. Cook over medium heat, stirring often for 5 minutes.
3. Turn heat to medium-high; add rhubarb, strawberries, and sugar, blending well.
4. Add orange rind and orange juice; bring to boil.
5. Reduce heat to simmer, cook, stirring often, for 10 minutes, or until rhubarb and apples have softened.
6. Taste and adjust, adding more sugar depending on the tartness of your rhubarb.
7. Remove from heat; cool to lukewarm.
8. Refrigerate until ready to serve.

Strawberry Ginger Slaw

This is a refreshing change of pace from the traditional cabbage slaw. For variation, toss in a handful of salted, shelled peanuts before serving.

Ingredients:

- ½   c. mayonnaise
- 2   Tbs. grape juice
- ⅛   tsp. ginger
- 4   c. cabbage, finely shredded
- ½   c. fresh or canned mandarin orange slices
- ½   c. fresh strawberries, hulled, sliced

Directions:

1. In small bowl, combine fruit juice and ginger; chill.
2. When ready to serve, toss cabbage, oranges, and strawberries with mixture until evenly coated.

Strawberry Delights Cookbook

A Collection of Strawberry Recipes
Cookbook Delights Series Book 15

Soups

Table of Contents

Page

Strawberry Orange Soup 274
Chilled Strawberry Mint Soup 274
Iced Strawberry Soup 275
Strawberry Kiwi Rhubarb Soup 276
Cool and Creamy Strawberry Soup 276
Strawberry Soup 277
Strawberry and Raspberry Soup............................... 278
Strawberry Yogurt Soup.. 278
Strawberry Rhubarb Soup 279
Strawberry and Champagne Soup.............................280
Strawberry Banana Soup...280
Cold Peach Strawberry Soup 281
Frosted Strawberry Lime Soup 282
Strawberry Wine Soup 282
Strawberry Coconut Milk Soup 283
Chilled Rhubarb and Strawberry Soup 284
Sweet and Sassy Strawberry Soup...............................284
Chilled Cantaloupe and Strawberry Soup......................285
Strawberry Bonbon Soup...286
Strawberry Tropical Soup 287
Strawberry Cherry Soup 288

Strawberry Orange Soup

This makes an attractively colored cold soup. It is wonderful on a hot summer day.

Ingredients:

½   c. water
1   Tbs. cornstarch
3   c. strawberries, sliced
1   c. sugar
1   Tbs. water
¾   c. rosé wine
1   c. fresh orange juice
1¼ c. sour cream

Directions:

1. In small cup, combine cornstarch with 1 tablespoon water.
2. In saucepan, combine strawberries, sugar, and water.
3. Bring to boil; simmer 5 minutes.
4. Stir in cornstarch mixture, wine, and juice.
5. Bring mixture to boil; cook, stirring constantly, until slightly thickened.
6. Cool 15 minutes.
7. Pour into a blender or food processor and purée.
8. Stir in sour cream; chill.
9. When chilled, serve garnished with sliced strawberries and mint leaves.

Chilled Strawberry Mint Soup

This is a refreshing fruit soup that makes a nice luncheon or brunch dish.

Ingredients:

1½ c. fresh strawberries, sliced
¾   c. sour cream

¾ c. heavy cream
2 Tbs. orange juice
2 Tbs. honey
1½ tsp. fresh mint leaves, finely chopped

Directions:

1. In food processor or blender, place strawberries, sour cream, heavy cream, orange juice, and honey; blend until smooth and stir in mint.
2. Taste for sweetness, if necessary, add more honey.
3. Refrigerate until well chilled.
4. Serve in cold soup bowls; top with strawberry slices or mint sprigs.

Iced Strawberry Soup

This is a refreshing soup with cucumbers and lemon yogurt. Serve with dainty sandwiches for a delightful afternoon tea on a hot summer's day. Rum or amaretto flavoring may be substituted for the rum, or use rum or amaretto syrup, and omit the sugar.

Ingredients:

2 c. strawberries, rinsed, hulled
1 med. English cucumber, peeled, cut into chunks
2 c. lemon yogurt
½ c. light rum
3 Tbs. fresh mint leaves, chopped
2 Tbs. sugar

Directions:

1. In blender, add strawberries and cucumber; purée.
2. Pour into a large bowl, set aside.
3. In blender, add yogurt, rum, mint leaves, and sugar; blend until smooth.
4. Add to bowl of strawberry mixture; stir to mix well, chill in refrigerator.
5. Serve ice cold; garnish with mint sprigs and lemon slices.

275

Strawberry Kiwi Rhubarb Soup

This is a nice cold soup that makes either a great beginning course to a meal or an intriguing finish.

Ingredients:

1	pt. fresh strawberries
3	c. rhubarb, cut into ½-inch pieces
1¼	c. orange juice
½	c. sugar, to taste
	sliced oranges
	sliced kiwi fruit
	additional strawberries

Directions:

1. In 3-quart saucepan, bring strawberries, rhubarb, and orange juice to a boil.
2. Reduce heat; cover and simmer 10 minutes.
3. Remove from heat; stir in sugar to taste.
4. In blender or food processor, blend half the fruit mixture at a time until smooth.
5. Refrigerate 1 hour, or until ready to serve.
6. When ready to serve, spoon into individual soup bowls and garnish with orange slices, kiwi, and strawberries.

Cool and Creamy Strawberry Soup

This is a great soup to prelude a meal, particularly when a pork dish is the main entrée.

Ingredients:

2	c. strawberries, sliced
1	c. sour cream
1	c. half and half cream
¼	c. sugar
½	tsp. vanilla extract
2	Tbs. brandy

Directions:

1. Place strawberries, sour cream, half and half, sugar, brandy, and vanilla in a blender.
2. Blend until smooth, 30 to 45 seconds.
3. Serve in chilled cups.
4. Garnish with sliced strawberries and mint sprigs.

Strawberry Soup

This makes an attractive, colored cold soup.

Ingredients:

    3   c. sliced strawberries
    1   c. sugar
    ½   c. water
    1   Tbs. cornstarch (or 2 tsp. arrowroot)
    1   Tbs. water
    ¾   c. rose wine
    1   c. fresh orange juice
    1¼   c. sour cream

Directions:

1. In large saucepan, combine strawberries, sugar, and water.
2. Bring to a boil; simmer 5 minutes.
3. In small bowl, stir cornstarch into the 1 tablespoon of water.
4. Stir in wine and juice.
5. Bring mixture to a boil.
6. Cook, stirring constantly, until slightly thickened.
7. Cool 15 minutes.
8. Pour into a blender or food processor and purée.
9. Stir in sour cream.
10. Chill.
11. Serve garnished with sliced strawberries and mint leaves.

Yields: 6 to 8 servings.

Strawberry and Raspberry Soup

This is a rich soup that would be great served in a cup at a luncheon.

Ingredients:

1	qt. fresh strawberries, rinsed, hulled, halved
3	c. fresh raspberries, rinsed
½	c. apple juice
¼	c. sugar
2	Tbs. cornstarch
1	c. water
1	Tbs. lemon juice
⅔	c. apple juice
½	c. plain yogurt
1	tsp. powdered sugar
½	tsp. vanilla extract

Directions:

1. In saucepan, place both berries, apple juice, and sugar. Let stand for 15 minutes.
2. Heat over low heat until boiling.
3. In small cup, combine cornstarch and water. Stir into fruit mixture.
4. Boil over low heat, stirring constantly, until fruit softens and soup is clear and thickened.
5. Remove from heat; stir in lemon juice. Chill.
6. Before serving, add ⅔ cup apple juice to make soup consistency; add more juice if needed.
7. In a small bowl, combine yogurt, sugar, and vanilla; serve with the soup.

Strawberry Yogurt Soup

This is a nicely flavored cold soup with just a hint of oranges and cinnamon.

Ingredients:

4	c. strawberries, rinsed, hulled

2   c. plain yogurt
½   c. orange juice
½   c. white sugar
½   c. water
½   tsp. ground cinnamon

Directions:

1. In blender, purée the strawberries until smooth.
2. Add yogurt, orange juice, sugar, and water, mixing until well blended.
3. Pour into serving bowl and refrigerate until chilled.
4. When ready to serve sprinkle the cinnamon on top.

Strawberry Rhubarb Soup

This is a delicious soup with a myriad of flavors.

Ingredients:

1   pt. strawberries, rinsed, hulled, sliced
1   lb. rhubarb, rinsed, trimmed, cut into ½ -inch pieces
1¼ c. orange juice
½   c. sugar
¼   c. orange sections, chopped
      whipped cream, sweetened

Directions:

1. Set aside 4 of the best slices of strawberries.
2. In 3-quart saucepan, over low heat, boil rhubarb, orange sections, strawberries, and orange juice, stirring constantly, until rhubarb softens.
3. Stir in sugar.
4. Remove from heat.
5. Cool.
6. Chill in refrigerator until ready to serve.
7. When ready to serve, pour into serving bowls.
8. Top with whipped cream and reserved strawberry slices.

Strawberry and Champagne Soup

This soup is unique with its blend of strawberries and champagne. Enjoy!

Ingredients:

2	pt. fresh ripe strawberries
2	bottles champagne
	sour cream
	lemon peel, finely grated

Directions:

1. Purée strawberries by pushing them through a sieve. This removes the seeds and skin, so do not use the blender.
2. Chill in the refrigerator.
3. In shallow crystal bowls, put an equal amount of cold purée. The bowls should rest on a bed of chopped ice, preferably inside a slightly larger crystal bowl.
4. To serve, pass iced champagne, stirring it into the bowl with the strawberry purée.
5. Note: The champagne must be opened at the table when you are ready for it, so that it is not flat.
6. Add sour cream and finely grated lemon peel if desired.

Strawberry Banana Soup

This soup is delicious with the strawberries and banana combination. Enjoy!

Ingredients:

2	c. fresh strawberries, sliced
1	sm. banana, thinly sliced
¼	c. sugar, divided
1	c. sour cream
1	c. whipping cream
¾	c. milk
¼	c. white wine

Directions:

1. In small bowl, combine 1 cup crushed strawberries, banana, and 2 tablespoons sugar; blend well and set aside.
2. In medium bowl, combine sour cream and remaining 2 tablespoons sugar.
3. Add whipping cream, milk, and wine.
4. Add strawberry mixture to sour cream mixture; whisk until well blended.
5. Fold in remaining strawberries.
6. Chill 2 hours.
7. Garnish each serving with a strawberry fan if desired.

Cold Peach Strawberry Soup

Try this delicious peach and strawberry soup. It is very refreshing on a hot summer day.

Ingredients:

2   peaches, sliced
2   c. strawberries, sliced
1   ctn. peach and strawberry yogurt (8 oz. ea.)
4   Tbs. sugar
4   Tbs. lemon juice
    fresh mint sprigs

Directions:

1. In blender or food processor, combine all ingredients except mint; process until smooth.
2. Pour into bowl.
3. Cover and refrigerate 2 to 3 hours, or until thoroughly chilled.
4. Spoon into soup bowls.
5. Garnish with mint as desired.
6. Note: You can also use extra strawberries to garnish.

Frosted Strawberry Lime Soup

This is a unique combination of flavors. It is great on a hot summer day.

Ingredients:

- 2 c. unsweetened strawberries
- ½ c. water
- ⅓ c. lime juice from concentrate
- ⅓ c. sugar
- 1 container sour cream or yogurt (8 oz.)
  strawberries, for garnish

Directions:

1. In blender container, combine strawberries, water, lime juice, and sugar; blend until smooth.
2. Pour into medium bowl; stir in sour cream; mix well.
3. Chill thoroughly; garnish with strawberries if desired.

Strawberry Wine Soup

This soup has a bit of spunk to it. Try this recipe and enjoy!

Ingredients:

- 1 qt. strawberries
- 1 c. sour cream
- 1 c. sugar
- 2½ c. water
- ½ c. red wine
- 6 strawberries, for garnish

Directions:

1. In blender container, add strawberries and blend until uniform.
2. Pour into medium bowl; add sour cream, sugar, water, and wine blending well.

Strawberry Coconut Milk Soup

The combination of strawberry and coconut make this a great soup for everyone to enjoy.

Ingredients:

3   c. white grape juice
½   c. sugar
1   lb. fresh strawberries, hulled, sliced in half
1   pc. fresh ginger, 1 x 1-inch, peeled, sliced
¾   c. coconut milk
2   c. whipping cream plus extra for garnish
1   Tbs. shredded toasted coconut
    juice of 1 lemon

Directions:

1. In large saucepan, over medium-high heat, combine grape juice with sugar.
2. Heat until sugar is dissolved.
3. Bring mixture to boil.
4. Add strawberries and ginger.
5. Simmer 1 to 2 minutes.
6. Remove pan from heat.
7. Allow mixture to infuse for 30 minutes.
8. After infusing, remove ginger slices and discard.
9. In blender or food processor, purée mixture until smooth.
10. Pass mixture through a sieve.
11. Add lemon juice.
12. Cool mixture to room temperature.
13. Stir whipping cream and coconut milk into the cooled strawberry mixture.
14. Cover and chill thoroughly.
15. To serve, spoon strawberry soup into bowls.
16. Swirl a little extra cream into each portion.
17. Sprinkle with toasted coconut.

Chilled Rhubarb and Strawberry Soup

Try this delicious soup. A scoop of Mascarpone cheese adds a luxurious texture.

Ingredients:

1	lb. rhubarb, sliced into 1-inch pieces
1	pt. strawberries, washed, hulled
2	c. orange juice
1	cinnamon stick, (2-4 inches long)
2	star anise pods
¼	c. sugar, to taste
3	Tbs. Grand Marnier or strawberry brandy
¼	c. Mascarpone
	freshly ground black pepper, for garnish

Directions:

1. In large pot, add rhubarb, strawberries, orange juice, cinnamon stick, and star anise.
2. Bring to boil; cook 10 to 15 minutes until rhubarb is tender.
3. Carefully remove cinnamon stick and star anise.
4. Add sugar; stir until dissolved. Taste; add more sugar if desired.
5. Cool slightly; pour into food processor; purée until smooth.
6. Strain soup through a sieve into another container.
7. Stir in Grand Marnier or strawberry brandy.
8. Refrigerate at least 2 hours until cold.
9. To serve, pour soup into small bowls.
10. Add some Mascarpone and pepper.

Sweet and Sassy Strawberry Soup

Enjoy this uniquely flavored strawberry soup. It is the perfect beginning or end to any meal during the hot summer.

Ingredients:

1½	c. strawberries, diced
1	Tbs. lemon juice

2	Tbs. lemon peel, grated
2	eggs, beaten
½	c. sugar
1	Tbs. vanilla extract
1	qt. buttermilk
1	c. strawberry ice cream

Directions:

1. In large bowl, sprinkle strawberries with sugar, lemon juice, and lemon peel. Add eggs, vanilla, and buttermilk.
2. Pour mixture into the bowl of a 9-cup food processor.
3. Add ½ cup of ice cream; blend mixture 1 to 2 minutes until ice cream is blended into the soup and liquid has become frothy. If you do not have a 9-cup processor, blend the soup in equal batches.
4. Transfer soup into a large crystal pitcher, cover and chill for a minimum of 4 hours.
5. Serve soup in champagne glasses and garnish with remaining ice cream, mint and additional zest if desired.

Chilled Cantaloupe and Strawberry Soup

This soup has a unique blend of flavors. Try this recipe for a refreshing soup on a hot summer day.

Ingredients:

1	lg. cantaloupe, peeled, chopped
3	c. strawberries, cleaned
1	c. orange juice
1	c. yogurt
½	c. champagne
	juice of 1 lemon
	fresh mint leaves, for garnish

Directions:

1. Place all ingredients except mint leaves in blender or food processor. Purée until smooth.
2. Chill and serve with fresh mint leaves.

Strawberry Bonbon Soup

Try this unique strawberry bonbon soup. This soup is a favorite of our family. For a festive presentation, serve in a clear glass dessert bowl or a martini glass with a strawberry over the rim.

Ingredients for soup:

- 2 c. strawberries, sliced
- 1 c. plain yogurt
- ¼ c. red grape juice or sweet and fragrant red wine (Muscat)
- 1 Tbs. sugar, or to taste
  sprigs of fresh mint and whole strawberries, for garnish

Ingredients for chocolate sauce:

- 1 oz. unsweetened baking chocolate
- 1 tsp. butter
- 3 Tbs. pure maple syrup
- 1 Tbs. cream or half-and-half

Directions for soup:

1. In blender, add all soup ingredients; purée.
2. Adjust the sweetening to taste.
3. Cover and refrigerate for 3 hours before serving.

Direction for chocolate sauce:

1. In the top pan of a double boiler, add chocolate and butter.
2. Stir over simmering water until melted.
3. Remove the top pan from the double boiler.
4. Whisk in the maple syrup and cream until smooth.
5. Serve immediately or set aside and bring to room temperature.
6. To serve, drizzle a swirl of chocolate sauce over bowls of the chilled soup.
7. Garnish with fresh mint and strawberries.

8. Note: This soup and the chocolate sauce will keep in separate covered containers in the refrigerator for up to 2 days.
9. When chilled, the sauce becomes firm; reheat in the microwave on high for about 30 seconds, or until softened; stir before using.

Yields: 2½ cups or 4 servings.

Strawberry Tropical Soup

This refreshing strawberry tropical soup has many different flavors to enjoy.

Ingredients:

3   c. strawberries
1   c. frozen cherries
4   c. frozen strawberry juice, diluted
2   Tbs. honey
½   c. fresh lime juice
½   c. sweet white wine
½   c. light cream
2   Tbs. cornstarch
2   Tbs. cold water
½   c. sour cream

Directions:

1. In small cup, mix cornstarch in 2 tablespoons of cold water.
2. In medium saucepan, simmer strawberry juice, honey, lime juice, and white wine until mixture thickens.
3. Remove from heat.
4. Stir occasionally as mixture cools.
5. Add strawberries and cream to the cooled mixture; blend until smooth.
6. Strain through a strainer.
7. Mix in thawed cherries.
8. To serve, add a dollop of sour cream to each serving.

Strawberry Cherry Soup

This is a traditional Dutch soup. It is perfect for breakfast on the go, soup alone, or with your favorite main dish.

Ingredients:

- ½   c. barley
- 6   c. water
- ½   c. sugar
- 1   pkg. frozen strawberries (10 oz.)
- ½   c. raisins
- 1   c. pitted cherries

Directions:

1. In large bowl, soak the barley in the water overnight; do not drain.
2. In large saucepan, over low heat, simmer barley for 1 hour.
3. Add sugar, strawberries, and raisins.
4. Simmer for another 30 minutes.
5. Add the cherries.
6. Simmer for another 15 minutes, or until the soup becomes relatively thick.
7. Allow to chill in the refrigerator and serve cold.
8. Note: This soup can be stored for at least one week in the refrigerator.
9. Amounts and types of fruits can be varied.

Did You Know? . . . .

Did you know the peak harvesting season in California runs from April through June, when up to 10 million pint baskets of strawberries are shipped daily?

Did you know that the Iroquois Indians grew strawberries? They used strawberry leaves to brew tea and the berries to season meats and soups.

Strawberry Delights Cookbook

A Collection of Strawberry Recipes
Cookbook Delights Series Book 15

Wines and Spirits

Table of Contents

Page

About Cooking with Alcohol 290
Irish Rose 290
Mexican Strawberry Rose 291
Sparkling Strawberry Mimosa.. 291
Strawberry Daiquiri.. 292
Strawberry Dream 292
Strawberry Fields 293
Strawberry Hummingbird 293
Strawberry Kiss 294
Strawberry Martini... 294
Strawberry Sangria 295
Strawberry Laced Punch 295
Strawberry Wine 296
Strawberry Liqueur... 297
Banana Berry Shot.. 297
Bloodhound Cocktail 298
Bourbon Cobbler 298
Banana Strawberry Peach Daiquiri 299
Spunky Lemonade.. 299
Strawberry Shortcake Drink 300
Strawberry Blonde 300
Batida Morango 301
Milky Way 301
Fruit Surprise 302
Blindside 302
Burning Sunshine Drink 302
Berry Patch... 303
Midsummer's Night Dream... 303
Strawberry Dawn Cocktail 304
Strawberry Coffee Drink 304

Strawberry Delights Cookbook

A Collection of Strawberry Recipes
Cookbook Delights Series Book 15

About Cooking with Alcohol

Some recipes in this cookbook contain, among other ingredients, liqueurs. It is for the purpose of obtaining desired flavor and achieving culinary appreciation, and not to be abused in any way. In cooking and baking, alcohol evaporates and only the flavor may be enjoyed. When mixed in cold, however, such as in desserts, caution must be exercised. These recipes are intended for people who may consume small amounts of alcohol in a responsible and safe manner.

I live in Washington State and we are proud of our wine production. Washington State is rapidly gaining prestige as a premier wine producer. Do enjoy the art of wine tasting and enjoy the completeness and uniqueness of each wine. It is an art to enjoy and savor in moderation.

If consumption of even small amounts of alcohol ingredients presents a problem, in whatever form, please substitute coffee flavor syrups, found in coffee sections of supermarkets. For example, instead of Southern Comfort liqueur, substitute with Irish Cream or Amaretto Syrup.

Karen Jean Matsko Hood

Irish Rose

This is a very refreshing drink. Enjoy!

Ingredients:

    1   oz. Tequila Rose strawberry cream liqueur
    1   oz. Bailey's Irish cream
    1   oz. brown Crème de Cacao

Directions:

    1. Pour ingredients into a stainless steel shaker over ice.
    2. Shake until completely cold. Strain into a chilled glass.

Mexican Strawberry Rose

This makes a festive and colorful drink for entertaining or just a get together with a couple of friends.

Ingredients:

- ⅔ oz. tequila
- ⅓ oz. strawberry liqueur
- 1½ oz. milk
- ½ oz. grenadine
- lime slices
- strawberry halves

Directions:

1. Place tequila and strawberry liqueur into a shaker; add milk and grenadine.
2. Cover; shake all ingredients together.
3. To serve, strain into ice filled glass with a slice of lime and strawberry half on toothpick.

Sparkling Strawberry Mimosa

My daughters enjoy an occasional Mimosa and this is a wonderful treat.

Ingredients:

- 2 oz. frozen strawberries, sliced
- 2 oz. orange juice
- 2 oz. chilled champagne
- whole fresh strawberries

Directions:

1. In blender, combine berries and juice; blend until smooth.
2. Pour into stemmed glass over ice.
3. Fill with champagne and garnish with whole, fresh strawberries.

Strawberry Daiquiri

Strawberry daiquiris are delightful and one of my favorites.

Ingredients:

- 5 strawberries
- 2 oz. light rum
- 1 oz. lime juice
- ½ oz. superfine sugar
- 1 c. ice

Directions:

1. Place strawberries in blender; blend at high speed until smooth.
2. Add rum, lime juice, and sugar, blending well.
3. Pour into a tall glass and serve with a straw.

Strawberry Dream

This is a great summer drink, and it is an easy one to prepare when you are tired after a day of working.

Ingredients:

- 5 strawberries, fresh
- 2 oz. vodka
- 1 oz. strawberry brandy
- 1 tsp. strawberry liqueur
   ginger ale

Directions:

1. In blender, add strawberries; blend well.
2. Add vodka, brandy, and strawberry liqueur; whirl quickly and pour over ice in shaker.
3. Shake well and pour into a highball glass.
4. Serve, topped with ginger ale.

Strawberry Fields

This is a smooth, delicious drink. Enjoy!

Ingredients:

- 2   shots Cointreau
- 1   shot strawberry vodka
- 1   shot vodka
- 2   shots strawberry liqueur
- 1   shot lime juice
-       ice
-       strawberries

Directions:

1. Shake all ingredients with ice in cocktail shaker.
2. Strain into cocktail glass.
3. Decorate with a strawberry on the glass rim.
4. You can also serve it with ice cubes in a rocks glass.

Strawberry Hummingbird

This delightful drink blends the flavors of strawberry rum, coffee cream, and bananas. Enjoy!

Ingredients:

- ½   banana
- 1   oz. cream
- 1   oz. rum cream liqueur
- 1   oz. rum and coffee liqueur
- ½   oz. strawberry syrup
-       crushed ice

Directions:

1. In blender, add banana and cream; blend until smooth.
2. Add liqueurs and strawberry syrup, blending well.
3. To serve, pour over crushed ice in a tall glass.

Strawberry Kiss

This is a pleasing tropical blend with additional flavors of strawberries and peaches.

Ingredients:

- 1   oz. strawberry liqueur
- 1   oz. peach schnapps
- 1   oz. orange juice
- 1   oz. pineapple juice
- 1   dash grenadine
- 1   splash cream
       strawberries, halved
       ice cubes

Directions:

1. Pour alcohol into glass over several ice cubes.
2. Add juices, followed by grenadine and cream.
3. Garnish with strawberry half.

Strawberry Martini

This is a unique twist on the classic martini and it is easy-to-make right at home for a refreshing drink.

Ingredients:

- 2   shots gin
- 1   dash dry vermouth
- 1   dash strawberry syrup
- 1   strawberry

Directions:

1. Stir together the gin, vermouth, and strawberry syrup.
2. Strain into chilled cocktail glass.
3. Decorate with a fresh strawberry.

Strawberry Sangria

Sangria is always fresh and easy to make.

Ingredients:

1   bottle red wine
1   pt. strawberries, washed, hulled, sliced
1   shot brandy
2   shots blue Curacao

Directions:

1. In large pitcher, combine wine, strawberries, and blue Curacao, mixing well.
2. Refrigerate at least 1 hour, or overnight.
3. Serve in chilled glasses.

Strawberry Laced Punch

This punch provides a festive color and delicious flavors to drinks for your special gathering.

Ingredients:

5   c. ice cubes
5   c. strawberry juice
1   c. lime juice
½   c. vodka
3   c. peach juice
1   c. white wine
1   c. rum
    lime or orange slices

Directions:

1. In blender, combine fruit juices with ice cubes; cover and blend until slushy. Stir in alcohol; mix thoroughly.
2. Pour mixture into punchbowl; float lime or orange slices in bowl if desired.

Strawberry Wine

The color of the strawberries makes a festive holiday addition. It is also enjoyable to make your own wine as a project.

Ingredients:

    4½ lb. strawberries
    1   gal. water
    2   lb. sugar
    1   tsp. acid blend (do acid test)
    ⅛   tsp. tannin
    ½   tsp. peptic enzyme
    1   tsp. yeast nutrient
    1   Campden tablet (plus more tablets for each rack)
    1   pkg. yeast, for wine

Directions:

1. Wash and remove stems and leaves.
2. Fill straining bag with strawberries.
3. Tie top, commence crushing and mashing.
4. In a bucket, place straining bag and leave there.
5. Add water, sugar, acid blend (do test), tannin, peptic enzyme, and yeast nutrient. Stir well.
6. Before adding yeast, you will need to sterilize the must.
7. Crush one Campden tablet and add to must.
8. Stir and cover for 24 hours.
9. Now you may add yeast.
10. Stir well, cover and stir every day for 4 to 5 days.
11. Siphon into your gallon jug, put rubber stopper on and airlock.
12. Siphon every 2 weeks and add 1 crushed Campden tablet every time you rack.
13. It will take about 2 to 3 months before wine is clear enough to bottle.
14. You can make more than one gallon if you just multiply out the recipe to however many gallons you want to make.
15. One pack of yeast works for 5 to 7 gallons.

Strawberry Liqueur

This is a very tasty and easy-to-make liqueur, and it makes a great gift.

Ingredients:

 1   pt. strawberries
 4   lemons
 1½ c. rock sugar
 1   bottle white liquor (or vodka)

Directions:

1. Wash strawberries and drain well.
2. Cut peels from lemons, removing as much of white as possible.
3. Cut lemons into 2 or 3 pieces.
4. Pour liquor into large clean glass jar or bottle.
5. Remove strawberry stems, dropping the hulled berries into the jar.
6. Add lemons and rock sugar.
7. Seal jar and leave in cool, dark place for 2 months, or until liqueur turns nice and red.
8. Strain to remove fruit, and transfer to clean bottles.

Banana Berry Shot

This is a simple yet flavorful drink to try.

Ingredients:

 1   part Crème de Banana
 1   part Strawberry schnapps
 1   part Crème de Cacao

Directions:

1. Pour each of the three ingredients into a shot glass.
2. Stir.

Bloodhound Cocktail

The combination of sweet and dry vermouth with gin and strawberries makes a smooth, spirited drink.

Ingredients:

- ½ oz. sweet vermouth
- ½ oz. dry vermouth
- 1 oz. gin
- 3 strawberries, crushed
   strawberries, whole
   lime wedges

Directions:

1. In shaker, add crushed ice and all ingredients except strawberries.
2. Shake well.
3. Strain into a cocktail glass.
4. Decorate with strawberries and lime wedges and serve.

Bourbon Cobbler

This is an easy-to-make bourbon cooler.

Ingredients:

- 1 tsp. sugar, superfine
- 3 oz. club soda
- 2 oz. bourbon
   pineapple wedge
   strawberries
   lime wedge

Directions:

1. In a large wine glass, dissolve sugar in the club soda.
2. Almost fill the glass with crushed ice.
3. Add the bourbon.
4. Garnish with a strawberry and fruit wedges.

Banana Strawberry Peach Daiquiri

This is a nice fruit variation of the usual strawberry daiquiri. Enjoy!

Ingredients:

2   oz. dark rum
1   oz. lime juice
2   Tbs. orange liqueur
2   c. ice
5   strawberries, fresh or frozen
1   banana, ripe, sliced
4   peach wedges, fresh or frozen

Directions:

1. In blender, place all ingredients except peach wedges.
2. Blend well.
3. Pour into tall glasses and garnish with peach wedges.
4. Serve.

Spunky Lemonade

This lemonade spiked with orange liqueur and vodka is delicious.

Ingredients:

1¼ oz. vodka
½   oz. orange liqueur
4   oz. lemonade
1   Tbs. strawberries, puréed

Directions:

1. In blender, add all ingredients and ice.
2. Blend until smooth.
3. Pour into a tall glass.
4. Garnish with a lemon wheel.

Strawberry Shortcake Drink

This is a creamy strawberry drink that makes a refreshing dessert drink.

Ingredients:

1   part strawberry schnapps
1   part sparkling lemon lime soda
1   Tbs. grenadine
1   c. cream

Directions:

1. In a tall, cold, glass, add schnapps and soda.
2. Add grenadine.
3. Stir gently.
4. Top with cream.

Strawberry Blonde

Strawberry liqueur combines with golden ginger ale for a refreshing, thirst quenching drink.

Ingredients:

1   oz. strawberry liqueur
1   tsp. sugar
1   strawberry, whole
    ginger ale

Directions:

1. Put a thin rim of sugar around a chilled cocktail glass.
2. Put crushed ice into glass.
3. Pour strawberry liqueur over ice; add ginger ale to fill.
4. Add strawberry for decoration.
5. Note: If you would like a non-alcoholic drink substitute the liqueur for strawberry syrup.

Batida Morango

If you have not tried Cachaca, you will need to try it with strawberries.

Ingredients:

- 2   oz. Cachaca
- ½   tsp sugar
- 1   c. ice, crushed
- 5   strawberries, very ripe

Directions:

1. Place all of the ingredients into a blender; blend well.
2. Pour into a wine glass and serve.

Milky Way

Strawberry and almond flavors combine with pineapple juice to make a very refreshing drink.

Ingredients:

- 6   parts gin
- 6   parts Amaretto
- 2   parts strawberry liqueur
- 3   parts strawberry syrup
  pineapple juice
  slices of apple, lemon, pineapple, for garnish

Directions:

1. Fill a highball glass to the rim with ice cubes.
2. Pour all ingredients except garnish into a shaker.
3. Fill the shaker with ice cubes.
4. Shake it until the shaker is very cold.
5. Strain the drink into the highball glass.
6. Top up with pineapple juice.
7. Garnish with apple or lemon slices and a pineapple leaf.

Fruit Surprise

This is a delicious fruit drink that is refreshing and easy to make.

Ingredients:

- 2 oz. strawberry schnapps
- 2 oz. orange juice
- 2 oz. cranberry juice
- club soda

Directions:

1. Pour schnapps, orange juice, and cranberry juice over ice in a highball glass.
2. Top with club soda and serve.

Blindside

This vodka drink is great with its citrus and strawberry flavors.

Ingredients:

- 2 oz. vodka
- 2 oz. orange juice
- 2 oz. grapefruit juice
- 1 oz. strawberry syrup

Directions:

1. In a large glass, pour strawberry syrup, orange juice, and grapefruit juice. Add vodka and stir.

Burning Sunshine Drink

Strawberry and pineapple combine to make an easy, cool drink.

Ingredients:

- 1½ oz. strawberry schnapps
- 4 oz. pineapple juice

Directions:

1. Pour over ice in highball glass, stir.
2. Garnish with a fresh strawberry.

Berry Patch

Crème de Cacao and berries and cream make a rich summer treat.

Ingredients:

½ oz. strawberry schnapps
½ oz. raspberry schnapps
½ oz. white Crème de Cacao
   lemon lime soda
   half and half cream

Directions:

1. Combine the schnapps and crème de cacao in a tall glass.
2. Fill the glass almost to the top with soda.
3. Top with cream and stir gently.

Midsummer's Night Dream

Cherry brandy adds a nice touch to this strawberry drink.

Ingredients:

2 oz. vodka
1 oz. cherry brandy
1 tsp. strawberry liqueur
5 fresh strawberries
   sparkling tonic water

Directions:

1. Add ice to a shaker.
2. In blender, add strawberries; purée. Pour into shaker.
3. Add vodka, brandy, and strawberry liqueur; shake well.
4. Pour into a highball glass; fill up with tonic water.

Strawberry Dawn Cocktail

Coconut and mint make this strawberry drink unique.

Ingredients:

1	oz. gin
1	oz. coconut rum
⅓	c. frozen strawberries
1	sprig mint

Directions:

1. Mix all ingredients in a cocktail shaker.
2. Pour into an unusual shaped glass.
3. Add crushed ice and garnish with a sprig of mint.

Strawberry Coffee Drink

Coffee flavor sets this strawberry drink apart from others. The vanilla schnapps adds a warm taste and fragrance.

Ingredients:

1	part strawberry cream liqueur
1	part vanilla schnapps
1	part coffee liqueur
1	part cream
1	splash grenadine syrup

Directions:

1. Pour all ingredients over ice in a shaker.
2. Shake well.
3. Strain.
4. Pour into a rocks glass.

Did You Know? . . . .

Did you know that in medieval times, strawberries were served at important functions to bring peace and prosperity?

Festival Information

California Strawberry Festival
When: May
Location: Strawberry Meadows of College Park
3250 South Rose Avenue, Oxnard, California

Florida Strawberry Festival
When: February
Location: 2202 West Reynolds Street, Plant City, Florida

Marysville Strawberry Festival
When: June, third weekend
Location: Marysville, Washington

Monterey Bay Strawberry Festival
When: August
Location: Watsonville, California

Pasadena Strawberry Festival
When: May
Location: Pasadena Fairgrounds, Pasadena, Texas

Ponchatoula Strawberry Festival
When: April
Location: 301 – N 6th Street, Ponchatoula, Louisiana

Strawberry Associations and Commissions

California Strawberry Commission
180 Westridge Dr. Suite 101
Watsonville, CA 95076
Mailing Address:
P.O. Box 269
Watsonville, CA 95077
Phone: 831-724-1301
Fax: 831-724-5973

Florida Strawberry Growers Association
13138 Lewis Gallagher Road
Dover, FL 33527
Mailing Address: P.O. Drawer 2550
Plant City, FL 33564
Telephone: 813-752-6822
Fax: 813-752-2167

North American Strawberry Growers Association
30 Harmony Way
Kemptville, Ontario K0G 1J0 Canada
Kevin Schooley-Executive Director
Phone: 613-258-4587
Fax: 613-258-9129
Email: kconsult@allstream.net

Oregon Strawberry Commission
4845 B SW Dresden Ave
Corvallis, OR. 97333
Phone: 541-758-4043
Fax: 541-758-4553

Washington Strawberry Commission
4430 John Luhr Road
Olympia WA 98506
Phone: 360-491-6567

U.S. and Metric Measurement Charts

Here are some measurement equivalents to help you with exchanges. There was a time when many people thought the entire world would convert to the metric scale. While most of the world has, America still has not. Metric conversions in cooking are vitally important to preparing a tasty recipe. Here are simple conversion tables that should come in handy.

U.S. Measurement Equivalents

A few grains/pinch/dash, (dry) = Less than ⅛ teaspoon
A dash (liquid) = A few drops
3 teaspoons = 1 tablespoon
½ tablespoon = 1½ teaspoons
1 tablespoon = 3 teaspoons
2 tablespoons = 1 fluid ounce
4 tablespoons = ¼ cup
5⅓ tablespoons = ⅓ cup
8 tablespoons = ½ cup
8 tablespoons = 4 fluid ounces
10⅔ tablespoons = ⅔ cup
12 tablespoons = ¾ cup
16 tablespoons = 1 cup
16 tablespoons = 8 fluid ounces
⅛ cup = 2 tablespoons
¼ cup = 4 tablespoons
¼ cup = 2 fluid ounces
⅓ cup = 5 tablespoons plus 1 teaspoon
½ cup = 8 tablespoons
1 cup = 16 tablespoons
1 cup = 8 fluid ounces
1 cup = ½ pint
2 cups = 1 pint
2 pints = 1 quart
4 quarts (liquid) = 1 gallon
8 quarts (dry) = 1 peck
4 pecks (dry) = 1 bushel
1 kilogram = approximately 2 pounds
1 liter=approximately 4 cups or 1quart

Approximate Metric Equivalents by Volume

U.S.	Metric
¼ cup	= 60 milliliters
½ cup	= 120 milliliters
1 cup	= 230 milliliters
1¼ cups	= 300 milliliters
1½ cups	= 360 milliliters
2 cups	= 460 milliliters
2½ cups	= 600 milliliters
3 cups	= 700 milliliters
4 cups (1 quart)	= .95 liter
1.06 quarts	= 1 liter
4 quarts (1 gallon)	= 3.8 liters

Approximate Metric Equivalents by Weight

U.S.	Metric
¼ ounce	= 7 grams
½ ounce	= 14 grams
1 ounce	= 28 grams
1¼ ounces	= 35 grams
1½ ounces	= 40 grams
2½ ounces	= 70 grams
4 ounces	= 112 grams
5 ounces	= 140 grams
8 ounces	= 228 grams
10 ounces	= 280 grams
15 ounces	= 425 grams
16 ounces (1 pound)	= 454 grams

Glossary

Aerate: A synonym for sift; to pass ingredients through a fine-mesh device to break up large pieces and incorporate air into ingredients to make them lighter.

Al Dente: "To the tooth," in Italian. The pasta is cooked just enough to maintain a firm, chewy texture.

Amaretto: A liqueur with a distinct flavor of almonds, though it is often made with apricot pits kernels.

Bake: To cook in the oven. Food is slowly cooked with gentle heat, which causes the natural moisture in the food to evaporate slowly, concentrating the flavor.

Baste: To brush or spoon liquid fat or juices over meat during roasting to add flavor and prevent it from drying out.

Beat: To make a mixture smooth by briskly stirring or whipping with a spoon, dork, sire whisk, rotary beater, or electric mixer.

Bias-Slice: To slice a food crosswise at a 45-degree angle.

Blanch: To boil briefly to loosen the skin of a fruit or a vegetable. After 30 seconds in boiling water, the fruit or vegetable should be plunged into ice water to stop the cooking action, and then the skin easily peels off.

Blend: Thoroughly combine all ingredients until very smooth and uniform.

Boil: To bring to the boiling point.

Braise: A cooking technique that requires browning meat in oil or other fat and then cooking slowly in liquid. The effect of braising is to tenderize the meat.

Bread: To coat food with crumbs (usually with soft or dry bread crumbs), sometimes seasoned.

Brew: To prepare (tea, coffee, etc.) by boiling, steeping, or the like.

Broil: To cook food directly under a heat source.

Brown: To quickly sauté, pan or oven broil, or grill, done either at the beginning or end of meal preparation. Browning enhances flavor, texture, and eye appeal.

Bundt Pan: The generic name for any tube baking pan having fluted sides (though it was once a trademarked name).

Campden Tablets: Used in winemaking to sanitize equipment and fermentation media and add free SO_2 to the must or wine.

Caramelize: To brown sugar over heat, with or without the addition of some water to aid the process. The temperature range in which sugar caramelizes is approximately 320 degrees F. to 360 degrees F.

Chill: To place in refrigerator to reduce temperature.

Clarify: To remove impurities from butter or stock by heating the liquid, then straining or skimming it.

Coat: To cover food evenly with flour, crumbs, or batter.

Cool: Allow to come to room temperature.

Core: To remove the inedible center of fruits such as pineapples.

Cream: To beat vegetable shortening, butter, or margarine, with or without sugar, until light and fluffy. This process traps in air bubbles, later used to create height in cookies and cakes.

Crimp: To create a decorative edge on a pie crust. On a double pie crust, this also seals the edges together.

Cruller: A twisted oblong pastry of doughnut dough, deep-fried and sugared or iced.

Crush: To condense a food to its smallest particles, usually using a mortar and pestle or a rolling pin.

Curd: A custard-like pie or tart filling flavored with juice and zest of citrus fruit, usually lemon, although lime and orange may be used, also.

Custard: A mixture of beaten egg, milk, and possibly other ingredients such as sweet or savory flavorings, which is cooked with gentle heat, often in a water bath or double boiler.

Cut In: To work butter into dry ingredients by chopping with knives or pastry blender.

Dash: A measure approximately equal to 1/16 teaspoon.

Deep-fry: To cook by submerging completely in hot oil.

Deglaze: To add liquid to a pan in which foods have been fried or roasted in order to dissolve the caramelized juices stuck to the bottom of the pan.

Direct Heat: A method of cooking that allows heat to meet food directly, such as grilling, broiling, or toasting.

Dollop: A spoonful of soft food, such as mashed potatoes or whipped cream. It may also mean a dash or "splash" of soda water, water, or other liquid if referring to liquid.

Dot: To sprinkle food with small bits of an ingredient such as butter to allow for even melting.

Dredge: To sprinkle lightly and evenly with sugar or flour.

Drippings: Used for gravies and sauces, drippings are the liquids left in the bottom of a roasting or frying pan after meat is cooked.

Drizzle: To pour a liquid such as a sweet glaze or melted butter in a slow, light trickle over food.

Dust: To sprinkle food lightly with spices, sugar, or flour for a light coating.

Dutch Process: A treatment used during the making of cocoa powder in which cocoa solids are treated with an alkaline solution to neutralize acidity. This process darkens the cocoa and develops a milder chocolate flavor.

Egg Wash: A mixture of beaten eggs (yolks, whites, or whole eggs) with either milk or water. Used to coat cookies and other baked goods to give them a shine when baked.

Fillet: To remove the bones from meat of fish for cooking.

Firm-Ball Stage: In candy making, the point where boiling syrup dropped in cold water forms a ball that is compact yet gives lightly to the touch.

Flan: An open pie filled with sweet or savory ingredients; also, a Spanish dessert of baked custard covered with caramel.

Flute: To create a decorative, scalloped, or undulating edge on a pie crust or other pastry.

Fold: To cut and mix lightly with a spoon to keep as much air in a mixture as possible.

Frittata: An unfolded omelet in which the eggs are mixed with vegetables, cheese, or other ingredients, cooked slowly over low heat, and then browned on top.

Ganache: A rich chocolate filling or coating made with chocolate, vegetable shortening, and possibly heavy cream. It is used to coat cakes or cookies and may be used as a filling for truffles.

Garnish: A decorative piece of an edible ingredient such as parsley, lemon wedges, croutons, or chocolate curls placed as a finishing touch to dishes or drinks.

Glaze: A liquid that gives an item a shiny surface. Examples are fruit jams that have been heated or chocolate thinned with melted vegetable shortening. Also, to cover a food with such a liquid.

Grate: To rub on a grater that separates the food into very fine particles.

Grease: To coat a pan, dish, or skillet with a thin layer of oil.

Grill: To cook over the heat source in the open air.

Hard-Ball Stage: In candy making, the point at which syrup has cooked long enough to form a solid ball in cold water.

Infusion: Extracting flavors by soaking them in liquid heated in a covered utensil. The term also refers to the liquid resulting from this process.

Julienne: To cut into long, thin strips.

Knead: To work dough with the heels of your hands in a pressing and folding motion until it becomes smooth and elastic.

Marble: To gently swirl one food into another.

Marinate: To combine flood with aromatic ingredients to add flavor. It can be used as the topping for pies or baked as cookies.

Medallion: A small round or oval piece of meat.

Meringue: Egg whites beaten until they are stiff, then sweetened.

Mince: To chop food into tiny, irregular pieces.

Mole Sauce: The generic term for several sauces used in Mexican cuisine, as well as for dishes based on these sauces. In English, it often refers to a specific sauce which is known in Spanish by the more specific name *mole poblano.*

Must: The combination of basic ingredients, both solid and liquid, from which wine is made.

Nonreactive Pan: Cookware that does not react chemically with foods, primarily acidic foods, is said to be "nonreactive. Glass, stainless steel, enamel, anodized aluminum, and permanent nonstick surfaces are basically nonreactive. Shiny aluminum is reactive.

Parchment: A heavy, heat-resistant paper used in cooking.

Peaks: The mounds made in a mixture. For example, egg whites that have been whipped to stiffness. Peaks are "stiff" if they stay upright or "soft" if they curl over.

Pesto: A sauce usually made of fresh basil, garlic, olive oil, pine nuts, and cheese. The ingredients are finely chopped and then mixed, uncooked, with pasta. Generally, the term refers to any uncooked sauce made of finely chopped herbs and nuts.

Pipe: To force a semi-soft food through a bag (either a pastry bag or a plastic bag with one corner cut off) to decorate food.

Poach: To simmer in liquid.

Poblano Chilies: Fresh dark green chilies, often called pasillas.

Pressure Cooking: A cooking method that uses steam trapped under a locked lid to produce high temperatures and achieve fast cooking time.

Ramekin: A small baking dish used for individual servings of sweet and savory dishes.

Reduce: To concentrate by boiling away excess liquid. This is best done in an uncovered, heavy-bottom pan over medium to medium-high heat.

Rolling Boil: A boil that does not stop bubbling when stirred.

Sauté: To brown or cook in a small amount of hot oil or butter.

Scald: To heat a liquid, usually a dairy product, until it almost boils.

Sift: To remove large lumps from a dry ingredient such as flour or confectioner's sugar by passing it through a fine mesh. This process also incorporates air into the ingredients, making them lighter.

Simmer: Cooking food in a liquid at a low enough temperature that small bubbles begin to break the surface.

Springform Pan: A pan that is round with high sides. The side rim expands when a clamp is opened, allowing it to separate from the base. This makes it easier to shape and then serve something like a cheesecake.

Steam: To cook over boiling water in a covered pan. This method helps foods keep their shape, texture, and nutritional value intact better than methods such as boiling.

Steep: To soak dry ingredients (tea leaves, ground coffee, herbs, spices, etc.) in liquid until the flavor is infused into the liquid.

Strain: To pass through a filtering agent such as a strainer; to draw off or remove by filtration.

Tomatillo: Green tomato-like vegetables with paper-thin husks.

Truss: To use string, skewers, or pins to hold together a certain food to maintain its shape while it cooks (usually applied to meat or poultry).

Unsweetened Chocolate: The ground up center (nib) of the cocoa bean.

Vinaigrette: A general term referring to any sauce made with vinegar, oil, and seasonings.

Whisk: To mix or fluff by beating; also refers to the utensil used for this action.

White Chocolate: A blend of cocoa butter, milk, sugar, and flavor. Not really "chocolate" since no chocolate solids other than cocoa butter are present. Similar to milk chocolate in composition.

Zest: The thin, brightly colored outer part of the rind of citrus fruits. It contains volatile oils, used as a flavoring.

Recipe Index of Strawberry Delights

Appetizers and Dips......................49
Cheesy Strawberry Salsa 53
Chocolate Candy Bar Fondue 56
Fruit and Cheese Quesadillas.......... 63
Grilled Fruit Antipasto Plate 52
Red White and Blue Strawberries...... 62
Strawberries with Sweet Cheese 54
Strawberry and Brie Bruschetta 61
Strawberry Ceviche 58
Strawberry Cheese Ball................... 56
Strawberry Cheese Ring.................. 57
Strawberry Chevre Spread 52
Strawberry Chicken Kabobs 64
Strawberry Coconut Crème Dip..... 62
Strawberry Dip.............................. 54
Strawberry Fruit Salsa and
   Cinnamon Crisps...................... 50
Strawberry Glazed Meatballs 51
Strawberry Pineapple Chicken Bites55
Strawberry Spring Rolls.................. 60
Strawberry Supreme Cheesecake Dip... 58
Beverages......................................65
Chocolate Strawberry Cordial Yogurt... 73
Chocolate Strawberry Smoothie 76
Coral Punch 69
Fresh Strawberry Punch................. 66
Strawberry and Huckleberry Milk-
   shake....................................... 68
Strawberry and Raspberry Milkshake.....69
Strawberry Frappe 70
Strawberry Frosty 76
Strawberry Fruit Shake................... 70
Strawberry Granita 72
Strawberry Ice 71
Strawberry Juice Cocktail 72
Strawberry Lemonade..................... 68
Strawberry Malted Milkshake.......... 74
Strawberry Milkshake..................... 74
Strawberry Slush........................... 75
Strawberry Smoothie...................... 66
Strawberry Yogurt Swirl.................. 67
Surprise Smoothie 75

Breads and Rolls 77
Strawberry Almond Bread 90
Strawberry Almond Muffins............ 84
Strawberry and Apple Muffins 91
Strawberry Bagels 80
Strawberry Banana Bread 85
Strawberry Bran Muffins 92
Strawberry Bread 80
Strawberry Cheesecake Muffins.......... 86
Strawberry Chocolate Chip Bread ... 87
Strawberry Crumpets 78
Strawberry Pecan Bread 79
Strawberry Rhubarb Hickory Nut
   Bread 82
Strawberry Scone Delight............... 88
Strawberry Scones 83
Strawberry Whole Wheat Bread 89

Breakfasts..93
Breakfast Strawberry Compote..... 101
Buckwheat Pancakes..................... 103
Buttermilk Pancakes....................... 97
Chocolate Strawberry Waffles 99
Crêpes 100
English Muffins 102
Finnish Soufflé 96
French Toast with Strawberries 95
German Pancakes Oven Style 100
Strawberry and Chocolate Breakfast
   Quiche 98
Strawberry Breakfast Chops.......... 105
Strawberry Breakfast Pizza............ 106
Strawberry Breakfast Puff 107
Strawberry Breakfast Sandwich....... 96
Strawberry Breakfast Sundae 104
Strawberry Crêpes 108
Strawberry Omelet 104
Streusel Filled Strawberry Coffee Cake
   94

Cakes 109
Ginger Orange Strawberry Shortcakes
   110
Strawberry and Huckleberry Cake 111
Strawberry Angel Cake................. 122
Strawberry Chiffon Cake............... 118
Strawberry Chocolate Mousse Cake ...
   115
Strawberry Jelly Roll Cake............. 114
Strawberry Peach Delight 112
Strawberry Pecan Roulade 113
Strawberry Pound Cake................. 117
Strawberry Shortcake Biscuits with
   Almonds.................................. 116
Strawberry Shortcake.................... 121
Strawberry Torte Ladyfinger Style. 120
Strawberry Torte Meringue Style .. 119
Strawberry Upside-Down Cake 124
Strawberry, Blueberry, and
   Raspberry Tart........................... 123

Candies 125
Chocolate Covered Strawberries ... 128
Chocolate Strawberry Truffles........ 131
Creamy Strawberry Drops 128
Strawberry Candy......................... 134
Strawberry Caramels 135
Strawberry Cream Candy............... 137
Strawberry Cream Eggs 127
Strawberry Delight Candy............. 133
Strawberry Divinity...................... 126
Strawberry Fudge 138
Strawberry Jujubes........................ 136
Strawberry Peanut Butter Bites..... 136
Strawberry Pecan Balls.................. 132
Strawberry Potato Candy.............. 132
Strawberry Salt Water Taffy 129
Strawberry Taffy 134
Strawberry White Chocolate
   Pretzels.................................... 130

Cookies......................**139**
Creamy Strawberry Sandwich
  Cookies.................... 141
Danish Strawberry Cookies 144
Fruit and Oat Bars...................... 143
Glazed Strawberry Kolache Cookies. 140
Strawberry Almond Candy Kiss
  Cookies 142
Strawberry Bars 154
Strawberry Cookies with Creamy
  Strawberry Frosting................. 152
Strawberry Fig Bars 150
Strawberry French Sugar Strips..... 147
Strawberry Heart Tarts 144
Strawberry Nut Drops 156
Strawberry Oatmeal Cookies 153
Strawberry Oats and Chips
  Cookies.................... 146
Strawberry Pecan Cookies 151
Strawberry Sugar Cookies............. 148
Strawberry Walnut Cookies.......... 149
White Chocolate Strawberry
  Fudgies 155

Desserts **157**
Baked Meringues with Strawberries.. 162
Bakewell Strawberry Tart.............. 166
Berry Parfait 180
Cheesecake Tart with Strawberries 174
Dark Chocolate Pavé with Strawberry
  Sauce................................... 176
Philadelphia Style Strawberry Ice
  Cream................................... 159
Strawberries and Cream............... 181
Strawberries in Balsamic Vinegar.. 178
Strawberries in Chocolate Cream
  Fruit Dip.............................. 165
Strawberry and Chocolate Tortilla 161
Strawberry and Raspberry Tart 182
Strawberry Cobbler 169
Strawberry Crêpes 179
Strawberry Dessert Soup 166
Strawberry Dessert 171
Strawberry Filling for Boston Cream
  Pie.. 180
Strawberry Flan 160
Strawberry Fool 165
Strawberry Hazelnut Flan............. 158
Strawberry Ice Cream 175
Strawberry Jam Bread Pudding..... 172
Strawberry Pineapple Ice Box
  Dessert.................................. 164
Strawberry Pudding...................... 170
Strawberry Rhubarb Cobbler........ 168
Strawberry Torte.......................... 173
Strawberry Yogurt Freeze.............. 167
Summer Strawberry Orange Cups 178

**Dressings, Sauces, and
  Condiments** **183**
Cranberry and Strawberry Relish.. 191
Strawberry Blueberry Sauce 192
Strawberry Butter 188
Strawberry Chutney 190

Strawberry Grand Marnier Sauce . 185
Strawberry Orange Chutney......... 190
Strawberry Orange Sauce 189
Strawberry Poppy Seed Dressing... 186
Strawberry Raspberry Sauce 189
Strawberry Rhubarb Sauce 188
Strawberry Sauce 192
Strawberry Sweetened Whipped
  Cream................................... 186
Strawberry Vinegar...................... 184
Sweet-Hot Strawberry Barbecue
  Sauce 184
Warm Double Strawberry Sauce... 187

Jams, Jellies, and Syrups **193**
A Basic Guide for Canning Jams,
  Jellies, and Syrups.................. 194
Citrus Strawberry Preserves 195
Freezer Strawberry Jam................. 198
Mango Strawberry Jam with
  Kiwifruit............................... 201
Rhubarb Strawberry Jam 204
Strawberry Apple Jelly 205
Strawberry Blueberry Jam............. 202
Strawberry Drink Mix Jelly 203
Strawberry Gooseberry Jam.......... 197
Strawberry Guava Jam 200
Strawberry Hedgerow Jam............ 196
Strawberry Huckleberry Jam 200
Strawberry Kiwi Jam 199
Strawberry Orange Jam 206
Strawberry Peach Jam................... 204
Strawberry Preserves 196
Strawberry Raspberry Jam 202
Strawberry Syrup.......................... 198

Main Dishes..............................**207**
Almond Dusted Strawberry Balsamic
  Chicken................................. 220
Chicken Strawberry Sauce Bake ... 209
Chicken with Strawberry Sauce 214
Grilled Shrimp with Strawberry
  Salsa..................................... 208
Grilled Tuna Steaks with Fresh
  Fruit 210
Pork Chops with Strawberry
  Mustard Glaze 210
Prawns, Peas, and Strawberries 213
Quesadillas with Strawberry Salsa..... 218
Sea Bass with Spicy Strawberry
  Sauce..................................... 214
Spiced Glazed Pork Tenderloin..... 216
Stir-Fried Scallops with
  Strawberries 219
Strawberry Glazed Ham 217
Strawberry Lemon Sole 212

Pies **221**
A Basic Cookie or Graham Cracker
  Crust 223
A Basic Recipe for Pie Crust......... 222
Amish Sour Cream Apple Strawberry
  Pie.. 228
Fresh Banana Strawberry Pie 232
Frosty Strawberry Cream Pie 234

314

Strawberry Cream Cheese Pie....... 233
Strawberry Cream Cheesecake Pie.... 230
Strawberry Cream Pie.................... 224
Strawberry Custard Pie................. 225
Strawberry Filling for Boston
    Cream Pie............................... 231
Strawberry Glazed Pie 230
Strawberry Ice Cream Pie 226
Strawberry Kiwi Pie..................... 229
Strawberry Rhubarb Pie 227

Preserving 235
A Basic Guide for Canning,
    Dehydrating, and Freezing 236
Canned Strawberries..................... 240
Dried Strawberries........................ 246
Frozen Strawberries 239
Strawberry and Apple Fruit
    Leather 240
Strawberry and Banana Fruit
    Leather 239
Strawberry and Blueberry Fruit
    Leather 246
Strawberry and Plum Rollups....... 241
Strawberry Fruit Rollup................ 243
Strawberry Honey 244
Strawberry Margarita Preserves..... 244
Strawberry Raspberry Fruit Leather.. 242
Strawberry Rhubarb Rollup.......... 242
Surprise Strawberry Apple Butter . 245

Salads..247
Chicken and Strawberry Salad...... 250
Double Strawberry Salad.............. 252
Fruit Salad with Poppy Seed
    Dressing.................................. 248
Gouda and Strawberry Salad 260
Molded Strawberry Cran-Orange
    Salad 260
Spinach, Asparagus, and Strawberry
    Salad.......................................251
Strawberry Ambrosia Salad........... 256
Strawberry and Avocado Salad 249
Strawberry and Brown Rice
    Salad....................................... 258
Strawberry and Spinach Salad....... 261
Strawberry Blueberry Salad.......... 253
Strawberry Chicken Salad............. 255
Strawberry Frog-Eye Salad 254
Strawberry Fruit Salad.................. 252
Strawberry Kiwi Salad 256
Strawberry Salad with Crystallized
    Almonds.................................. 259
Strawberry Salad.......................... 262
Tropical Compote 257

Side Dishes 263
Asparagus with Strawberry
    Vinaigrette.............................. 270
Creamed Strawberry Rice............. 270
Hot Fruit Casserole 267
Hot Spiced Strawberries 264
Patriotic Layered Gelatin Mold 268
Strawberry Fruit Stuffing.............. 264
Strawberry Ginger Carrots............ 265

Strawberry Ginger Slaw................ 272
Strawberry Kiwi Sorbet 269
Strawberry Nut Rice..................... 266
Strawberry Pecan Stuffing............. 271
Strawberry Rhubarb Applesauce ... 272

Soups 273
Chilled Cantaloupe and Strawberry
    Soup 285
Chilled Rhubarb and Strawberry
    Soup 284
Chilled Strawberry Mint Soup 274
Cold Peach Strawberry Soup 281
Cool and Creamy Strawberry
    Soup 276
Frosted Strawberry Lime Soup...... 282
Iced Strawberry Soup 275
Strawberry and Champagne Soup.... 280
Strawberry and Raspberry Soup.... 278
Strawberry Banana Soup 280
Strawberry Bonbon Soup 286
Strawberry Cherry Soup............... 288
Strawberry Coconut Milk Soup.... 283
Strawberry Kiwi Rhubarb Soup ... 276
Strawberry Orange Soup 274
Strawberry Rhubarb Soup 279
Strawberry Soup 277
Strawberry Tropical Soup 287
Strawberry Wine Soup 282
Strawberry Yogurt Soup............... 278
Sweet and Sassy Strawberry Soup . 284

Wines and Spirits.......................289
About Cooking with Alcohol 290
Banana Berry Shot........................ 297
Banana Strawberry Peach Daiquiri ... 299
Batida Morango 301
Berry Patch.................................. 303
Blindside 302
Bloodhound Cocktail 298
Bourbon Cobbler 298
Burning Sunshine Drink 302
Fruit Surprise 302
Irish Rose 290
Mexican Strawberry Rose 291
Midsummer's Night Dream.......... 303
Milky Way 301
Sparkling Strawberry Mimosa....... 291
Spunky Lemonade......................... 299
Strawberry Blonde........................ 300
Strawberry Coffee Drink 304
Strawberry Daiquiri...................... 292
Strawberry Dawn Cocktail 304
Strawberry Dream 292
Strawberry Fields......................... 293
Strawberry Hummingbird 293
Strawberry Kiss 294
Strawberry Laced Punch............... 295
Strawberry Liqueur....................... 297
Strawberry Martini....................... 294
Strawberry Sangria 295
Strawberry Shortcake Drink 300
Strawberry Wine 296

Reader Feedback Form

Dear Reader,

We are very interested in what our readers think. Please fill in the form below and return it to:

Whispering Pine Press International, Inc.
c/o Strawberry Delights Cookbook
P.O. Box 214, Spokane Valley, WA 99037-0214
Phone: (509) 928-8700 | Fax: (509) 922-9949
Email: sales@whisperingpinepress.com
Publisher Websites: www.WhisperingPinePress.com
www.WhisperingPinePressBookstore.com
Blog: www.WhisperingPinePressBlog.com

Name: _____

Address: _____

City, St., Zip: _____

Phone/Fax: (____) _____ / (____) _____

Email: _____

Comments/Suggestions: _____

_____

_____

_____

_____

A great deal of care and attention has been exercised in the creation of this book. Designing a great cookbook that is original, fun, and easy to use has been a job that required many hours of diligence, creativity, and research. Although we strive to make this book completely error free, errors and discrepancies may not be completely excluded. If you come across any errors or discrepancies, please make a note of them and send them to our publishing office. We are constantly updating our manuscripts, eliminating errors, and improving quality.

Please contact us at the address above.

About the Cookbook Delights Series

The *Cookbook Delights Series* includes many different topics and themes. If you have a passion for food and wish to know more information about different foods, then this series of cookbooks will be beneficial to you. Each book features a different type of food, such as avocados, strawberries, huckleberries, salmon, vegetarian, lentils, almonds, cherries, coconuts, lemons, and many, many more.

The *Cookbook Delights Series* not only includes cookbooks about individual foods but also includes several holiday-themed cookbooks. Whatever your favorite holiday may be, chances are we have a cookbook with recipes designed with that holiday in mind. Some examples include *Halloween Delights, Thanksgiving Delights, Christmas Delights, Valentine Delights, Mother's Day Delights, St. Patrick's Day Delights,* and *Easter Delights.*

Each cookbook is designed for easy use and is organized into alphabetical sections. Over 250 recipes are included along with other interesting facts, folklore, and history of the featured food or theme. Each book comes with a beautiful full-color cover, ordering information, and a list of other upcoming books in the series.

Note cards, bookmarks, and a daily journal have been printed and are available to go along with each cookbook. You may view the entire line of cookbooks, journals, cards, posters, puzzles, and bookmarks by visiting our website at www.strawberrydelights.net, or you can email us with your questions and your comments to: sales@whisperingpinepress.com.

Please ask your local bookstore to carry these sets of books.

To order, please contact:

Whispering Pine Press International, Inc.
c/o Strawberry Delights Cookbook
P.O. Box 214, Spokane Valley, WA 99037-0214
Phone: (509) 928-8700 | Fax: (509) 922-9949
Email: sales@whisperingpinepress.com
Publisher Websites: www.WhisperingPinePress.com
www.WhisperingPinePressBookstore.com
Blog: www.WhisperingPinePressBlog.com
SAN 253-200X

We Invite You to Join the Whispering Pine Press International, Inc., Book Club!

Whispering Pine Press International, Inc.
c/o Strawberry Delights Cookbook
P.O. Box 214, Spokane Valley, WA 99037-0214
Phone: (509) 928-8700 | Fax: (509) 922-9949
Email: sales@whisperingpinepress.com
Publisher Websites: www.WhisperingPinePress.com
www.WhisperingPinePressBookstore.com
Blog: www.WhisperingPinePressBlog.com

Buy 11 books and get the next one free, based on the average price of the first eleven purchased.

How the club works:

Simply use the order form below and order books from our catalog. You can buy just one at a time or all eleven at once. After the first eleven books are purchased, the next one is free. Please add shipping and handling as listed on this form. There are no purchase requirements at any time during your membership. Free book credit is based on the average price of the first eleven books purchased.

Join today! Pick your books and mail in the form today!

Yes! I want to join the Whispering Pine Press International, Inc., Book Club! Enroll me and send the books indicated below.

<u>Title</u>	<u>Price</u>
1. _____	_____
2. _____	_____
3. _____	_____
4. _____	_____
5. _____	_____
6. _____	_____
7. _____	_____
8. _____	_____
9. _____	_____
10. _____	_____
11. _____	_____

Free Book Title: _____

Free Book Price: _____ Avg. Price: _____ Total Price: _____

Credit for the free book is based on the average price of the first 11 books purchased.

(Circle one) Check | Visa | MasterCard | Discover | American Express

Credit Card #: _____ Expiration Date: _____

Name: _____

Address: _____

City: _____ State: _____ Country: _____

Zip/Postal: _____ Phone: (_____) _____

Email: _____

Signature_____

Whispering Pine Press International, Inc.
Fundraising Opportunities

Fundraising cookbooks are proven moneymakers and great keepsake providers for your group. Whispering Pine Press International, Inc., offers a very special personalized cookbook fundraising program that encourages success to organizations all across the USA.

Our prices are competitive and fair. Currently, we offer a special of 100 books with many free features and excellent customer service. Any purchase you make is guaranteed first-rate.

Flexibility is not a problem. If you have special needs, we guarantee our cooperation in meeting each of them. Our goal is to create a cookbook that goes beyond your expectations. We have the confidence and a record that promises continual success.

Another great fundraising program is the *Cookbook Delights Series* Program. With cookbook orders of 50 copies or more, your organization receives a huge discount, making for a prompt and lucrative solution.

We also specialize in assisting group fundraising— Christian, community, nonprofit, and academic among them. If you are struggling for a new idea, something that will enhance your success and broaden your appeal, Whispering Pine Press International, Inc., can help.

For more information, write, phone, or fax to:

Whispering Pine Press International, Inc.
P.O. Box 214
Spokane Valley, WA 99037-0214
Phone: (509) 928-8700 | Fax: (509) 922-9949
Email: sales@whisperingpinepress.com
Publisher Websites: www.WhisperingPinePress.com
www.WhisperingPinePressBookstore.com
Blog: www.WhisperingPinePressBlog.com
Book Website: www.StrawberryDelights.net
SAN 253-200X

Personalized and/or Translated Order Form for Any Book by Whispering Pine Press International, Inc.

Dear Readers:

If you or your organization wishes to have this book or any other of our books personalized, we will gladly accommodate your needs. For instance, if you would like to change the names of the characters in a book to the names of the children in your family or Sunday school class, we would be happy to work with you on such a project. We can add more information of your choosing and customize this book especially for your family, group, or organization.

We are also offering an option of translating your book into another language. Please fill out the form below telling us exactly how you would like us to personalize your book.

Please send your request to:

Whispering Pine Press International, Inc.
c/o Strawberry Delights Cookbook
P.O. Box 214, Spokane Valley, WA 99037-0214
Phone: (509) 928-8700 | Fax: (509) 922-9949
Email: sales@whisperingpinepress.com
Publisher Websites: www.WhisperingPinePress.com
www.WhisperingPinePressBookstore.com
Blog: www.WhisperingPinePressBlog.com

Person/Organization placing request: _____

Date_____ Phone: (____) _____

Address_____ Fax: (____) _____

City_____ State_____ Zip: _____

Language of the book: _____

Please explain your request in detail: _____

_____

_____

_____

_____

_____

Strawberry Delights Cookbook
A Collection of Strawberry Recipes

How to Order

Get your additional copies of this book by returning an order form and your check, money order, or credit card information to:

Whispering Pine Press International, Inc.
c/o Strawberry Delights Cookbook
P.O. Box 214, Spokane Valley, WA 99037-0214
Phone: (509) 928-8700 | Fax: (509) 922-9949
Email: sales@whisperingpinepress.com
Publisher Websites: www.WhisperingPinePress.com
www.WhisperingPinePressBookstore.com
Blog: www.WhisperingPinePressBlog.com

Customer Name: _____

Address: _____

City, St., Zip: _____

Phone/Fax: _____

Email: _____

- -

Please send me _____ copies of _____

_____ at $_____ per copy
and $4.95 for shipping and handling per book, plus $2.95 each for additional books. Enclosed is my check, money order, or charge my account for $_____.

☐ Check ☐ Money Order ☐ Credit Card

(Circle One) MasterCard | Discover | Visa | American Express
☐☐☐☐ ☐☐☐☐ ☐☐☐☐ ☐☐☐☐

Expiration Date: _____

_____
Signature
_____
Print Name

Whispering Pine Press International, Inc.
Your Northwest Book Publishing Company
P.O. Box 214
Spokane Valley, WA 99037-0214 USA
Phone: (509) 928-8700 | Fax: (509) 922-9949
Email: sales@whisperingpinepress.com
Publisher Websites: www.WhisperingPinePress.com
www.WhisperingPinePressBookstore.com

Shop Online:
www.whisperingpinepressbookstore.com
Fax orders to: (509)922-9949

Gift-wrapping, Autographing, and Inscription
We are proud to offer personal autographing by the author. For a limited time this service is absolutely free!
Gift-wrapping is also available for $4.95 per item.

1. Sold To

Name: _____
Street/Route: _____
_____
City: _____
State: _____ Zip: _____
Country: _____
Gift message: _____
_____
Email address: _____
Daytime Phone: (_ _) _ _ _-_ _ _ _
   *Necessary for verifying orders
   Home Phone: (_ _) _ _ _-_ _ _ _
   Fax: (_ _) _ _ _-_ _ _ _

2. Ship To

☐ Is this a new or corrected address?
☐ Alternative Shipping Address
☐ Mailing Address

Name: _____
Address: _____
_____
City: _____
State: _____ Zip: _____
Country: _____
Email address: _____

3. Items Ordered

ISBN # /Item #	Size	Color	Qty.	Title or Description	Price	Total

4. Method Of Payment

☐ Visa ☐ MasterCard ☐ Discover ☐ American Express
☐ Check/Money Order   Please make it payable to Whispering Pine Press International, Inc. (No Cash or COD's)

Expiration Date

Account Number ____ / ____
                Month Year

☐☐☐☐ ☐☐☐☐ ☐☐☐☐ ☐☐☐☐

Signature_____
              Cardholder's signature
Printed Name_____
              Please print name of cardholder
Address of Cardholder_____
_____

5. Shipping & Handling

Continental US
US Postal Ground: For books please add $4.95 for the first book and $2.95 each for additional books. All non-book items. add 15% of the Subtotal. Please allow 1-4 weeks for delivery.
US Postal Air: Please add $15.00 shipping and handling. Please allow 1-3 days for delivery.

Alaska, Hawaii, and the US Territories
By Ship: Please add 10% shipping and handling (minimum charge $15.00). Please allow 6-12 weeks for delivery.
By Air: Please add 12% shipping and handling (minimum charge $15.00). Please allow 2-6 weeks for delivery.

International
By Ship: Please add 10% shipping and handling (minimum charge $15.00). Please allow 6-12 weeks for delivery.
By Air: Please add 12% shipping and handling (minimum charge $15.00). Please allow 2-6 weeks for delivery.
FedEx Shipments: Add $5.00 to the above airmail charges for overnight delivery.

Subtotal	
Gift wrap $4.95 Each	
For delivery in WA add 8.7% sales tax.	
Shipping See chart at left	
6. Total	

About the Author and Cook

Karen Jean Matsko Hood has always enjoyed cooking, baking, and experimenting with recipes. At this time Hood is working to complete a series of cookbooks that blends her skills and experience in cooking and entertaining. Hood entertains large groups of people and especially enjoys designing creative menus with holiday, international, ethnic, and regional themes.

Hood is publishing a cookbook series entitled the *Cookbook Delights Series*, in which each cookbook emphasizes a different food ingredient or theme. The first cookbook in the series is *Apple Delights Cookbook*. Hood is working to complete another series of cookbooks titled *Hood and Matsko Family Cookbooks*, which includes many recipes handed down from her family heritage and others that have emerged from more current family traditions. She has been invited to speak on talk radio shows on various topics, and favorite recipes from her cookbooks have been prepared on local television programs.

Hood was born and raised in Great Falls, Montana. As an undergraduate, she attended the College of St. Benedict in St. Joseph, Minnesota, and St. John's University in Collegeville, Minnesota. She attended the University of Great Falls in Great Falls, Montana. Hood received a B.S. Degree in Natural Science from the College of St. Benedict and minored in both Psychology and Secondary Education. Upon her graduation, Hood and her husband taught science and math on the island of St. Croix in the U.S. Virgin Islands. Hood has completed postgraduate classes at the University of Iowa in Iowa City, Iowa. In May 2001, she completed her Master's Degree in Pastoral Ministry at Gonzaga University in Spokane, Washington. She has taken postgraduate classes at Lewis and Clark College on the North Idaho college campus in Coeur d'Alene, Idaho, and Taylor University in Fort Wayne, Indiana. Hood is working on research projects to complete her Ph.D. in Leadership Studies at Gonzaga University in Spokane, Washington.

Hood resides in Greenacres, Washington, along with her husband, sixteen children, and foster children. Her interests include writing, research, and teaching. She previously has volunteered as a court advocate in the Spokane juvenile court system for abused and neglected children. Hood is a literary advocate for youth and adults.

Her hobbies include cooking, baking, collecting, photography, indoor and outdoor gardening, farming, and the cultivation of unusual flowering plants and orchids. She enjoys raising several specialty breeds of animals including Babydoll Southdown, Friesen, and Icelandic sheep, Icelandic horses, bichons frisés, cockapoos, Icelandic sheepdogs, a Newfoundland, a Rottweiler, a variety of Nubian and fainting goats, and a few rescue cats. Hood also enjoys bird-watching and finds all aspects of nature precious.

She demonstrates a passionate appreciation of the environment and a respect for all life. She also invites you to visit her websites.

www.KarenJeanMatskoHood.com
www.KarenJeanMatskoHoodBookstore.com
www.KarenJeanMatskoHoodBlog.com
www.KarensKidsBooks.com
www.KarensTeenBooks.com

www.HoodFamilyBlog.com
www.HoodFamily.com

Author's Social Media

Please Follow the Author on **Twitter:** @KarenJeanHood
Friend her on **Facebook:** Karen Jean Matsko Hood Author Fan Page
Google Plus Profile: Karen Jean Matsko Hood
Pinterest.com/KarenJMHood

www.ingramcontent.com/pod-product-compliance
Lightning Source LLC
Chambersburg PA
CBHW031235090426
42742CB00007B/210